HOW TO START A BUSINESS IN MARYLAND, VIRGINIA, OR THE DISTRICT OF COLUMBIA

James Burk

Mark Warda
Attorneys at Law

SPHINX® PUBLISHING
AN IMPRINT OF SOURCEBOOKS, INC.®
NAPERVILLE, ILLINOIS
www.SphinxLegal.com

First Edition, 2003

Published by: **Sphinx® Publishing, An Imprint of Sourcebooks, Inc.®**

<u>Naperville Office</u>
P.O. Box 4410
Naperville, Illinois 60567-4410
630-961-3900
Fax: 630-961-2168
www.sourcebooks.com
www.SphinxLegal.com

This publication is designed to provide accurate and authoritative information in regard to the subject matter covered. It is sold with the understanding that the publisher is not engaged in rendering legal, accounting, or other professional service. If legal advice or other expert assistance is required, the services of a competent professional person should be sought.

From a Declaration of Principles Jointly Adopted by a Committee of the American Bar Association and a Committee of Publishers and Associations

This product is not a substitute for legal advice.

Disclaimer required by Texas statutes.

Library of Congress Cataloging-in-Publication Data
Burk, James.
    How to start a business in Maryland, Virginia or the District of Columbia / by James Burk and Mark Warda.-- 1st ed.
        p. cm.
    Includes bibliographical references.
    ISBN 1-57248-359-8
    1. Business enterprises--Law and legislation--Maryland--Popular works. 2. Business law--Maryland. 3. Business enterprises--Law and legislation--Virginia--Popular works. 4. Business law--Virginia. 5. Business enterprises--Law and legislation--Washington (D.C.)--Popular works. 6. Business law--Washington (D.C.) I. Warda, Mark. II. Title.
KF1355.Z95 B86 2003
346.752'065--dc22
                                    2003016480

Printed and bound in the United States of America.
VHG Paperback — 10 9 8 7 6 5 4 3 2

ACKNOWLEDGMENTS

Writing a book of this sort is, by its nature, a collaborative effort.

I am very grateful for the magnificent support I received from my associate Richard Lehmann who reviewed the Virginia law portions of the work and who always comes through; and to my wife Katherine, whose research skills continue to amaze me. I am also appreciative of the support of my law partner Alan Reedy, whose thoughtful comments are always a source of wisdom to me; and to Herb Rubenstein, my friend and colleague, who graciously reviewed the Maryland law sections of the work.

James Burk

Washington, D.C.

CONTENTS

Using Self-Help Law Books

Before using a self-help law book, you should realize the advantages and disadvantages of doing your own legal work and understand the challenges and diligence that this requires.

The Growing Trend

Rest assured that you won't be the first or only person handling your own legal matter. For example, in some states, more than seventy-five percent of the people in divorces and other cases represent themselves. Because of the high cost of legal services, this is a major trend and many courts are struggling to make it easier for people to represent themselves. However, some courts are not happy with people who do not use attorneys and refuse to help them in any way. For some, the attitude is, "Go to the law library and figure it out for yourself."

We write and publish self-help law books to give people an alternative to the often complicated and confusing legal books found in most law libraries. We have made the explanations of the law as simple and easy to understand as possible. Of course, unlike an attorney advising an individual client, we cannot cover every conceivable possibility.

Cost/Value Analysis

Whenever you shop for a product or service, you are faced with various levels of quality and price. In deciding what product or service to buy, you make a cost/value analysis on the basis of your willingness to pay and the quality you desire.

When buying a car, you decide whether you want transportation, comfort, status, or sex appeal. Accordingly, you decide among such choices as a Neon, a Lincoln, a Rolls Royce, or a Porsche. Before making a decision, you usually weigh the merits of each option against the cost.

When you get a headache, you can take a pain reliever (such as aspirin) or visit a medical specialist for a neurological examination. Given this choice, most people, of course, take a pain reliever, since it costs only pennies; whereas a medical examination costs hundreds of dollars and takes a lot of time. This is usually a logical choice because it is rare to need anything more than a pain reliever for a headache. But in some cases, a headache may indicate a brain tumor and failing to see a specialist right away can result in complications. Should everyone with a headache go to a specialist? Of course not, but people treating their own illnesses must realize that they are betting on the basis of their cost/value analysis of the situation. They are taking the most logical option.

The same cost/value analysis must be made when deciding to do one's own legal work. Many legal situations are very straight forward, requiring a simple form and no complicated analysis. Anyone with a little intelligence and a book of instructions can handle the matter without outside help.

But there is always the chance that complications are involved that only an attorney would notice. To simplify the law into a book like this, several legal cases often must be condensed into a single sentence or paragraph. Otherwise, the book would be several hundred pages long and too complicated for most people. However, this simplification necessarily leaves out many details and nuances that would apply to special or unusual situations. Also, there are many ways to interpret most legal questions. Your case may come before a judge who disagrees with the analysis of our authors.

Therefore, in deciding to use a self-help law book and to do your own legal work, you must realize that you are making a cost/value analysis. You have decided that the money you will save in doing it yourself outweighs the chance that your case will not turn out to your satisfaction. Most people handling their own simple legal matters never have a problem, but occasionally people find that it ended up costing them more to have an attorney straighten out the situation than it would have if they had hired an attorney in the beginning. Keep this in mind while handling your case, and be sure to consult an attorney if you feel you might need further guidance.

Local Rules
The next thing to remember is that a book which covers the law for the entire nation, or even for an entire state, cannot possibly include every procedural difference of every jurisdiction. Whenever possible, we provide the exact form needed; however, in some areas, each county, or even each judge, may require unique forms and procedures. In our state books, our forms usually cover the majority of counties in the state, or provide examples of the type of form which will be required. In our national books, our forms are sometimes even more general in nature but are designed to give a good idea of the type of form that will be needed in most locations. Nonetheless, keep in mind that your state, county, or judge may have a requirement, or use a form, that is not included in this book.

You should not necessarily expect to be able to get all of the information and resources you need solely from within the pages of this book. This book will serve as your guide, giving you specific information whenever possible and helping you to find out what else you will need to know. This is just like if you decided to build your own backyard deck. You might purchase a book on how to build decks. However, such a book would not include the building codes and permit requirements of every city, town, county, and township in the nation; nor would it include the lumber, nails, saws, hammers, and other materials and tools you would need to actually build the deck. You would use the book as your guide, and then do some work and research involving such matters as whether you need a permit of some kind, what type and grade of wood are available in your area, whether to use hand tools or power tools, and how to use those tools.

Before using the forms in a book like this, you should check with your court clerk to see if there are any local rules of which you should be aware, or local forms you will need to use. Often, such forms will require the same information as the forms in the book but are merely laid out differently or use slightly different language. They will sometimes require additional information.

Changes in the Law
Besides being subject to local rules and practices, the law is subject to change at any time. The courts and the legislatures of all fifty states are constantly revising the laws. It is possible that while you are reading this book, some aspect of the law is being changed.

In most cases, the change will be of minimal significance. A form will be redesigned, additional information will be required, or a waiting period will be extended. As a result, you might need to revise a form, file an extra form, or wait out a longer time period; these types of changes will not usually affect the outcome of your case. On the other hand, sometimes a major part of the law is changed, the entire law in a particular area is rewritten, or a case that was the basis of a central legal point is overruled. In such instances, your entire ability to pursue your case may be impaired.

Again, you should weigh the value of your case against the cost of an attorney and make a decision as to what you believe is in your best interest.

INTRODUCTION

The decision to start a new business is both scary and exciting. Small businesses provide most of the new employment opportunities in our economy. From the high tech corridors of Northern Virginia, to the bioscience labs of the Maryland suburbs, there is flurry of entrepreneurial activity in the District of Columbia, Maryland, and Virginia.

Each year many thousands of new businesses are registered in the three states—corporations, partnerships, limited liability companies, and proprietorships. Choosing the right type of entity for your new business is the first step of many.

This book will give you the basic steps to get started and take your business to the next level. An extensive list of publications appears in the section entitled *For Further Reference* and there are numerous references to helpful Internet sites throughout the book. As little as ten years ago, information on starting and operating a business was scarce. There were plenty of general works on sales and marketing but precious few on the mechanics of actually starting a business. In large measure, the Internet and the publishing industry has changed that situation.

The wealth of information now available is both empowering and daunting. We have tried to write this book in a non-technical, non-legalistic manner while giving adequate emphasis to state and federal laws that impact your business and its operations. If you do not follow the laws of your state and applicable federal laws, your progress can be slowed or stopped by government fines, civil judgments, or even criminal penalties.

This book is intended to give you the basics for opening a business in the District of Columbia, Maryland, or Virginia. Questions will inevitably arise that are not covered by this book or for which you need additional information. For specific problems and planning strategies, you should consult with competent legal counsel—preferably an attorney who specializes in business law matters. For accounting issues you should consult with a certified public accountant (CPA) who likewise specializes in the needs of small businesses.

For a complete picture of the start-up business, you should probably read through this entire book. Much of the information is rather dry reading and we suggest you imagine you are learning the fundamental rules of a game so that you can become a knowledgeable player at a higher level—somewhat like learning the piano scales in order to one day play a Beethoven sonata.

You should also be aware that laws have a way of changing on a frequent basis as do the forms that are included in this book. The state and federal Internet sites referenced in this book are the easiest places to obtain the most current version of all forms. Many forms have a revision date in their header or footer so it is a good idea to check the date for the most recent form.

The current issues in the business community are focused on integrity and compliance. Integrity and compliance begin on *day one* of your business. This book will give you the tools to be legally compliant—the integrity piece is up to you.

I DECIDING TO START A BUSINESS

If you are reading this book, then you have probably made a serious decision to take the plunge and start your own business. Hundreds of thousands of people make the same decision each year and many of them become very successful. Many of them also fail. Knowledge can only help your chances of success. You need to know why some succeed while others fail. Some of what follows may seem obvious, but to someone wrapped up in a new business idea, some of this information is occasionally overlooked.

Know Your Strengths

The last thing a budding entrepreneur wants to hear is that he or she is not cut-out to run his or her own business. Those "do you have what it takes" quizzes are ignored with the fear that the answer might be one the entrepreneur does not want to hear. But even if you lack some skills you can be successful if you know how to obtain them.

You should consider all of the skills and knowledge that running a successful business requires and decide whether you have what it takes. If you do not, it does not necessarily mean you are doomed to be an employee all your life.

Perhaps you just need a partner who has the skills you lack. Perhaps you can hire someone with the skills you need or you can structure your business to avoid areas where you are weak. If those options do not work, maybe you can learn the skills.

For example, if you are not good at dealing with employees (either you are too passive and get taken advantage of, or too tough and scare them off) you can:

✪ handle product development yourself and have a partner or manager deal with employees;

✪ take seminars in employee management; or,

✪ structure your business so that you don't need employees. (Either use independent contractors or set yourself up as an independent contractor.)

Here are some of the factors to consider when planning your business.

✪ If it takes months or years before your business turns a profit, do you have the resources to hold out? Businesses have gone under or have been sold just before they were about to take off, and staying power is an important ingredient to success. It has been said that you should have the resources to last without revenues for at least twelve months, longer if your business requires product development.

✪ As an alternative to financing with your own money, you can sell equity in your company to get the necessary capital to progress. Keep in mind that stock sales are regulated by federal and state securities laws that must be observed.

✪ Are you willing to put in a lot of overtime to make your business a success? Owners of businesses do not set their own hours; the business sets them for the owner. Many business owners work long hours seven days a week; However, they typically enjoy running their business more than family picnics or fishing.

✪ Are you willing to do the dirtiest or most unpleasant work of the business? Emergencies come up and employees are not always dependable. You might need to mop up a flooded room, spend a weekend stuffing 10,000 envelopes, or work Christmas if someone calls in sick.

✪ Do you know enough about the product or service? Are you aware of the trends in the industry and what changes new technology might bring? Think of the people who started typesetting or printing businesses just before type was replaced by laser printers.

✪ Do you know enough about accounting and inventory to manage the business? Do you have a good head for business? Some people naturally know how to save money and do things profitably. Others are in the habit of buying the best and the most expensive of everything. The latter can be fatal to a struggling new business.

✪ Are you good at managing employees?

✪ Do you know how to sell your product or service? You can have the best product on the market but people do not know about it. If you are a wholesaler, shelf space in major stores is hard to get, especially for a new company without a record, a large line of products, or a large advertising budget.

✪ Do you know enough about getting publicity? The media receives thousands of press releases and announcements each day and most are thrown away. Do not count on free publicity to put your name in front of the public.

Know Your Business

Not only do you need to know the concept of a business, but also you need the experience of working in a business. Maybe you always dreamed of running a bed and breakfast or having your own pizza place. Have you ever worked in such a business? If not, you may have no idea of the day-to-day headaches and problems of the business. For example, do you really know how much to allow for theft, spoilage, and unhappy customers?

You might feel silly taking an entry-level job at a pizza place when you would rather start your own, but it might be the most valuable preparation you could have. A few weeks of seeing how a business operates could mean the difference between success and failure.

Working in a business as an employee is one of the best ways to be successful at running such a business. New people with new ideas who work in old industries have been known to revolutionize them with obvious improvements that no one before dared to try.

Do the Math

Conventional wisdom says you need a business plan before committing yourself to a new venture, but many businesses are started successfully without a formal business plan. A person has a great concept, they put it on the market, and it takes off. However, at the very least, you need to do some basic calculations to see if the business can make a profit. Here are some examples:

If you want to start a retail shop, figure out how many people are in close enough proximity to become customers, and how many other stores will be competing for those customers. Visit some of those other shops and see how busy they are. Without giving away your plans to compete, ask some general questions like *how's business?* and maybe they will share their frustrations or successes.

Whether you sell a good or a service, calculate to find out the potential profit. For example, if you plan to start a house painting company, find out what you will have to pay to hire painters; what it will cost you for the insurance; what bonding and licensing you will need; and what the advertising will cost. Determine how many jobs you can do per month and what other painters are charging. In some industries in different areas of the country, there may be a large margin of profit or there may be virtually no profit.

Determine if there is a demand for your product or service. Suppose you have designed a beautiful new kind of candle. All your friends say you should open a shop because everyone will want them, but before making a hundred of them and renting a store, bring a few to craft shows or flea markets and see what happens.

Figure out what the income and expenses would be for a typical month of your new business. List monthly expenses such as rent, salaries, utilities, insurance, taxes, supplies, advertising, services, and other overhead. Then calculate how much profit you will average from each sale. Next, figure out how many sales you will need to cover your overhead and divide by the number of business days in the month. Can you reasonably expect that many sales? How will you get those sales?

Most types of businesses have trade associations, that often have figures on how profitable its members are. Some even have start-up kits for people wanting to start businesses. One good source of information on such organizations is the *Encyclopedia of Associations* published by Gale Research Inc. The book is a comprehensive source of detailed information on over 135,000 nonprofit membership organizations worldwide. It is available on the Internet at **http://library.dialog.com/bluesheets/html/bl0114.html** and is also available in many library reference sections. Producers of products for the trade often give assistance to small companies getting started to win their loyalty. Contact the largest suppliers of the products your business will need and see if they can help.

Sources for Further Guidance

The following offices offer free or low-cost guidance for new businesses.

SCORE The Service Corps of Retired Executives is a resource partner with the US Small Business Administration and is dedicated to the formation, growth, and success of small business. SCORE is comprised of a network of volunteer business executives and professionals who provide advice, troubleshooting and counseling.

For more information contact SCORE at their website:

www.score.org

**Washington Metro Area
SCORE Offices**

Washington

District of Columbia: Score #1
SCORE Office
1110 Vermont Avenue N.W., 9th
Floor
Washington, D.C. 20005
202-606-4000 ext. 287
Monday to Friday 9 am to 3 pm
www.scoredc.org
dcscore@hotmail.com

Suburban Maryland

Montgomery County
Montgomery County Chamber of
Commerce
51 Monroe Street Suite 1609
Rockville, MD 20850
301-738-0015
Thursday 1 pm to 3 pm, by appoint-
ment

Silver Spring Chamber of Commerce
Lee Plaza, 8601 Georgia Avenue,
Suite 203
Silver Spring, MD 20910
301-565-3777
Thursday 2 to 5 pm

Wheaton-Kensington Chamber of
Commerce
2401 Blueridge Avenue, Suite 101
Wheaton, MD 20902
301-949-0080
Wednesday 9 am to 3 pm

Suburban Virginia

Arlington
Arlington Central Library
1015 North Quincy Street
Arlington, VA 22202
703-228-5984
Tuesday 1 to 5 pm

Fairfax County
Central Fairfax Chamber of
Commerce
3975 University Drive, Suite 350
Fairfax, VA 22030
703-591-2450
Tuesday 10 am to 3 pm

Fairfax County Chamber of
Commerce
8230 Old Courthouse Road, Suite
350
Vienna, VA 22182
703-749-0400
Thursday 9:30 am to 2:30 pm

Fairfax County Economic Development
Authority
8300 Boone Boulevard, Suite 450
Vienna, VA 22182
703-790-0600
First Friday of each Month 9:30 am
to 12:30 pm

Reston
1763 Fountain Drive
Reston, VA 20190
703-707-9045
Every Friday 12:00 noon to 3:00 pm,
by appointment

Herndon
Herndon-Dulles Chamber of
Commerce
730 Eldon Street
Herndon, VA 20172
703-437-5556
Thursday 10:00 am to 12:00 noon,
by appointment

Score Offices in Virginia

Bristol: SCORE #196
Bristol Chamber of Commerce
20 Volunteer Parkway
P.O. Box 519
Bristol, VA 24203-0519
423-989-4423

Central Virginia: SCORE #494
Chamber of Commerce Center
E. Market & Fifth Streets, Suite 200
P.O. Box 865
Charlottesville, VA 22902-0865
434-295-6712

Peninsula: SCORE #100
Virginia Peninsula Chamber of
Commerce
1919 Commerce Drive, Suite 320
P.O. Box 7269
Hampton, Virginia 23666
757-262-2000
score100@seva.net

Greater Lynchburg: SCORE #529
Federal Building
1100 Main Street, Room 102
Lynchburg, VA 24504-1700
434-846-3235

Greater Prince William: SCORE #530
Prince William County Greater
Manassas Chamber of Commerce
8963 Center Street
Manassas, VA 20110
703-368-6600

Martinsville: SCORE #540
Martinsville Chamber of Commerce
115 Broad Street
P.O. Box 709
Martinsville, VA 24114-0709
276-632-6401
mhccoc@neocom.net

Hampton Roads: SCORE #60
Federal Building
200 Granby Street, Room 737
Norfolk, VA 23510
757-441-3733
scorehr60@whro.net

Richmond: SCORE #12
Federal Building
400 North 8th Street, Suite 1150
P.O. Box 10126
Richmond, VA 23240-0126
804-7712400 ext. 131
scorechapter12@yahoo.com

Roanoke: SCORE #26
Federal Building
250 Franklin Road S.W.
Room 716
Roanoke, VA 24011
540-857-2834

Shenandoah Valley: SCORE #427
Waynesboro Chamber of Commerce
301 West Main Street
Waynesboro, VA 22980
540-949-4423
score427@intelos.net

Williamsburg: SCORE #549
Williamsburg Chamber of Commerce
421 North Boundary Street
Williamsburg, VA 23185
757-229-6511
wacc@wmbg.com

Score Offices in Maryland
Annapolis: SCORE # 390
Southern Maryland SCORE
2525 Riva Road, Suite 110
Annapolis, MD 21401
410-266-9553
www.hometown.aol.com/score390
score390@aol.com

Baltimore: SCORE # 3
City Crescent Building
10 South Howard Street, 6th Floor
Baltimore, MD 21201
410-962-2233
www.scorebaltimore.org

Bel Air
Harford County Chamber of
Commerce
108 S. Bond St.
Bel Air, MD 21014
Call first: 410-838-2020

Cockeysville
Cockeysville Library
9833 Greenside Drive
Cockeysville, MD 21030
Thursday 2:30 p.m. to 4:30 p.m.
Call first: 410-887-7750

Columbia
Howard County Resource Center
9250 Bendix Road, North
Columbia, MD 21045
Call first: 410-313-6550

Frederick: SCORE #632
Frederick Chamber of Commerce
43A South Market Street
Frederick, MD 21701
301-662-8723
Fax: 301-846-4427
www.fred.net/score
score632@fred.net

Hagerstown: SCORE #539
Hagerstown SCORE
111 W. Washington Street
Hagerstown, MD 21742
Phone: 301-739-2015, Ext. 103
www.scorehagerstown.org
info@ScoreHagerstown.org

Harford County,
Harford County Community College
401 Thomas Run Rd.
Bel Air, MD 21015
Edgewood Hall
Call first: 410-836-4237

Harford County Public Library
100 E. Pennsylvania Ave.
Bel Air, MD 21014
Thursday 5:30 to 7:30 pm
Friday 2:30 to 4:30 pm
Call first: 410-638-3151

Pikesville
Pikesville Library
1301 Reisterstown Rd.
Reisterstown, MD 21208
Monday evenings 7:00 p.m. to 8:30 p.m.
Call first: 410-887-1234

Towson
Towson Library
320 York Rd.
Baltimore, MD 21204
Fridays 2:30 p.m.-4:30 p.m.
Call first: 410-887-6166

Towson
Baltimore County Resource Center
102 W. Pennsylvania Avenue Suite 101
Towson, MD 21204
Call first: 410-825-8612

Offices of Economic Development

Offices of Economic Development are created by governmental bodies to assist in the coordination, planning, supervision, and execution of matters relating to economic development in state or District of Columbia. Specific mandates and limitations may exist as to the roles and functions of various Offices of Economic Development and you should contact the office in your area for further information.

Washington, DC
Office of the Deputy Mayor for Planning and Economic Development
John A. Wilson Building
1350 Pennsylvania Avenue, NW, Suite 317
Washington, DC 20004
202-727-6365
http://dcbiz.dc.gov/main.shtm

Virginia
Fairfax County Economic Development Authority
8300 Boone Boulevard, Suite 450
Vienna, VA 22182-2633
703-790-060
www.fairfaxcountyeda.org

The Alexandria Economic Development Partnership, Inc.
1729 King Street, Suite 410
Alexandria, VA 22314
703-739-3820
www.alexecon.org

Arlington County Department of Economic Development
1100 North Glebe Road, Suite 1500,
Arlington, VA 22201
703-228-0800
commteam@arlingtonvirginiausa.com
www.smartplace.org/small_bus/small-bus.html

Loudoun County Department of
Economic Development
1 Harrison Street, S.E., 5th Floor
Leesburg, VA 20177
703-777-0426
good4biz@loudoun.gov
www.loudoun.gov/business
    /home.htm

Prince William County Department of
Economic Development
10530 Linden Lake Plaza, Suite 105
Manassas, VA 20109-6434
703-392-0330, 800-334-9876
econdev@pwcgov.org
www.pwcecondev.org

Maryland
Montgomery County Business
Resource Center
Rockville Regional Library
101 Monroe St, 15th Floor
Rockville, MD 20850
Business Hours: Monday-Friday
10am-5pm
By Appointment: Monday-Friday
8:30am-5pm
240-777-2041
www.montgomerycountymd.gov

Prince George's County Economic
Development Corporation
Prince George's County Small
Business Assistance Center (SBAC)
4640 Forbes Blvd., Suite 200
Lanham, MD 20706
301-306-5682
tmiles@pgcedc.com
www.pgcedc.com

**Local
Government
Websites**

The following websites may be of help in answering questions about doing
business in the Washington area:

Washington, DC:
www.dc.gov

Fairfax County, Virginia:
www.co.fairfax.va.us

Alexandria, Virginia:
http://ci.alexandria.va.us/

Arlington County, Virginia:
www.co.arlington.va.us

Loudoun County, Virginia:
www.loudoun.gov

Prince William County, Virginia:
www.co.prince-william.va.us

Montgomery County, Maryland:
www.montgomerycountymd.gov

Prince George's County, Maryland:
www.goprincegeorgescounty.com

Small Business Development Centers

America's Small Business Development Center (SBDC) Network is the Federal Government's largest and most productive small business management and technical assistance program. In partnership with Congress, the SBA, and other partners, the SBDC network consists of almost one thousand service centers nationwide. It is unique in that it combines public and private resources to help over 1.25 million American entrepreneurs start, manage, and grow their own businesses. The SBDC can be reached on the Web at:

www.asbdc-us.org

Washington, DC
Howard University
Washington, D.C. Small Business
Development Center
Howard University School of
Business
2600 6th Street, NW , Room 128
(Georgia Avenue & Fairmont Street,
NW)
Washington, DC 20059
202-806-1550
www.bschool.howard.edu/SBDC

Virginia
Virginia Department of Business
Assistance
707 E. Main Street, Suite 300
Richmond, Virginia 23219
804-371-8200
www.dba.state.va.us

George Mason Enterprise Center
4031 University Drive, Suite 200
Fairfax, VA 22030-7700
703-993-4223
www.dba.state.va.us

Maryland
Maryland Small Business
Development Center
7100 Baltimore Ave., Suite 401
College Park, MD 20740
301-403-8300
www.mdsbdc.umd.edu

Chambers of Commerce

Local, state and national chamber of commerce organizations can provides valuable assistance to a starting business. The organizations are made up of members with similar interest and promote business interests, act as a resource for growth and development, and provide a forum for business owners to connect and network.

Washington, DC
United States Chamber of Commerce
1615 H Street, NW
Washington, DC 20062-2000
Main Number: 202-659-6000
Customer Service: 800-638-6582
www.uschamber.com
custsvc@uschamber.com

D.C. Chamber of Commerce
1213 K St NW
Washington, DC 20005
202-638-6764
www.dcchamber.org

Greater Washington Board of Trade
1129 20th St NW, #200
Washington, DC 20036
202-857-5910

National Black
Chamber Of Commerce, Inc.
1350 Connecticut Avenue NW,
Suite 825
Washington, DC 20036
202-466-6888
www.nationalbcc.org

Northern Virginia
Virginia Chamber of Commerce
9 South 5th Street
Richmond, VA 23219
804-644-1607
www.vachamber.com

Alexandria Chamber of Commerce
801 N Fairfax Street, Ste 402
Alexandria, VA 22314
703-549-1000
www.alexchamber.com

Arlington Chamber of
Commerce, Inc.
2009-14th St North, Ste 111
Arlington, VA 22201
703-525-2400
www.arlingtonchamber.org

Central Fairfax
Chamber of Commerce
3975 University Dr, Suite 350
Fairfax, VA 22030
703-591-2450
www.cfcc.org

Culpeper County
Chamber of Commerce
109 S Commerce St
Culpeper, VA 22701
540-825-8628
www.culpepervachamber.com

Fairfax County
Chamber of Commerce
8230 Old Courthouse Rd, #350
Vienna, VA 22182
703-749-0400

Fredericksburg Area
Chamber of Commerce
PO Box 7476
Fredericksburg, VA 22404
540-373-9400
www.fredericksburgchamber.org

Front Royal-Warren County
Chamber of Commerce
414 East Main St
Front Royal, VA 22630
540-635-3185
www.frontroyalchamber.com

Greater Falls Church
Chamber of Commerce
417 W Broad St, Suite 207
Falls Church, VA 22040
703-532-1050
www.fallschurchchamber.org

Greater Richmond
Chamber of Commerce
PO Box 12280
Richmond, VA 23241
804-648-1234
www.grcc.com

Herndon Dulles
Chamber of Commerce
PO Box 327
Herndon, VA 20172
703-437-5556
www.herndoncc.org

Loudoun County
Chamber of Commerce
PO Box 1298
Leesburg, VA 20177
703-777-2176
www.loudounchamber.org

Mount Vernon-Lee
Chamber of Commerce
8804-D Pear Tree Village Ct.
Alexandria, VA 22309
703-660-6602
http://MtVernon-LeeChamber.org

Prince William County-Greater
Manassas Chamber of Commerce
PO Box 495
Manassas, VA 20108
703-368-4813
www.pwcgmcc.org

Prince William Regional
Chamber of Commerce
4320 Ridgewood Center Dr
Woodbridge, VA 22192
703-590-5000
www.RegionalChamber.org

U.S. Lebanese Chamber of
Commerce
8000 Towers Cresent Dr, #1350
Vienna, VA 22182

Vienna-Tysons Regional
Chamber of Commerce
513 Maple Ave W, 2nd Floor
Vienna, VA 22180
703-281-1333
www.viennacc.org

Virginia Peninsula
Chamber Of Commerce
1919 Commerce Drive, Suite 320
Hampton, VA 23666
757-762-2000

Williamsburg Area
Chamber of Commerce
PO Box 3620
Williamsburg, VA 23187
757-229-6511
www.williamsburgcc.com

Winchester-Frederick County
Chamber of Commerce
2 North Cameron St, Suite 200
Winchester, VA 22601
540-662-4118
www.winchesterva.org

Maryland
Maryland Chamber of Commerce
60 West Street, Suite 100
Annapolis, MD 21401
410-269-0642
www.mdchamber.org/index2.html

Baltimore County
Chamber of Commerce
102 W Pennsylvania Avenue, Ste 101
Towson, MD 21204
410-825-6200
www.baltimorecountychamber.com

Baltimore/Washington Corridor
Chamber
312 Marshall Ave, #104
Laurel, MD 20707-4824
301-725-4000
www.baltwashchamber.org

Calvert County
Chamber of Commerce
120 Dares Beach Road
P.R. Box 9
Prince Frederick, MD 20678
410-535-2577

Carroll County
Chamber of Commerce
PO Box 871
Westminster, MD 21158
410-848-9050
www.carrollcountychamber.org

Chamber of Commerce Of Frederick
County, Inc
43 A S Market St
Frederick, MD 21701
301-662-4164
www.frederickchamber.org

Charles County Chamber of
Commerce
6360 Crain Hwy
La Plata, MD 20646
301-932-6500
www.cccc-md.org

Gaithersburg-Germantown
Chamber of Commerce
4 Professional Drive, Ste 132
Gaithersburg, MD 20879
301-840-1400
www.ggchamber.org

Greater Bethesda-Chevy Chase
Chamber of Commerce
7910 Woodmont Avenue, Suite 1204
Bethesda, MD 20814
301-652-4900
www.bccchamber.org

Greater Silver Spring
Chamber of Commerce
8601 Georgia Avenue, Ste 203
Silver Spring, MD 20910
301-565-3777
www.gsscc.org/prod

Hagerstown-Washington County
Chamber of Commerce
111 W Washington Street
Hagerstown, MD 21740
301-739-2015
www.hagerstown.org

Montgomery County Chamber of
Commerce
51 Monroe Street, Suite 1609
Rockville, MD 20850
301-258-9000
www.montgomery-chamber.com

Prince George's Chamber Of
Commerce
4640 Forves Blvd, Suite 130
Lanham, MD 20806
301-731-5000
301-731-5013
www.pgcoc.org

Rockville Chamber of Commerce
255 Rockville Pk, #L10
Rockville, MD 20850
301-424-9300

West Anne Arundel County
Chamber of Commerce
8373 Piney Orchard Pkwy, #100
Odenton, MD 21113
410-672-3422
www.waaccc.org

2 | CHOOSING THE FORM OF YOUR BUSINESS

The five most common forms for a business are sole proprietorship, partnership, corporation, limited partnership, and limited liability company. The reasons for choosing among these are wide-ranging because no one form of business is right for everyone. This chapter attempts to explain in brief detail some of the characteristics, advantages, and disadvantages of each. The chapter also details some of the basic operational requirements for corporations.

Proprietorship

Characteristics   A proprietorship involves one person conducting business in his or her own name or under a fictitious name.

Advantages   Simplicity is the main advantage. There is no organizational expense and no extra tax forms or reports. You simply file *Schedule C* with your federal *Form 1040 Individual Income Tax Return* and applicable state income tax returns.

Disadvantages   The proprietor is personally liable for all debts and obligations. Also, the business does not continue after the proprietor's death. All profits are directly taxable, which is certainly a disadvantage for the proprietor, and business affairs are easily mixed with personal affairs.

General Partnership

Characteristics   This involves two or more people carrying on a business together and sharing the profits and losses.

Advantages   Partners can combine expertise and assets. A general partnership allows liability to be spread among more persons. Also, the business can continue after the death of a partner if bought out by a surviving partner.

Disadvantages   Each partner is *jointly and severally* liable for other partners' actions within the scope of the business. This means that if your partner harms a customer or signs a million-dollar credit line in the partnership name, you can be personally liable for any and all of it. Even if left in the business, all profits are taxable. All parties share control, and the death of a partner may result in liquidation. In a general partnership, it is often hard to get rid of a bad partner.

Corporation

Characteristics   A corporation is an *artificial legal person* that carries on business through its officers for its shareholders. In Maryland, Virginia, and the District of Columbia, one person may form a corporation and be the sole shareholder and officer. This legal person carries on business in its own name and shareholders are not necessarily liable for its acts. Laws concerning corporations are covered in Maryland Corporations and Associations Code (Md. Corp and Assn. Code) Sec. 2, District of Columbia Code (D.C. Code) Sec. 29, and the Code of Virginia (Va. Code) Sec. 13.1.

An *S corporation* is a corporation that has filed *Internal Revenue Service (IRS) Form 2553* choosing to have all profits taxed to the shareholders, rather than to the corporation. An S corporation files a tax return but pays no federal or state tax. The profit shown on the S corporation tax return is reported on the owners' tax returns.

A *C corporation* is any corporation that has not elected to be taxed as an S corporation. A C corporation pays income tax on its profits. Therefore, when *dividends* are paid to shareholders they are taxed twice, once for the corporation and once when they are paid to the shareholders. In Maryland, Virginia, and the

District of Columbia, a C corporation must also pay corporate income tax. In Maryland, the corporate tax rate is 7.0%; in D.C., it is 9.5%; and, in Virginia, it is 6.0%.

A *professional service corporation* or *professional corporation* is a corporation formed by a professional such as a doctor, lawyer, or accountant. Maryland, Virginia, and the District of Columbia have special rules for professional corporations that differ slightly from those of other corporations. There are also special tax rules for professional corporations. Any professional seeking to form an entity for their professional services should consult with an attorney specializing in the formation of professional entities.

A *nonprofit corporation* is usually used for organizations such as churches and condominium associations. However, with careful planning, some types of businesses can be set up as nonprofit corporations and save a lot in taxes. While a nonprofit corporation cannot pay dividends, it can pay its officers and employees fair salaries. Some of the major nonprofit organizations pay their officers well over $100,000 a year. Rules for nonprofit corporations are included in Md. Corp. and Assn. Code Sec. 5, D.C. Code Sec. 29 Ch. 3 and Va. Code Sec. 13.1, Ch. 10. Additional information on non-profit corporations can be found on the state websites.

Advantages

If properly organized, shareholders have no liability for corporate debts and lawsuits, and officers usually have no personal liability for their corporate acts. The existence of a corporation may be perpetual. There are tax advantages allowed only to corporations. It is prestigious to own a corporation.

Corporations have two other excellent advantages—capital may be raised by issuing stock and it is easy to transfer ownership upon death. A small corporation can be set up as an S corporation to avoid corporate taxes but still retain corporate advantages. Some types of businesses can be set up as nonprofit corporations that provide significant tax savings.

Disadvantages

The start-up costs for forming a corporation are a disadvantage. Additionally, there are certain formalities such as *annual meetings*, separate bank accounts, and tax forms. Unless a corporation registers as an S corporation, it must pay federal income tax separate from the tax paid by the owners, and must pay state income taxes.

Limited Partnership

Characteristics   A *limited partnership* has characteristics similar to both a corporation and a partnership. There are *general partners* who have the control and personal liability, and there are *limited partners* who only put up money and whose liability is limited to what they paid for their share of the partnership (like corporate stock). A new type of limited partnership, a *limited liability limited partnership*, allows all partners to avoid liability.

Advantages   Capital can be contributed by limited partners who have no control of the business or liability for its debts.

Disadvantages   A great disadvantage is high start-up costs. Also, an extensive partnership agreement is required because general partners are personally liable for partnership debts and for the acts of each other. (One solution to this problem is to use a corporation as the general partner.)

Limited Liability Company

Characteristics   A *Limited Liability Company (LLC)* is like a limited partnership without general partners. It has characteristics of both a corporation and a partnership—none of the partners have liability and all can have some control. LLC law also allows *Professional Limited Liability Companies*, which are used for medical, law, and accounting practices.

Advantages   The limited liability company offers the tax benefits of a partnership with the protection from liability of a corporation. While both a corporation and an LLC offer a business owner protection from business debts, the LLC also offers protection of the company's assets from the debts of an owner. It offers more tax benefits than an S corporation because it may pass through more depreciation and deductions, have different classes of ownership, have an unlimited number of members, and have aliens (persons from out of state) as members.

Disadvantages   A disadvantage is that an extensive *Operating Agreement* needs to be drafted to allocate profits and losses of the company and define control. Another perceived disadvantage is that all profits and losses are deemed distributed on the last day of the tax year but many companies need to retain some funds to meet current expenses. As a result, some owners may be charged with income they have not actually received. Most well drafted operating agreements provide for a mandatory *tax distribution* to cover the taxes due on the phantom income.

Start-up Procedures

Proprietorship

In a proprietorship, all accounts, property, and licenses are taken in the name of the owner. (See Chapter 3 for using a *fictitious name*.)

Partnership

To form a general partnership, a written agreement should be prepared to spell out rights and obligations of the parties. It may be registered, but this is not required and generally not done. Most accounts, property, and licenses can be in either the partnership name or that of the partners. For more information and for books on the subject, see *For Further Reference* at the end of this book. The principal disadvantage of a general partnership is that all partners are liable for the debts of the partnership personally and their personal assets can be reached by a judgment creditor. Generally, it is better to avoid the general partnership format if you are an individual.

Corporation

To form a corporation, *articles of incorporation* must be filed in Maryland with the State Department of Assessments; in the District of Columbia with the Department of Consumer and Regulatory Affairs; and, in Virginia with the State Corporation Commission, along with the appropriate filing fees. An organizational meeting is then held. At the meeting, directors are appointed, officers are elected, stock is issued and other formalities are complied with in order to avoid the corporate entity being set aside later and treated as though it never was formed. Licenses and accounts are titled in the name of the corporation. One or more persons may form a for-profit or nonprofit corporation in Maryland and Virginia. In the District of Columbia, for a nonprofit, three directors are required. The references at the end of this book have more specific information.

Limited Partnership

A *certificate of limited partnership agreement* must be drafted and filed in Maryland with the State Department of Assessments; in the District of Columbia with the Department of Consumer and Regulatory Affairs; and, in Virginia with the State Corporation Commission along with the appropriate filing fees. In addition, a more extensive limited partnership agreement should be drafted and signed by all partners. Because of the complexity of *securities laws* and the criminal penalties for violation, it is advantageous to have an attorney organize a limited partnership.

Limited Liability Company

One or more persons may form a limited liability company by filing *articles of organization* in Maryland with the State Department of Assessments; in the District of Columbia with the Department of Consumer and Regulatory Affairs; and, in Virginia with the State Corporation Commission along with the appropriate filing fees. Licenses and accounts are in the name of the company. A limited liability company is taxed like a partnership but affords all of the protection of a corporation.

Helpful Resources

Information on entity formation requirements may be found on state websites. For Maryland, information may be found at **www.dat.state.md.us**; for the District of Columbia at **www.dcra.dc.gov**; and, for Virginia at **www.state.va.us/scc**.

Operational Procedures

The following are general rules for operating new corporations. These are general guidelines and are not intended to be all-inclusive. In addition, various statutory requirements may vary from state to state.

Bylaws

The *bylaws* of a corporation are a separate document from the articles of incorporation, and usually deal with matters of procedure. The bylaws are considered a contract between the stockholders, directors, and officers, and typically contain the terms that are not required in the articles of incorporation regarding the regulation of their rights and the affairs of the corporation.

The bylaws usually state the place and time of the annual meetings of the stockholders and directors, and detail the procedures for notifying these individuals of these meetings. The bylaws also will define what makes up a voting majority and a quorum for the purposes of the corporation. The procedures for calling special meetings are usually described, as is the standard order of business. The bylaws are also the place where the specific duties of the officers of the corporation described.

While many of these terms could be otherwise stated in the articles of incorporation, it is usually easier to adopt them as bylaws. Since bylaws are drafted by the directors and adopted by the shareholders as their internal operating procedure, the directors may draft changes to the bylaws at any time. The shareholders must then adopt the changes. Neither the bylaws nor any amendments to them are filed with the Secretary of State.

If a corporation functions without bylaws, the articles of incorporation become the sole document that regulates the affairs of the corporation. Since amendments to the articles of incorporation require more procedure and cost, it is advisable for a corporation to adopt bylaws as a way of maintaining some flexibility in the functions of the corporation.

Initial Corporate Reports

Many states require an initial report to be filed with the state within thirty to ninety days of the formation of the corporation. These reports generally require a list of officers and directors of the corporation and are usually mailed to the *registered agent*. (For more information, contact your state's corporation commission.)

Annual Corporate Reports

Corporations are required to make an annual filing with a state agency in their state of incorporation and any state in which they are qualified to do business as a foreign entity. These reports are mailed to the registered agent and generally require a representative of the corporation to provide an updated list of officers, directors, and resident agent. Failure to file these annual reports can result in termination of the corporate charter.

In Maryland, a corporation needs to file a *Personal Property Return* with the Department of Assessments and Taxation. In the District of Columbia, a corporation needs to file an *Annual Report for Foreign and Domestic Corporation* with the Department of Consumer and Regulatory Affairs. In Virginia, a Corporation needs to file an *Annual Corporate Report* with the Virginia State Corporation Commission. It is important to note that you are required to file these reports even if you do not receive them in the mail from the state.

Minutes of Meetings

The *minutes* of a corporation's meetings provide a complete record of corporate formalities, and provide decisive proof that the corporation was functioning properly. *Put it in writing* should be the corporation's adage. In small corporations especially, it is too easy to make important decisions during the day over the telephone, during coffee breaks, or on the golf course, and neglect to record them. Writing down these decisions, however, is essential.

Even if you feel that you are too busy managing the corporation to attend to the detail of the corporate minutes, you need to realize that accurate, written reports of your corporate proceedings may be your only defense should a problem arise.

Without accurate minutes, a judge or an IRS agent may disallow many of the corporation's actions, including executive compensation and bonuses, retirement plans, and dividend disbursements.

The minutes of any meeting should show that the meeting was *properly called*, and that everyone there received adequate *notice* as required by the corporate bylaws. If a written notice of the meeting was sent out, a copy should be included, and if no notice was given, the appropriate *waiver of notice* should accompany the minutes. The minutes should be *signed* by all attending, indicating agreement that the minutes accurately reflect what took place in the meeting.

For every action that is taken during a meeting, the minutes should show that the matter was properly introduced, seconded, discussed, and agreed to by a voting majority as defined in the bylaws. The complete text of any resolution, contract, report, or other document adopted or ratified in a meeting also should appear in the minutes.

There is no standard format for minutes, but such items as the time, date, and place of the meeting, along with a list of all attending should be included. All actions by the board of directors should be recorded. Although minutes should be specific, they need not record every word of debate on every subject. They should concentrate on final decisions rather than discussion.

Required Meetings

Stockholders and directors are required to conduct *annual meetings*. The meetings must be documented within the corporate records. Most states allow the annual meetings to be held at a designated time and place either within or without of the state's boundaries. If you have incorporated in another state, review the laws pertaining to annual meetings in that state.

Stockholder's Meeting   Any business requiring stockholder approval may be addressed at the annual stockholders' meeting. The main topic of business is that of electing a board of directors to serve for the upcoming year. In addition, stockholders should adopt a resolution endorsing actions taken by the board of directors during the past year.

The text of any resolution adopted by the stockholders should be recorded in the minutes along with other documents that relate to the resolution. Actions taken on behalf of the corporation without a meeting must be authorized in writing by stockholders holding a majority of the voting power.

Director's Meeting

The primary purpose of the directors' meeting is to make the decisions that have been delegated to the directors by the stockholders. Directors should also use this opportunity to ratify actions they may have taken by resolution since their last meeting. Copies of resolutions adopted by the board of directors for the time period between meetings should be attached to the minutes providing comprehensive records of corporate formalities. The directors are also given responsibility in their meeting to elect officers for the following year.

Steps to Take before Meetings

The following should be done to make your meetings more productive and to comply with legal requirements.

- ✪ *Send the annual report to the stockholders.* In a small company, this may simply be a financial statement that details the profit and loss, and assets and liabilities of the corporation. The accuracy of all financial documents should be attested to by either the treasurer or company accountant. This step is not required for a small company that has no stockholders outside the family; however, it is always a good idea to provide this information annually to the stockholders anyway.

- ✪ *Have an agenda.* Regardless of the number of items to be discussed and whatever the number of stockholders or directors of the corporation, it is a good idea to go through the motions of putting an agenda together. The presence of an agenda notifies everyone involved of the topics of discussion for the meeting.

- ✪ *Update the list of stockholders.* If there have been any changes or transfers of stock, make sure the corporate books reflect the current situation. Where there are many stockholders, this list is required to verify voting rights of those attending the meetings.

- ✪ *Notify stockholders.* Stockholders must be notified in writing of any meetings usually no less than ten days or more than sixty days before the meeting is held. This notification must include the time, place, and purpose for the meeting.

✪ *Issue proxy statement.* When the notifications are sent out, it is a good idea to include proxy statements that will allow stockholders who will be unable to attend the meeting to participate by designating someone else to cast their votes for them.

✪ *Prepare yourself to answer questions.* Small corporations will usually be able to anticipate controversial topics, but larger corporations can be *blind-sided* by stockholders who may be unknown to any of the officers and directors. When a large number of stockholders will be present, it is a good idea to arrange for your attorneys and accountants to be at the meeting with any documentation they may need to consult. This material is likely to include all corporate records, contracts, leases, and tax data.

Steps to Take after Meetings

Once the meeting is concluded, the following should take place.

✪ *Write and distribute the meeting's minutes.* File your corporate minutes with your corporate records. The minutes should contain accurate and specific records about all decisions made during the meeting, and should be attested to by those attending.

✪ *Follow up on all approved actions.* Some actions taken in a meeting may not take effect until the Secretary of State is notified. This includes any changes to the articles of incorporation.

Resolutions

The use of resolutions provides another way to manage the formalities of a corporation. By definition, a resolution is a document that records actions that the directors (or in some cases, stockholders) *resolve* to take on behalf of the corporation. Resolutions may be included as part of the minutes of either directors or stockholders meetings, or they may be included separately into a *Resolutions* section of the corporate record book.

Most state corporate codes allow the board of directors to take an action without an official directors meeting, as long as all the directors sign a resolution in support of the action, and that resolution is ratified at the next meeting and filed with the minutes. The stockholders also may take action without a meeting as long as at least a majority of the voting rights consent in writing to the action.

In other words, a corporation can conduct nearly all of its business with resolutions. Simply keep the corporate resolutions in chronological order, and you will maintain a complete record of all the corporate activities. Then at each annual meeting, the shareholders will ratify all of the actions taken by resolution by the board of directors. You may find this method of maintaining corporate formalities to be much simpler and faster, and equally effective as holding special meetings and recording their minutes.

The typical resolution will contain the following:

- ✪ an indication as to whose resolution it is (i.e., directors or stockholders);

- ✪ the name of the corporation;

- ✪ the state of incorporation;

- ✪ an indication that the resolution contains the direction of at least a majority of those empowered to make decisions at this level;

- ✪ the text of the resolution itself;

- ✪ the date of the adoption of the resolution; and,

- ✪ the signatures of all of the individuals who have approved the resolution.

Money

Avoid combining personal funds or expenditures with those of the corporation. Separating the corporation's account from a personal account allows for ease in record keeping and bookkeeping. In addition, for tax purposes, it is necessary to put adequate explanations on corporate checks along with cash tickets and receipts for each transaction. Refrain from using a corporate check for personal expenses.

Signing Documents

When signing invoices, receipts, contracts or other documents on behalf of the corporation, always put the corporate name followed by the individual's name and title. Note the following example:

> ABC Corporation
> By: _____
> Jane Doe, President

By this, public notice is given that the named individual is signing on behalf of the corporation. This formality precludes *piercing the corporate veil.* By signing as an individual, the signor may be held liable for a corporate obligation.

Proxy

A proxy is an authorization given by the stockholder allowing the voting rights attached to the stockholder's shares to be exercised by a second party. Most states require that all proxies be written. A proxy is generally valid for six (6) months unless the following conditions exist: (a) the stockholder specifically states the time period for which a proxy is to be enforced, or (b) the proxy is coupled with an interest. In either case, the validity of a proxy cannot exceed the number of years in the applicable statute. A proxy is termed *irrevocable* if it is expressly stated and is coupled with an interest.

Bank Accounts

In order to open a bank account you will need to obtain, at a minimum, a federal tax ID number for your corporation. This number is obtained by filing **IRS FORM SS-4**. (see form 12, p.249.) The SS-4 can be submitted by fax and a tax number will be returned by fax—instructions are on the form. The form can also be obtained online at **www.irs.gov**. A sample filled-in form is included in Appendix A.

The bank will also require a *corporate resolution,* which is a standardized form normally provided by your bank. If you are incorporated in another state, you will have to qualify your *Foreign Corporation* in the state where you are opening the bank account.

Sale or Issue of Stock

In most corporations, the stock or equity issued to shareholders is *common voting stock.* There are other classes of stock such as *preferred* and *non-voting common* which are not discussed here. Initial stock being issued to the founders should be issued by the corporation as soon after incorporation as possible and should be so stated in the minutes.

Restricted Legend Language

All stock issued should carry the following legend, which is usually printed on the back of the certificate:

[Type on front of certificate:]

SUBJECT TO RESTRICTIONS APPEARING
ON BACK OF THIS CERTIFICATE

[Type on back of certificate:]

RESTRICTED LEGEND

The shares of stock represented by this certificate have not been registered under the Securities Act of 1933, as amended, and may not be sold or otherwise transferred without compliance with the registration provisions of the Act or unless the availability of an exemption from such registration provisions has been established, or unless sold pursuant to Rule 144 of the Securities Act of 1933.

Remember that all sales of stock constitute the sale of a security and applicable federal and state securities laws must be observed. Generally, this means that all investors should be supplied with a private placement memorandum and the company must make any filings required by federal or state securities laws on a timely basis.

Foreign Nationals

Persons who are neither citizens nor legal permanent residents of the United States are still free to start any type of business organization. The type that would be most advantageous would be the LLC because it allows foreign owners (unlike an S corporation) and it avoids corporate taxation (unlike a C corporation).

Two legal issues that foreign persons should be concerned with when starting a business are their *immigration status* and the *proper reporting* of the business's foreign owners.

Immigration Status

The ownership of a U.S. business does not automatically confer rights to enter or remain in the United States. Different types of *visas* are available to investors and business owners and each of these has strict requirements.

A visa to enter the United States may be permanent or temporary. *Permanent visas* for business owners usually require investments of $500,000 to $1,000,000 that result in the creation of new jobs. However, there are ways to obtain visas for smaller investments if structured right. For more information on this area you should consult an immigration attorney, or visit the Immigration and Naturalization website at:

www.bcis.gov

Temporary visas may be used by business owners to enter the U.S.; however, these are hard to obtain because in most cases the foreign person must prove that there are no U.S. residents qualified to take the job.

Reporting

United States businesses that own real property and are controlled by foreigners are required to file certain federal reports under the *International Investment Survey Act*, the *Agricultural Foreign Investment Disclosure Act*, and the *Foreign Investment in Real Property Tax Act (FIRPTA)*. If these laws apply to your business, you should consult an attorney who specializes in foreign ownership of U.S. businesses.

BUSINESS COMPARISON CHART

	Sole Proprietorship	General Partnership	Limited Partnership	Limited Liability Co.	Corporation C or S	Nonprofit Corporation
Liability Protection	No	No	For limited partners	For all members	For all shareholders	For all members
Taxes	Pass through	Pass through	Pass through	Pass through	S corps. pass through C corps. pay tax	None on Corp. Employees pay on wages
Minimum # of members	1	2	2	1	1	3
Startup fee	None	*MD $11[1] *DC $150[2] *VA $25[3]	MD $50 DC $70 VA $100	MD $50 DC $150 VA $100	*MD $40[4] *DC $185[5] *VA $75[6]	MD $40 DC $70 VA $75
Annual fee	None	MD $0 DC $150 VA $0	MD $0 DC $150 VA $50	MD $0 DC $185 VA $50	MD $100 *DC $185[5] *VA[7]	MD $0 DC $70 VA $50
Diff. classes of ownership	No	Yes	Yes	Yes	S corps. No C corps. Yes	No ownership Diff. classes of membership
Survives after Death	No	No	Yes	Yes	Yes	Yes
Best for	One person low-risk business or no assets	Low-risk business	Low-risk business with silent partners	All types of businesses	All types of businesses	Charitable, educational, religious, scientific

See following page for footnotes.

(1) *Filing for a General Partnership in Maryland is optional.*

(2) *Filing for a General Partnership in DC is required.*

(3) *Filing for a General Partnership in Virginia is optional. The fee for registration is paid every five years.*

(4) *Maryland minimum fee is $40. Fee is for up to 5,000 shares at no par value or $100,000. There is also an optional $50 expedite fee.*

(5) *D.C. minimum fee is $185. $150 filing fee plus initial license fee ($35 minimum for up to $100,000 worth of authorized stock).*

(6) *Virginia minimum fee is $75. $25 filing fee plus $50 charter fee for up to 25,000 shares or fraction thereof; additional $50 for each 25,000 shares or fraction thereof up to 1,000,000. If more than 1,000,000 shares, then the maximum fee is $2,500.*

(7) *Virginia minimum annual fee is $100 for up to 5,000 authorized shares and increases $30 for each additional 5,000 authorized shares up to a maximum of $1,700.*

Business Start-up Checklist

❏ Make your plan
- ❏ Obtain and read all relevant publications on your type of business
- ❏ Obtain and read all laws and regulations affecting your business
- ❏ Calculate whether your plan will produce a profit
- ❏ Plan your sources of capital
- ❏ Plan your sources of goods or services
- ❏ Plan your marketing efforts

❏ Choose your business name
- ❏ Check other business names and trademarks
- ❏ Reserve your name and register your trademark

❏ Choose the business form
- ❏ Prepare and file organizational papers
- ❏ Prepare and file fictitious name if necessary

❏ Choose the location
- ❏ Check competitors
- ❏ Check zoning

❏ Obtain necessary licenses
- ❏ City ❏ County
- ❏ State ❏ Federal

❏ Choose a bank
- ❏ Checking
- ❏ Credit card processing
- ❏ Loans

❏ Obtain necessary insurance
- ❏ Worker's Comp ❏ Automobile
- ❏ Liability ❏ Health
- ❏ Hazard ❏ Life/Disability

❏ File necessary federal tax registrations

❏ File necessary state tax registrations

❏ Set up a bookkeeping system

❏ Plan your hiring
- ❏ Obtain required posters
- ❏ Obtain or prepare employment application
- ❏ Obtain new hire tax forms
- ❏ Prepare employment policies
- ❏ Determine compliance with health and safety laws

❏ Plan your opening
- ❏ Obtain all necessary equipment and supplies
- ❏ Obtain all necessary inventory
- ❏ Do all necessary marketing and publicity
- ❏ Obtain all necessary forms and agreements
- ❏ Prepare your company policies on refunds, exchanges, returns

3 | NAMING YOUR BUSINESS

Before deciding upon a name for your business, you should be sure that no one else is using it already. Many business owners have spent thousands of dollars on publicity and printing, only to throw it all away because another company owned the name. A company that owns a name can take you to court and force you to stop using that name. The company can also sue you for damages if it thinks your use of the name cost it financial loss.

Preliminary Considerations

Even if you will be running a small local shop with no plans for expansion, you should at least check out whether the name has been *trademarked*. If someone else is using the same name anywhere in the country and has registered it as a federal trademark, they can sue you if you use it. If you plan to expand or to deal nationally, then you should do a thorough search of the name.

To see if someone has registered a fictitious or corporate name in your state that is the same as, or confusingly similar to, the one you have chosen, you should call or check your state's website at:

✪   for Maryland—**www.sdatcert3.resiusa.org/ucc-charter/CharterSearch_f.asp;**

✪   for the District of Columbia call the Department of Consumer and Regulatory Affairs at 202-442-4400; or,

✪   for Virginia—**www.state.va.us/scc/division/clk/diracc.htm.**

To do a national search, you should check trade directories and phone books of major cities. These can be found at many libraries and are usually reference books that cannot be checked out. You can also check with Thomson & Thomson to do a comprehensive trademark, copyright, title, and domain name search. They can be found at:

www.thomson-thomson.com

If you have a computer with Internet access, you can use it to search all of the yellow page listings in the U.S. at a number of sites at no charge. One website, **www.yellowpages.com**, offers free searches of yellow pages for all states at once.

To be sure that your use of the name does not violate someone else's trademark rights, you should have a trademark search done of the mark in the *United States Patent and Trademark Office (USPTO)*. In the past, this required a visit to their offices or the hiring of a search firm for over a hundred dollars. Now the trademark records are online and can be searched at **www.uspto.gov/main/trademarks.htm.** If you do not have access to the Internet you might be able to search at a public library or have one of their employees order an online search for you for a small fee. If this is not available to you, you can have the search conducted through a firm, such as Government Liason Services. They can be reached at:

Government Liaison Services, Inc.
200 N. Glebe Road Suite 321
Arlington, VA 22203
703-524-8200

They also offer searches of 100 trade directories and 4800 phone books.

No matter how thorough your search is, there is no guarantee that there is not a local user somewhere with rights to the mark. If, for example, you register a name for a new chain of restaurants and later find out that someone in Tucumcari, New Mexico, has been using the name longer than you, that person will still have the right to use the name, but just in that local area. If you do not want that restaurant to cause confusion with your chain, you can try to buy it out. Similarly, if you are operating a small business under a unique name and a law firm in New York writes and offers to buy the right to your name, you can assume that some large corporation wants to start a major expansion under your name.

The best way to make sure someone else does not already own a name you are using is to make up a name. Names such as Xerox, Kodak and Exxon were made up and did not have any meaning prior to their use. But remember that there are millions of businesses and even a name you make up may already be in use. Do a search anyway.

Fictitious Names

In Maryland, the District of Columbia, and Virginia, as in most states, unless you do business in your own legal name, you must register the name you are using, called a *fictitious name*. When you use a fictitious name, you are *doing business as* (d/b/a) whatever name you choose. The name must be registered with the state in Maryland and the District of Columbia, and with state and county in Virginia.

A *fictitious name registration* is good for five years in Maryland and two years in the District of Columbia. In Virginia, *registration of a fictitious trade name* is valid indefinitely and only lapses if you dissolve it.

Not every name must be registered. If your name is John Doe and you are operating a masonry business, you may operate your business as John Doe, Mason without registering it. But any other use of a name should be registered, such as:

Doe Masonry	Doe Masonry Company
Doe Company	Monument Masonry

Example: Legally, you would use the full name "John Doe d/b/a Doe Masonry."

You cannot use the words, *corporation, incorporated, corp.,* or *inc.* unless you are a corporation. However, corporations do not have to register the name they are using unless it is different from their registered corporate name.

Attorneys and professionals licensed in Maryland, the District of Columbia, and Virginia do not have to register the names under which they practice their profession.

As discussed previously, you should do some research to see if the name you intend to use is already being used by anyone else. Even persons who have not registered a name can acquire some legal rights to the name through mere use.

Some businesses have special requirements for registration of their fictitious names. For example, prior to obtaining its license from the state, a private investigative agency must obtain permission from the state for the use of its proposed name. Other businesses may have similar requirements. See Chapter 6 for a list of state regulated professions with references to the laws that apply to them.

(Appendix B has blank fictitious name applications for Maryland, the District of Columbia, and Virginia.)

Entity Names

A corporation does not have to register a fictitious name if it is using its legal name. The name of a corporation must contain one of the following words: *Incorporated, Inc., Company, Co., Corporation, Corp., Limited,* or *Ltd.* A Limited Liability Company name must contain one of the following words: *L.L.C., LLC,* or *Limited Liability Company*. And finally, a Limited Partnership name must contain one of the following words: *L.P., LP,* or *Limited Partnership*.

If the name of the entity does not contain one of the above words it will be rejected. It will also be rejected if the name used by it is already taken or is similar to the name of another entity, or if it uses a forbidden word such as *Bank* or *Trust*.

If a name you pick is taken by another company, you may be able to change it slightly and have it accepted. For example, if there is already a Tri-City Upholstery, Inc., and it is in a different county, you may be allowed to use Tri-City Upholstery of Arlington County, Inc. But, even if this is approved by the state, you might get sued by the other company if your business is close to theirs or there is a likelihood of confusion.

Also, do not have anything printed until your corporate papers are returned to you. Sometimes a name is approved over the phone and rejected when submitted. Once you have chosen a corporate name and know it is available, you should immediately register your corporation. If you are not ready to file yet, you can *reserve* the name with the state for a small fee.

If a corporation wants to do business under a name other than its corporate name, it can register a fictitious name such as *Doe Corporation d/b/a Doe Industries*. But if the name used leads people to believe that the business is not a corporation, the right to *limited liability* may be lost. If you use such a name, it should always be accompanied by the corporate name.

Professional Associations

Professionals such as attorneys, doctors, dentists, life insurance agents, and architects can form corporations, limited liability companies, or other entities in which to practice. These are better than general partnerships because they protect the professional from the malpractice of his or her co-workers.

By law, a *professional corporation* cannot use the usual corporate designations Inc., Corp., or Co. In Maryland, a professional corporation name must use the words *Professional Corporation*, *Professional Association*, *Chartered*, or an abbreviation thereof. In the District of Columbia, the words *Professional Corporation*, the abbreviation *P.C.*, or the word *Chartered* must be used. In Virginia, the words *Professional Corporation* or the abbreviation *P.C.* must be used.

A professional LLC in the District of Columbia or Virginia can use the words *Professional Limited Company*, or the abbreviations *P.L.L.C.* or *PLLC*.

Domain Names

With the Internet changing so rapidly, all of the rules for Internet names have not yet been worked out. Originally, the first person to reserve a name owned it, and enterprising souls bought up the names of most of the fortune 500 corporations. Then a few of the corporations went to court and the rule was developed that if a company had a trademark for a name, that company could stop someone else from using it if the other person did not have a trademark.

More recently, Congress made it illegal for *cybersquatters* to register the names of famous persons and companies.

You cannot yet get a trademark merely for using a domain name. Trademarks are granted for the use of a name *in commerce*. Once you have a valid trademark, you will be safe using it for your domain name.

In the 1980s, several now familiar top-level domains (TLDs) were introduced. These are the last three letters of the URL (uniform resource locator) such as .com, .edu, .gov, and .org. In 2001, several new TLDs were introduced including .biz, .info, and .name.

If you wish to protect your domain name, the best thing to do at this point is to get a trademark for it. To do this, you would have to use it on your goods or services. The following section gives some basic information about trademarks. To find out if a domain name is available, go to:

www.whois.net

or

www.networksolutions.com

Trademarks

As your business builds *goodwill*, its name will become more valuable and you will want to protect it from others who may wish to copy it. To protect a name used to describe your goods or services, you can register it as a trademark or a service mark with the Secretary of State if you are doing business in Maryland; the State Corporation Commission if you are in Virginia; or, federally with the United States Patent and Trademark Office, which is also where you would file for the District of Columbia.

A trademark is a word, phrase, symbol or design, or a combination of words, phrases, symbols or designs, that identifies and distinguishes the source of the goods of one party from those of others. A *service mark* is the same as a trademark, except that it identifies and distinguishes the source of a service rather than a product.

The name of your business is protected when you incorporate. A particular corporate name can only be registered by one company in each state. Any business name you use to market and identify your products or services may also be protected by registering the trademark.

Trademarks that are unusually creative are known as inherently distinctive marks. Typically, these marks consist of the following:

- ✪ unique logos or symbols, such as McDonalds golden arches;

- ✪ made-up words (coined or arbitrary marks), such as Exxon or Kodak;

- ✪ words that evoke images in the context of their usage (fanciful marks), such as Hungry Man dinners;

- ✪ words that are surprising in the context of their usage (arbitrary marks), such as The Gap for a clothing store; or,

- ✪ words that suggest qualities about a product or service (suggestive or evocative marks), such as Slim Fast for diet food products.

State Registration   State registration would be useful if you only expect to use your trademark within the state where you are incorporated. Federal registration would protect your mark anywhere in the country and is generally more advisable. The registration of a mark gives you exclusive use of the mark for the types of goods for which you register it. The only exception is persons who have already been using the mark. You cannot stop people who have been using the mark prior to your registration.

The procedure for state registration is simple and the cost is $50 in Maryland and $30 in Virginia. (The District of Columbia does not have trademark registration). In Maryland, check the availability of the name on the Secretary of State's website at:

www.sos.state.md.us/sos/admin2/html/trade.html

Before a mark can be registered, it must be used *in commerce*. For goods, this means it must be used on the goods themselves, or on containers, tags, labels, or displays of the goods. For services, it must be used in the sale or advertising of the services. The use must be in an actual transaction with a customer. A sample mailed to a friend is not an acceptable use.

For questions about filing trademarks in Maryland, call the Secretary of State at 410-974-5531. In Virginia, call the State Corporation Commission Securities & Retail Franchising Division at 804-371-9051. To file in the District of Colubia, follow the procedures for federal registration, discussed below.

Federal Registration   For federal registration, the procedure is a little more complicated. There are two types of applications depending upon whether you have already made actual use of the mark or whether you merely have an intention to use the mark in the future. For a trademark that has been in use, you must file an application form along with specimens showing actual use and a drawing of the mark that complies with all of the rules of the United States Patent and Trademark Office.

For an *Intent to Use* application you must file two separate forms—one when you make the initial application and the other after you have made actual use of the mark—as well as the specimens and drawing. Before a mark can be entitled to federal registration the use of the mark must be in *interstate commerce* (commerce with another state). The fee for registration is $335, but if you file an *Intent to Use* application there is a second fee of $150 for the filing after actual use. For more information on how to register a federal trademark, see

www.uspto.gov

You can also have your trademark registration handled by an attorney specializing in *intellectual property* (patents, trademarks, and copyrights). The costs generally include a search and filing of the application. An attorney can be helpful when you have to deal with the comments and requests, which are often sent from the USPTO after the filing, and must be addressed before the trademark is allowed.

4 | FINANCING YOUR BUSINESS

The way to finance your business is determined by the rate of growth for your business and how much risk of failure you can handle. Letting the business grow with its own income is the slowest but safest way to grow. Taking out a personal loan against your house to expand quickly is the fastest but riskiest way to grow.

Growing with Profits

Many successful businesses have started out with little money and used the profits to grow. If you have another source of income to live on (such as a job or a spouse) you can plow all the income of your fledgling business into growth. This route is sometimes known as *bootstrapping*.

Some businesses start as hobbies or part-time ventures on the weekend while the entrepreneur holds down a full time job. Many types of goods or service businesses can start this way. Even some multi-million dollar corporations, such as Apple Computer, started out this way.

This allows you to test your idea with little risk. If you find you are not good at running that type of business, or the time or location was not right for your idea, all you lose is the time you spent and your start-up capital.

However, a business can only grow so big from its own income. In many cases, as a business grows, it gets to a point where the orders are so big that money must be borrowed to produce the product to fill them. With this kind of order, there is the risk that if the customer cannot pay or goes bankrupt, the business will also go under. At such a point, a business owner should investigate the credit worthiness of the customer and weigh the risks. Some businesses have grown rapidly, some failed, and others have decided not to take the risk and stayed small. You can worry about that down the road.

Using Your Savings

If you have savings you can tap to get your business started, that is one of your the best sources. You will not have to pay high interest rates and you will not have to worry about paying someone back.

Home Equity

If you have owned your home for several years, it is possible that the equity has grown substantially and you can get a second mortgage to finance your business. If you have been in the home for many years and have a good record of paying your bills, some lenders will make second mortgages that exceed the equity. Just remember, if your business fails, you may lose your house.

Retirement Accounts

Be careful about borrowing from your retirement savings. There are tax penalties for borrowing from or against certain types of retirement accounts. Also, your future financial security may be lost if your business does not succeed.

Having Too Much Money and Too Little Sense

It probably does not seem possible to have too much money with which to start a business, but many businesses have failed for that reason. With plenty of start-up capital available, a business owner does not need to watch expenses and can become wasteful. Employees get used to lavish spending. Once the money runs out and the business must run on its own earnings, it fails.

Starting with the bare minimum forces a business to watch its expenses and be frugal. It necessitates finding the least expensive solutions to problems that crop up and creative ways to be productive.

Borrowing Money

It is extremely tempting to look to others to get the money to start a business. The risk of failure is less worrisome and the pressure is lower, but that is a problem with borrowing. If it is others' money, you do not have quite the same incentive to succeed as if everything you own is on the line.

Actually, you should be even more concerned when using the money of others. Your reputation should be more valuable than the money itself, which can always be replaced.

Family   Depending on how much money your family can spare, it may be the most comfortable or most uncomfortable source of funds for you. If you have been assured a large inheritance and your parents have more funds than they need to live on, you may be able to borrow against your inheritance without worry. It will be your money anyway and you need it much more now than you will ten or twenty or more years from now. If you lose it all, it is your own loss.

However, if you are borrowing your widowed mother's source of income, asking her to cash in a CD she lives on to finance your get-rich-quick scheme, you should have second thoughts about it. Stop and consider all the real reasons your business might not take off and what your mother would do without the income.

Friends   Borrowing from friends is like borrowing from family members. If you know they have the funds available and could survive a loss, you may want to risk it. If they would be loaning you their only resources, do not chance it.

Financial problems can be the worst thing for a relationship, whether it is a casual friendship or a long-term romantic involvement. Before you borrow from a friend, try to imagine what would happen if you could not pay it back and how you would feel if it caused the end of your relationship.

The ideal situation is if your friend were a co-venturer in your business and the burden would not be totally on you to see how the funds were spent. Still, realize that such a venture will put extra strain on the relationship.

Banks   In a way, a bank can be a more comfortable party from which to borrow because you do not have a personal relationship with them as you do with a friend or family member. If you fail, they will write your loan off rather than disown you. But a bank can also be the least comfortable party to borrow from because they will demand realistic projections and pressure you to perform. If you do not meet their expectations, they may call your loan just when you need it most.

The best thing about a bank loan is that they will require you to do your homework. You must have plans that make sense to a banker. If they approve your loan, you know that your plans are at least reasonable.

Bank loans are not cheap or easy. You will be paying a good interest rate, and you will have to put up collateral. If your business does not have equipment or receivables, they may require you to put up your house and other personal property to guarantee the loan. If that is not enough, you and your partners, directors, and possibly principal shareholders will most likely have to sign personally on the loans.

Banks are a little easier to deal with when you get a *Small Business Administration (SBA)* loan. That is because the SBA guarantees that it will pay the bank if you default on the loan. SBA loans are obtained through local bank branches.

You may also seek financing from a *Small Business Investment Corporation (SBIC)*, which is a privately owned investment fund licensed by the SBA. Investments by SBIC's have contributed to growth of companies such as FedEx, Intel, Callaway Golf, America Online and Outback Steakhouse. Information on SBICs can be found at:

www.sba.gov/INV/overview.html

Credit Cards   Borrowing against a credit card is one of the fastest growing ways of financing a business, but it can be one of the most expensive ways. The rates can go higher than twenty percent, but many cards offer lower rates and some people are able to get numerous cards. Some successful businesses have used the personal credit cards to get off the ground or to weather through a cash crunch. However, if the business does not begin to generate the cash to make the payments, you could soon end up in bankruptcy. A good strategy is only to use credit cards for a long-term asset like a computer or for something that will quickly generate cash, like buying inventory to fill an order. Do not use credit cards to pay expenses that are not generating revenue.

Getting a Rich Partner
One of the best business combinations is a young entrepreneur with ideas and ambition and a retired investor with business experience and money. Together they can supply everything the business needs.

To find such a partner, be creative. You should have investigated the business you are starting and know others who have been in such businesses. Have any of them had partners retire over the last few years? Are any of them planning to phase out of the business?

If you find a partner, it is very important that you have a *written agreement* that clearly defines, among other things, ownership percentages, capital contributions, and the rights of the partners if one of them dies or wants to sell their interest. This type of agreement is often called a *buy-sell agreement* or a *founders agreement*. The buy-out provisions can be funded by a life insurance policy, which eases the out of pocket cash requirements for the company.

Developing a Business Plan

As you commence your new business, it would behoove you to sit down and develop a business plan for your company. A business plan allows you to address the essential issues of your new business, such as defining the unique aspects of your product or service and planning to capture a share of the market. The financial statement accompanying the plan will give you and possibly investors a road map of the next three to five years of your business.

You are encouraged to initially write your own business plan. If you need assistance in getting started there are a variety of business plan software products such as *Biz Plan Builder 8* (**www.JIAN.com**) as well as numerous examples on the Internet. If you feel you need to work on the plan, there are a variety of business plan consultants who can assist you in completing the final product. The SBA website is also helpful, at:

www.sba.gov/starting_business/planning/basic.html

Selling Shares of Your Business

Passive investors are one of the best sources of capital for your business. Often, you can retain full control of the business and if it happens to fail you have no obligation to them. Unfortunately, few silent investors are interested in new businesses. It is only after you have proven your concept to be successful and built up a rather large enterprise, that you will be able to attract such investors.

A typical way to obtain money from investors is to sell stock to them. For this, the best type of business entity is the corporation. It gives you almost unlimited flexibility in the number and kinds of shares of stock you can issue. Selling membership interests in a limited liability company or limited partnership interests in a limited partnership are also legitimate ways to raise capital for your business.

Understanding Securities Laws

When you sell *equity* (stock), *partnership interests*, or *membership interests* in your business you must comply with the federal and state laws and regulations regarding the sale of *securities*. Both the state and federal governments have long and complicated laws dealing with the sales of securities. There are also hundreds of court cases attempting to explain what these laws mean. A thorough explanation of this area of law is beyond the scope of this book.

Basically, securities have been held to exist in any case, in which a person provides money to someone with the expectation that he or she will get a profit through the efforts of that person. This can apply to any situation where someone buys stock in or makes a loan to your business. What the laws require is disclosure of the risks involved, and in some cases, registration of the securities with the government. There are exemptions from registration, such as if the securities are sold to a limited number of people in a private offering with no general advertising. On the federal side, one of the principal exemptions is known as *Regulation D* or *Reg. D.*

Raising capital from the sale of your company's securities is a time honored means to raise capital. There are basically two types of offerings—public and private. The *public offering* requires a registration statement to be filed, reviewed, and approved by the *Securities and Exchange Commission (SEC)* in Washington, DC and usually one or more state securities agencies. The public offering is quite time consuming and expensive but the amounts of capital raised can be quite large.

The *private offering* is the means used by most new business to raise their initial capital. It is far less costly than a public offering and is not subject to the review process of the SEC and state agencies. The sale is accomplished through the use of an offering document known as a private placement memorandum or confidential offering document, which is prepared by securities counsel. There are federal and state filings required when sales are made. You should consult a specialist in securities laws before issuing any security. You can often get an introductory consultation at a reasonable rate to learn your options. (see **www.washingtonpractice.com**). Please remember, a business plan, by itself, is not a proper offering documents to sell securities. For information on federal securities regulations visit:

www.SEC.gov

Using the Internet to Find Capital

At the present time, you cannot offer securities over the Internet in a private placement transaction unless you restrict access to the offer to certain high net worth individuals known as *accredited investors* and you pre-screen those individuals so that viewing the offer is by password access only. You can offer securities on the Internet if you file for a public offering with the SEC and the states and observe other somewhat complicated rules regarding Internet sales.

The Internet does have some sources of capital listed. Be cautious about paying upfront fees to any broker. Most legitimate brokers receive a commission or fee based upon results delivered not promised. The following organizations' websites may be helpful:

America's Business Funding Directory	www.businessfinance.com
Angel Capital Electronic Network (SBA)	www.sba.gov
Inc. Magazine	www.inc.com
NVST	www.nvst.com
The Capital Network	www.thecapitalnetwork.com

5 | LOCATING YOUR BUSINESS

The right location for your business will be determined by what type of business it is and how fast you expect it to grow. For some types of businesses, the location will not be important to your success or failure, and in others it will be crucial.

Working out of Your Home

Many small businesses get started out of the home. Chapter 6 discusses the legalities of home businesses. This section discusses the practicalities.

Starting a business out of your home can save you the rent, electricity, insurance, and other costs of setting up at another location. For some people this is ideal, and they can combine their home and work duties easily and efficiently. For other people, it is a disaster. A spouse, children, neighbors, television, and household chores can be so distracting that no other work gets done.

Since residential rates are usually lower than business lines, many people use their residential telephone line to conduct business or add a second residential line. However, if you wish to be listed in the yellow pages, you will need to have a business line in your home. If you are running two or more types of businesses, you can probably add their names as additional listings on the original number and avoid paying for another business line.

You also should consider whether the type of business you are starting is compatible with a home office. For example, if your business mostly consists of making phone calls or calling clients, then the home may be an ideal place to run it. If your clients need to visit you or you will need daily pickups and deliveries by truck, then the home may not be a good location. This is discussed in more detail in the next chapter.

Choosing a Retail Site

For most types of retail stores the location is of prime importance. Such things to consider are how close it is to your potential customers, how visible it is to the public, and how accessible it is to both cars and pedestrians. The attractiveness and safety should also be considered.

Location would be less important for a business that was the only one of its kind in the area. For example, if there were only one moped parts dealer or Armenian restaurant in a metropolitan area, people would have to come to wherever you are if they want your products or services. However, even with such businesses, keep in mind that there is competition. People who want moped parts can order them by mail and restaurant customers can choose another type of cuisine.

You should look up all the businesses similar to yours in the phone book and mark them on a map. For some businesses, like dry cleaners, you would want to be far from the others. But for other businesses, like antique stores, you would want to be near the others. (Antique stores usually do not carry the same things, they do not compete, and people like to go to an antique district and visit all the shops.)

Choosing Office, Manufacturing, or Warehouse Space

If your business will be the type where customers will not come to you, then locating it near customers is not as much of a concern and you can probably save money by locating away from the high traffic, central business districts. However, you should consider the convenience for employees and not locate in an area that would be unattractive to them, or too far from where they would likely live.

For manufacturing or warehouse operations, you should consider your proximity to a post office, trucking company or rail line. Where several sites are available you might consider which one has the earliest or most convenient pick-up schedule for the carriers you plan to use.

Leasing a Site

A lease of space can be one of the biggest expenses of a small business so you should do a lot of homework before signing one. There are a lot of terms in a commercial lease that can make or break your business. The most critical are zoning restrictions, signage, ADA compliance, expansion, renewal, guaranty, duty to open, and sublease.

Zoning Restrictions

Before signing a lease, you should be sure all your business functions are allowed by the *zoning* of the property.

In some shopping centers, existing tenants have guarantees that other tenants do not compete with them. For example, if you plan to open a restaurant and bakery you may be forbidden to sell carry out baked goods if the supermarket has a bakery and a *noncompete* clause.

Signage

Zoning laws, sign laws, and property restrictions regulate business signs. If you rent a hidden location with no possibility for adequate *signage*, your business will have a lot smaller chance of success than with a more visible site or much larger sign.

ADA Compliance   The *Americans with Disabilities Act (ADA)* requires that *reasonable accommodations* be made to make businesses accessible to the handicapped. When a business is remodeled many more changes are required than if no remodeling is done. When renting space you should be sure that it complies with the law, or that the landlord will be responsible for *compliance*. Be aware of the full costs you will bear.

Expansion   As your business grows, you may need to expand your space. You should know your options before you sign the lease. Perhaps you can take over adjoining units when those leases expire.

Renewal   Location is a key to success for some businesses. If you spend five years building up a clientele, you do not want someone to take over your locale at the end of your lease. Therefore, you should have a *renewal clause* on your lease. Usually this allows an increase in rent based on inflation.

Guaranty   Most landlords of commercial space will not rent to a small corporation without a *personal guaranty* of the lease. This is a very risky thing for a new business owner to do. The lifetime rent on a long term commercial lease can be hundreds of thousands of dollars and if your business fails the last thing you want to do is be personally responsible for five years of rent.

Where space is scarce or a location is hot, a landlord can get the guarantees demanded and there is nothing you can do about it (except perhaps set up an asset protection plan ahead of time). But where several units are vacant or the commercial rental market is soft, often you can negotiate out of the personal guaranty. If the lease is five years, maybe you can get away with a guaranty of just the first year. Give it a try.

Duty to Open   Some shopping centers have rules requiring all shops to be open certain hours. If you cannot afford to staff it the whole time required or if you have religious or other reasons that make this a problem, you should negotiate it out of the lease or find another location.

Sublease   At some point you may decide to sell your business, and in many cases the location is the most valuable aspect of it. For this reason you should be sure that you have the right to either *assign* your lease or to *sublease* the property. If this is impossible, one way around a prohibition is to incorporate your business before signing the lease and then when you sell the business, sell the stock. But some lease clauses prohibit transfer of *any interest* in the business, so read the lease carefully.

Buying a Site

If you are experienced with owning rental property you will probably be more inclined to buy a site for your business. If you have no experience with real estate, you should probably rent and not take on the extra cost and responsibility of property ownership.

One reason to buy your site is that you can build up equity. Rather than pay rent to a landlord, you can pay off a mortgage and eventually own the property.

Separating the Ownership

One risk in buying a business site is that if the business encounters financial difficulties, the creditors pursue the building as well. For this reason most people who buy a site for their business keep the ownership out of the business. For example, the business will be a corporation and the real estate will be owned personally by the owner or by a trust unrelated to the business.

Expansion

Before buying a site you should consider the growth potential of your business. If it grows quickly will you be able to expand at that site or will you have to move? Might the property next door be available for sale in the future if you need it? Can you get an *option* on it?

If the site is a good investment whether or not you have your business then by all means buy it. But if its main use is for your business, think twice.

Zoning

Some of the concerns when buying a site are the same as when renting. You will want to make sure that the zoning permits the type of business you wish to start, or that you can get a *variance* without a large expense or delay. Be aware that just because a business is now using the site does not mean that you can expand or remodel the business at that site. Check with the zoning department and find out exactly what is allowed.

Signs

Signs are another concern. Some cities have regulated signs and do not allow new or larger ones. Some businesses have used these laws to get publicity. For example, a car dealer who was told to take down a large number of American flags on his lot filed a federal lawsuit and rallied the community behind him.

ADA Compliance

ADA compliance is another concern when buying a commercial building. Find out from the building department if the building is in compliance or determine what needs to be done to put it in compliance. If you remodel, the requirements may be stricter.

NOTE: *When dealing with public officials, keep in mind that they do not always know what the law is, or do not accurately explain it. They often try to intimidate people into doing things that are not required by law. Read the requirements yourself and question the officials if they seem to be interpreting it wrong. Seek legal advice if officials refuse to reexamine the law or move away from an erroneous position.*

Consider that keeping public officials happy may be worth the price. If you are already doing something they have overlooked, do not make an issue over a little thing they want changed, or they may subject you to a full inspection or audit.

Checking Governmental Regulations

When looking for a site for your business, you should investigate the different governmental regulations in your area. For example, a location just outside the city or county limits might have a lower licensing fee, a lower sales tax rate, and less strict sign requirements.

6 LICENSING YOUR BUSINESS

Governmental licenses, permits, and zoning regulations are a part of any business. Ignoring these requirements can cost you your business as well as result in criminal penalties.

Occupational Licenses and Zoning

The District of Columbia requires all businesses that make over $2000 a year to register and obtain a *Master Business License*. Maryland and Virginia require *occupational business licenses* that are obtained from various state agencies. Businesses that do work in Maryland, Virginia, and the District of Columbia, such as builders, must obtain a license from each jurisdiction in which they do work. (However, this may not have to be done until you actually begin a job in a particular jurisdiction.)

Be sure to find out if zoning allows your type of business before buying or leasing property. The licensing departments will check the zoning before issuing your license.

If you will be preparing or serving food, you will need to check with the local health department to be sure that the premises complies with their regulations. In some areas, if food has been served on the premises in the past, there is no problem getting a license. If food has never been served on the premises, then the property must comply with all the newest regulations. This can be very costly.

Home Businesses

The local jurisdictions that surround the District of Columbia do not have special laws regulating home-based business. However, people wanting to start a new business out of their home should consult the local and state government to ascertain the business license and zoning requirements or restrictions for home businesses in general and their occupation or business in particular. Problems sometimes arise when people attempt to start a business in their home and have not consulted the local zoning laws. Using common sense as to what types of business are appropriate for operating in a home could save many problems with authorities and neighbors too.

If a person regularly parks commercial trucks and equipment on his or her property, has delivery trucks coming and going, or allows employees to park along the street, there will probably be complaints from neighbors and the authorities will probably take legal action. But if a person's business consists merely of making phone calls out of the home and keeping supplies there, the problem may never become an issue.

Maryland or Virginia state business licenses are granted to occupations and businesses by various state agencies. A state license does not necessarily mean that you can set up shop in your home.

For hundreds of years people performed income-producing activities in their homes. Court battles with the government are expensive and probably not worth the effort for a small business. The best course of action is to keep a low profile. Using a post office box for the business is sometimes helpful in diverting attention away from the residence.

Maryland Start-Up Information

Business Licensing and Startup Information

The State of Maryland Business Website is **www.mdbusiness.state.md.us**. Under the heading *Business Assistance*, there are connections to helpful pages for *Starting a Business* and *Small Business Assistance*. You can download or print the *Guide to Legal Aspects of Doing Business in Maryland*.

The State of Maryland *Business License Information System (BLIS)* is available online at **www.blis.state.md.us/client/Blis.jsp**. Use it to determine which state-issued licenses and permits are needed for your business. After determining your licensing needs, check with the following three governmental bodies to determine what additional licenses may be needed to operate a business in Maryland.

Maryland Department of Assessments and Taxation (MDAT).

✪   For a legal entity, such as a corporation, LLC, LLP, LP, business trust or foreign corporation, call MDAT at 410-767-1340. Stock corporations must also contact the Maryland Office of the Attorney General at 410-576-6300.

✪   To *register a general partnership or sole proprietorship*, call 410-767-4991.

✪   To obtain a *trade name application* for *doing business as (DBA)*, call 410-767-1340.

✪   For *personal property assessment* questions, call 410-767-1170.

✪   To *reserve a business name* for future use, call 410-767-1340.

Maryland Comptroller of the Treasury.

Comptroller of Maryland
Revenue Administration Center
Annapolis, Maryland 21411-0001

Use the **COMBINED REGISTRATION APPLICATION** (see form 2, p.217) or go online to register for the tax accounts you need at:

https://interactive.marylandtaxes.com/comptrollercra.

Additional registrations are required in written form for motor fuel, alcohol and tobacco taxes. The forms can be printed or downloaded from the above web page.

Maryland Clerk of the Circuit Court Offices.

Check with the Clerk's Office in your county to determine if you need a business license. You can refer to the following website for information regarding the Maryland State Division of Occupational and Professional Licensing:

www.dllr.state.md.us/license/occprof/lawindex.htm

Montgomery and Prince George's Counties

In Montgomery County and Prince George's County, licenses are handled in the following manner.

Business licenses in *Montgomery County* consist of a trader (a store front that buys and sells inventory), a vendor's license of several types, non-profit benefits such as performances or festivals, an agricultural producer wanting to sell produce along right-of-ways, construction (new homes from the ground up and commercial buildings), electricians and electrical contractors, sign installers, vending machines, cigarette sales, plumbers, gas fitters, and soda fountains. Merchants engaged in motor vehicle repair, maintenance, or towing must also be licensed.

Renewal of all business licenses are in March of each year. Businesses must have their new license posted by May 1st of every year.

For further information, contact the Division of Consumer Affairs at 240-777-3636, and the Montgomery County Circuit Court at:

Montgomery County Circuit Court
License Department, Room 111
50 Maryland Avenue
Rockville, Maryland 20850
240-777-9460
www.montgomerycountymd.gov/mc/judicial/circuit/services
/crtclerk/license/license.html

The Clerk of the Circuit Court Business License Department issues licenses and accepts renewals of Licenses for Maryland businesses located with Prince George's County. For more information, contact:

Licensing Division
County Administration Building, Room L 15
14741 Governor Oden Bowie Drive
Upper Marlboro, Maryland 20772.
www.goprincegeorgescounty.com

Virginia Start-Up Information

Licensing   The official Commonwealth of Virginia (Virginia Information Providers Network) website is **www.vipnet.org/cmsportal**. Go to the site and follow directions to the step-by-step guide to starting a business in Virginia. First click on the "Business and Employment" link and then click on "Starting a Business." Additionally, you can use this Web page for business and professional resources:

www.vipnet.org/cmsportal/employment_850/professional_941/index.html

The *Commonwealth of Virginia License and Permit Guide* website, **www.dba.state.va.us/licenses**, is used to locate the state agency that regulates businesses by type or activity. It has connections to each agency and directions there for licenses and fees. The *Business Registration Guide* was compiled by the State Corporation Commission, the VA Employment Commission, and the Department of Taxation to help new businesses with licensing and registering a business in Virginia. It is available at:

www.state.va.us/scc/division/clk/brg.htm

Fairfax County. The following information must be supplied to the Fairfax County Department of Tax Administration in order to obtain a business license: the owner's name, trade name, business address, nature (description) of business, estimated first year gross receipts, and start date. You should also check with the Zoning Administration Division (Zoning Permit Review Branch) of the Department of Planning and Zoning to determine if regulatory permits are required for your place of business. The address is:

Zoning Administration Division
Department of Planning and Zoning
12055 Government Center Parkway, Second Floor, Suite 250
Fairfax, Virginia, 22035
703-222-1082 or 703-222-5504

There is no cost associated with the issuance of an actual business license. However, there is a tax that must be paid prior to issuance of said license. This tax is determined by multiplying the gross receipts or gross purchases (if wholesale) of the business by an assigned tax rate. The tax rate is determined by the *nature of the business.* Current tax rates are as follows:

- gross receipts/purchases $10,000 and under are not required to file for a business license;

- gross receipts/purchases between $10,001—$50,000 pay a flat fee of $30.00;

- gross receipts/purchases between $50,001—$100,000 pay a flat fee of $50.00; and,

- for gross receipts/purchases over $l00,001, the tax rate is determined by the business classification.

Refer to **www.co.fairfax.va.us/dta/bpol_rate_schedule.htm** or **www.co.fairfax .va.us/dta/bpol.htm** for more information about business classifications and rates.

Regardless of gross income/purchases, if the business has tangible personal property, and that property was located in Fairfax County on January 1st of the current year, a *Return of Business Tangible Personal Property* is required to be filed by May 1st of the current year with the Department of Tax Administration.

Arlington County. The *Guide for Starting a Business* is available at **www.smart-place.org/small_bus/guide.html**. It contains most of the information you might need for starting a business in Arlington County and also the State information for Virginia, including site and zoning considerations, licenses and occupancy permits, various taxes, registration, etc. The tax rates for obtaining a business license are similar if not the same as those for Fairfax County. For more information on doing business in Arlington, contact:

Arlington Economic Development
1100 North Glebe Road, Suite 1500
Arlington, Virginia 22201
703-228-0800
Fax: 703-228-3574
Arlington@smartplace.org.

Loudoun County. As with Fairfax and Arlington, there is a business tax that must be paid before the issuance of a business license in Loudoun County. Most businesses, including home-based ones, are subject to a gross receipts tax and a personal property tax on business equipment. You are required to register your business with the *Commissioner of the Revenue* within thirty days of commencing business. The tax for the first year of business is $30 for most businesses. After that, the tax is based on the previous year's gross receipts. For more information contact:

Commissioner of the Revenue
1 Harrison Street, SE, First Floor
Leesburg, VA 20175
703-777-0260
www.loudoun.gov/cor/home.htm
cor@loudoun.gov

The City of Alexandria. The *Guide to Establishing a Business in the City of Alexandria* is available on the City of Alexandria website at the following address: **www.ci.alexandria.va.us/city/busguide/pdf/bus_guide01.pdf**. This online booklet contains most of the information you will need to start a business in Alexandria. It also has information about tax saving business incentives for starting or moving your business to Alexandria.

District of Columbia Start-Up Information

Under a new law, the *Master Business License and Registration Program* requires that all businesses that generate more than $2,000 in annual gross receipts in the District of Columbia must obtain a *Master Business License*. These businesses include the self-employed, profit and non-profit, individuals, organizations, and associations, whether located in commercial or residential neighborhoods, in the home, office, or even out of a briefcase. Visit **http://mblr.dc.gov/main.shtm** to read about the regulations and apply online for a license.

You can visit the District of Columbia website at **www.dc.gov** or go directly to the business startup page at **http://brc.dc.gov/whattodo/business** to see a checklist for starting your profit or non-profit business and tips for obtaining financing or registering a trade name.

Federal Licenses

Currently, few businesses require federal registration. If you are in any of the types of businesses listed below, you should check with the listed federal agency.

Radio or television stations or manufacturers of equipment emitting radio waves:

Federal Communications Commission
1919 M Street, NW
Washington, DC 20550
www.fcc.gov

Manufacturers of alcohol, tobacco or firearms:

Bureau of Alcohol, Tobacco and Firearms, Treasury Department
1200 Pennsylvania Ave., NW
Washington, DC 20226
www.atf.treas.gov

Securities brokers and providers of investment advice:

Securities and Exchange Commission
450—5th Street NW
Washington, DC 20549
www.sec.gov

Manufacturers of drugs and processors of meat:

Food and Drug Administration
5600 Fishers Lane
Rockville, MD 28057
www.fda.gov

Interstate carriers:

Surface Transportation Board
12th St. & Constitution Ave. NW
Washington, DC 20423
www.stb.dot.gov

Exporting:

Bureau of Export Administration
Department of Commerce
14th St. & Constitution Ave., NW
Washington, DC 20220
www.bxa.doc.gov

7 | CONTRACT LAWS

As a business owner, you need to know the basics of forming a simple contract for your transactions with both customers and vendors. There is a lot of erroneous information out there about what is the law. Relying on such information can cost you money. This chapter will give you a quick overview of the principles that apply to your transactions and the pitfalls to avoid. If you face more complicated contract questions, you should consult a law library or an attorney familiar with small business law.

Traditional Contract Law

A contract is not legal unless three elements are present: *offer*, *acceptance*, and *consideration*. As a business owner, the important things to remember about a contract are as follows.

- ✪ If you make an offer to someone, it may result in a binding contract, even if you change your mind or find out it was a bad deal for you.

- ✪ Unless an offer is accepted and both parties agree to the same terms, there is no contract.

✪ A contract does not always have to be in writing. Some laws require certain contracts to be in writing, but as a general rule an oral contract is legal. The problem is in proving that the contract existed.

✪ Without *consideration* (the exchange of something of value or mutual promises) there is not a valid contract.

Additionally, some of the most important rules for the business owner are as follows.

✪ *An advertisement is not an offer.* Suppose you put an ad in the newspaper offering "New IBM computers only $1995," but there is a typo in the ad and it says "$19.95." Can people come in and say, "I accept, here's my $19.95," creating a legal contract? Fortunately, no. Courts have ruled that the ad is not an offer that a person can accept. It is an invitation to make an offer, which the business can accept or reject.

✪ *The same rule applies to the price tag on an item.* If someone switches price tags on your merchandise, or if you accidentally put the wrong price on it, you are not required by law to sell it at that price. If you intentionally put the wrong price, however, you may be liable under the *bait and switch* law. Many merchants honor a mistaken price just because refusing to would constitute bad will and might result in the loss of a customer.

✪ *When a person makes an offer, several things may happen.* It may be accepted, creating a legal contract. It may be rejected. It may expire before it has been accepted. Or, it may be withdrawn before acceptance. A contract may expire either by a date made in the offer ("This offer remains open until noon on January 29, 2004") or after a *reasonable* amount of time. What is reasonable is a legal question that a court must decide. If someone makes you an offer to sell goods, clearly you cannot come back five years later and accept. Can you accept a week later or a month later and create a legal contract? That depends on the type of goods and the circumstances.

✪ *A person accepting an offer cannot add any terms to it.* If you offer to sell a car for $1,000, and the other party says they accept as long as you put new tires on it, there is no contract. An acceptance with changed terms is considered a rejection and a counteroffer.

✪ *When someone rejects your offer and makes a counteroffer, a contract can be created by your acceptance of the counteroffer.*

These rules can affect your business on a daily basis. Suppose you offer to sell something to one customer over the phone, and five minutes later another customer walks in and offers you more for it. To protect yourself, you should call the first customer and withdraw your offer before accepting the offer of the second customer. If the first customer accepts before you have withdrawn your offer, you may be sued if you have sold the item to the second customer.

There are a few exceptions to the basic rules of contracts.

✪ *Consent to a contract must be voluntary.* If it is made under a threat, the contract is not valid. If a business refuses to give a person's car back unless they pay $200 for changing the oil, the customer could probably sue and get the $200 back.

✪ *Contracts to do illegal acts or acts against public policy are not enforceable.* If an electrician signs a contract to put illegal wiring in a house, the customer could probably not force him to fulfill the contract because the court would refuse to require an illegal act.

✪ *If either party to an offer dies, then the offer expires and cannot be accepted by the heirs.* If a painter is hired to paint a portrait, and dies before completing it, his wife cannot finish it and require payment. However, a corporation does not die, even if its owners die. If a corporation is hired to build a house and the owner dies, the heirs may take over the corporation and finish the job and require payment.

✪ *Contracts made under misrepresentation are not enforceable.* For example, if someone tells you a car has 35,000 miles on it and you later discover it has 135,000 miles, you may be able to *rescind* the contract for *fraud* and *misrepresentation*. However, if the seller knew the car has 135,000 miles on it, and you assumed it had 35,000 but did not ask, you probably could not rescind the contract.

✪ *A contract may be rescinded a mutual mistake was made.* For example, if both you and the seller thought the car had 35,000 miles on it and both relied on that assumption, the contract could be rescinded.

Statutory Contract Law

The previous section discussed the basics of contract law. These laws are not usually stated in the statutes, but judges have used these legal principles to decide cases over the past few hundreds of years. In recent times, legislatures have made numerous exceptions to these principles. In most cases, these laws have been passed when the legislature felt that the traditional law was not fair. An important example is the *Statute of Frauds*.

Statute of Frauds   *Statute of Frauds* state the circumstances in which a contract must be *in writing* to be valid. Some people believe a contract is not valid unless it is in writing, but that is not so. Only those types of contracts mentioned in the statutes of frauds must be in writing. Oral contracts are valid, but much harder to prove in court than one that is in writing. It is always a good idea to write things down.

In general, *Statute of Frauds* require that contracts must be in writing in the following situations:

- ✪ sales of any interest in real estate;

- ✪ leases of goods or real estate over one year;

- ✪ guarantees of debts of another person;

- ✪ sales of goods of over $500;

- ✪ sales of personal property of over $5,000;

- ✪ agreements that take over one year to complete; and,

- ✪ sales of securities.

Due to the alleged unfair practices by some types of businesses, laws have been passed controlling the types of contracts they may use. Most notable among these are health clubs and door-to-door solicitations. The laws covering these businesses usually give the consumer a certain time to cancel the contract. These laws are described in Chapter 12.

Preparing your Contracts

Before you open your business, you should obtain or prepare the contracts or policies you will use in your business. In some businesses, such as a restaurant, you will not need much. Perhaps you will want a sign near the entrance stating "shirt and shoes required" or "diners must be seated by 10:30 p.m."

However, if you are a building contractor or a similar business, you will need detailed contracts to use with your customers. If you do not clearly spell out your rights and obligations, you may end up in court and lose thousands of dollars in profits.

An attorney who is experienced in the subject can best prepare an effective contract to meet the needs of your business. However, since this may be too expensive for your new operation, you may want to go elsewhere. You may want to look at contracts from trade associations, legal form books, and other businesses like yours. You should obtain as many different contracts as possible, compare them, and decide which terms are most comfortable for you.

In addition, you can find legal forms at **www.uslegalforms.com** and **www.legallawforms.com**. Legal forms software can be found at **www.lawbookshop.com**. Keep in mind that preprinted forms can only get you so far—they are not specifically designed for your particular situation. All knowledgeable contact lawyers will tell you to be cautious, because drafting a contract is as much an art as a science.

8 | INSURANCE

Few laws require you to have insurance, but if you are uninsured, you may face liability that can ruin your business. You should be aware of the types of insurance available and weigh the risks of a loss against the cost of a policy.

Be aware that there can be a wide range of prices and coverage in insurance policies. You should get at least three quotes from different insurance agents and ask each one to explain the benefits of his or her policy.

Workers' Compensation

To protect yourself from litigation, you may wish to carry workers' compensation insurance even if it is not required.

This insurance can be obtained from most insurance companies and is not expensive, at least for low-risk occupations. If you have such coverage, you are protected against potentially ruinous claims by employees or their heirs in case of accident or death.

For high-risk occupations such as roofing, worker's compensation insurance can be very expensive, sometimes thirty to fifty cents for each dollar of payroll. For this reason, construction companies often try to gain exemption through hiring independent contractors or through hiring only a few employees and making them officers of the business. The requirements for the exemptions are strict, however, and anyone intending to obtain an exemption should first check with an attorney specializing in workers' compensation to be sure to do it right.

Maryland   The Maryland workers' compensation law requires employers to acquire insurance to pay compensation to employees for work-related injuries, occupational diseases, or deaths, regardless of fault. It makes no difference if the employer, the injured employee, a co-worker, or a non-employee is to blame. This *no-fault* compensation is the employee's only remedy against the employer. The injured employee may not sue the employer in an attempt to recover greater compensation. The compensation includes:

- ✪   medical and rehabilitation expenses;

- ✪   a percentage of lost wages; and,

- ✪   an amount for impairment of earning capacity.

The cost of the insurance varies with the accident rate of the industry and of the specific employer. Thus, an employer has a financial incentive to keep a safe and healthy work environment, to hire competent and careful employees, and to train and discipline them in on the job safety and health practices.

Failing to have workers' compensation insurance is a misdemeanor and is subject to punishment by fine between $500 and $5,000 or by imprisonment for not more than one year or both.

The entire cost of workers' compensation insurance must be paid by the employer. It is a misdemeanor to deduct the amount of the premiums from the employee's wages.

If an employee has an accident that results in disability for more than three days, the employer is responsible for reporting the accident to the *Workers' Compensation Commission* within ten days of the accident. The employer must use the *First Report of Injury* form that can be obtained from:

Maryland Workers' Compensation Commission
10 East Baltimore Street
Baltimore, Maryland 21202-1641
410-864-5100 or 800-492-0479

Copies of this report must also be sent to your insurance company and to the Department of Labor at:

Maryland Department of Labor
Licensing & Regulation
Division of Labor & Industry
1100 North Eutaw Street, Suite 611
Baltimore, MD 21201
www.dllr.state.md.us.

Employers may obtain coverage for their employees in one of the following three ways.

1. The employer may insure with the *State Accident Fund*, which is a non-profit self-supporting agency of the State of Maryland. For more information, contact:

Injured Workers' Insurance Fund
8722 Loch Raven Boulevard
Towson, MD 21268-2235
410-494-2000

2. The employer may insure with any company authorized to write this coverage in the state. To obtain a directory of licensed insurance companies, contact:

Insurance Commissioner
525 St. Paul Place
Baltimore, Maryland 21202-2272
410-468-2020

3. The employer may *self-insure* with the prior permission of the Maryland Workers' Compensation Commission. For more information, contact:

Director of Self Insurance
Maryland Workers' Compensation Commission
10 East Baltimore Street
Baltimore, Maryland 21201
410-864-5292
www.wcc.state.md.us

Virginia   Virginia law requires every employer who regularly employs three or more full-time or part-time employees to purchase and maintain workers' compensation insurance. Employers with fewer than three employees may voluntarily acquire insurance. Employers who fail to purchase workers' compensation insurance can be fined up to $5000. A notice of benefits must be posted (VWC Form 1).

Insurance may be acquired in approximately the same ways as in Maryland. Contact the northern Virginia office of the Virginia Workers' Compensation Commission for more specific information:

Alexandria Regional Office
Workers' Compensation Commission
520 King Street, Second Floor
Alexandria, Virginia 22314
P.O. Box 20246
Alexandria, Virginia 22320
703-518-8055

The Virginia Workers' Compensation Plan is administered by the *National Council on Compensation Insurance*. For additional assistance in obtaining coverage, call NCCI at 407-998-6356. The Independent Insurance Agents of Virginia is available at **www.iiaa.org**. Click on the "Other States" tab at the top and then select "VA" from the map.

If an employee is injured, An *Employer's Accident Report* (VWC Form 3) must be filed with the insurance carrier, who in turn will report the injury to the Commission. The employer will then provide the employee with a panel of three doctors from which to choose a treating physician.

District of Columbia

Employers in the District of Columbia are required to have workers' compensation insurance if they have one or more employees. The employer is also required to post a *Notice of Compliance*, found at **http://does.dc.gov/frames /Notice%20of%20Compliance.shtm**. The Workers' Compensation Program (WCP) processes claims and monitors the payment of benefits to injured employees in the District of Columbia. It also administers a fund for special or second injuries that provides benefits for uninsured employers or for workers whose injury combines with a previous disability. An insurance surcharge that covers this fund is collected quarterly.

Every employer should file an Employer's First Report of Injury (OWC-8) with the WCP as soon as an injury is brought to his or her attention or within 10 days. Failure to file has a $1000 fine. Copies of posters and claim forms are available from:

DC Department of Employment Services
Labor Standards Bureau
Office of Workers' Compensation
77 P Street, NE, 2nd floor
Washington, DC 20002
(202) 671-1000
http://does.dc.gov/services/wkr_comp.shtm.

Liability Insurance

There are many things to think about when starting and running a business today, and among the most important are the amounts and types of insurance to carry. Without proper protection, a business can face financial ruin in the event of a property loss or a lawsuit resulting from its activities. In most cases, you are not required to carry liability insurance. Most states require businesses to carry liability insurance on all motor vehicles.

Liability insurance can be divided into two main areas: coverage for injuries on your premises and by your employees, and coverage for injuries caused by your products or services.

Coverage for the first type of injury is usually very reasonably priced. Injuries in your business or by your employees (such as in an auto accident) are covered by standard premises or auto policies. But coverage for injuries by products may be harder to find and more expensive. If insurance is unavailable or unaffordable, you can go without and use a corporation and other asset protection devices to protect yourself from liability.

The best way to find out if insurance is available for your type of business is to check with other businesses. If there is a trade group for your industry, their newsletter or magazine may contain ads for insurers.

Umbrella Policy   As a business owner you will be a more visible target for lawsuits even if there is little merit to them. Lawyers know that a nuisance suit is often settled for thousands of dollars. Because of your greater exposure you should consider getting a *personal umbrella policy*. This is a policy that covers you for claims of up to a million—or even two or five million dollars and is very reasonably priced.

Hazard Insurance

One of the worst things that can happen to your business is a fire, flood, or other disaster. With lost customer lists, inventory, and equipment, many businesses have been forced to close after such a disaster.

The premium for such insurance is usually reasonable and could protect you from loss of your business. You can even get *business interruption insurance,* which will cover your losses while your business is getting back on its feet.

Home Business Insurance

There is a special insurance problem for home businesses. Most homeowner and tenant insurance policies do not cover business activities. In fact, under some policies you may be denied coverage if you used your home for a business.

If you merely use your home to make business phone calls and send letters, you will probably not have a problem and not need extra coverage. But if you own equipment, or have dedicated a portion of your home exclusively to the business, you could have a problem. Check with your insurance agent for the options that are available to you.

If your business is a sole proprietorship, and you have, say, a computer that you use both personally and for your business, it would probably be covered under your homeowners' policy. But if you incorporate your business and buy the computer in the name of the corporation, coverage might be denied. If a computer is your main business asset you could get a special insurance policy in the company name covering just the computer. One company that offers such a policy is Safeware at 800-800-1492 or on the Web at:

www.safeware.com

Automobile Insurance

If you or any of your employees will be using an automobile for business purposes, be sure that such use is covered. Sometimes a policy may include an exclusion for business use. Check to be sure your liability policy covers you if one of your employees causes an accident while running a business errand.

Health Insurance

While new businesses can rarely afford health insurance for their employees, the sooner they can obtain it, the better chance they will have to find and keep good employees. Those starting a business usually need insurance for themselves (unless they have a working spouse who can cover the family) and they can sometimes get a better rate under a small business package.

Employee Theft

If you fear that employees may steal from your business, you may want to have them bonded. This means that you pay an insurance company a premium to guarantee employees' honesty, and if they cheat you, the insurance company pays you damages. This can cover all existing and new employees.

9 YOUR BUSINESS AND THE INTERNET

The Internet has opened up a world of opportunities for businesses. A few years ago getting national visibility cost a fortune. Today a business can set up a Web page for a few hundred dollars and, with some clever publicity and a little luck, millions of people around the world will see it.

But this new world of publicity has new legal issues and new liabilities. Not all of them have been addressed by laws or by the courts. Before you begin doing business on the Internet, you should know the existing rules and the areas where legal issues exist.

Domain Names

A *domain name* is the address of your website. For example, **www.apple.com** is the domain name of Apple Computer Company. The last part of the domain name, the ".com" (or "dot com") is the *top level domain*, or TLD. The .com designation is the most popular, but others are currently available in the United States, including .net and .org. (Originally .net was only available to network service providers and .org only to nonprofit organizations, but regulations have eliminated those requirements.) Other endings include .biz, .tv, .cc, .info, and .us. You can determine the availability of a domain name at:

www.networksolutions.com

If you want to know who owns a particular registered name, go to the section called *WHOIS* or go to **www.whois.net**.

It may seem like most words have been taken as a dot-com name, but if you combine two or three short words or abbreviations, a nearly unlimited number of possibilities are available. For example, if you have a business dealing with automobiles, most likely someone has already registered automobile.com and auto.com. But you can come up with all kinds of variations, using adjectives or your name, depending on your type of business:

autos4u.com	joesauto.com	autobob.com
myauto.com	yourauto.com	onlyautos.com
greatauto.com	autosfirst.com	usautos.com
greatautos.com	firstautoworld.com	4autos.com

When the Internet first began, some individuals realized that major corporations would soon want to register their names. Since the registration was easy and cheap, people registered names they thought would ultimately be used by someone else.

At first, some companies paid high fees to buy their names from the registrants. But one company, Intermatic, filed a lawsuit instead of paying. The owner of the mark they wanted had registered numerous trademarks, such as **britishairways.com** and **ussteel.com**. The court ruled that since Intermatic owned a trademark on the name, the registration of their name by someone else violated that trademark and that Intermatic was entitled to it.

Since then, people have registered names that are not trademarks, such as CalRipkin.com, and have attempted to charge the individuals with those names to buy their domain. As a result, Congress stepped in and passed the *Anti-Cybersquatting Consumer Protection Act*. This law makes it illegal to register a domain with no legitimate need to use it.

This law helped a lot of companies protect their names, but then some companies started abusing it and tried to stop legitimate users of similar names. This is especially likely against small companies. Two organizations have been set up to help small companies protect their domains: the *Domain Defense Advocate* and the *Domain Name Rights Coalition*. Their websites are:

www.ajax.org/dda
www.domain-name.org

Registering a domain name for your own business is a simple process. There are many companies that offer registration services. For a list of those companies, visit the site of the *Internet Corporation for Assigned Names and Numbers (ICANN)* at **www.icann.org**. You can link directly to any member's site and compare the costs and registration procedures required for the different top-level domains.

Web Pages

There are many new companies eager to help you set up a website. Some offer turnkey sites for a low flat rate such as **www.Digibelly.com**. Custom sites can cost tens of thousands of dollars. If you have plenty of capital you may want to have your site handled by one of these professionals. However, setting up a website is a fairly simple process, and once you learn the basics you can handle most of it in-house.

If you are new to the Web, you may want to look at the following sites, which will familiarize you with the Internet jargon and give you a basic introduction to the Web:

www.learnthenet.com
www.webopedia.com

Site Setup   There are seven steps to setting up a website:

❂   purpose;

❂   design;

✪ content;

✪ structure;

✪ programming;

✪ testing; and,

✪ publicity.

Whether you do it yourself, hire a professional site designer, or use a college student, the steps toward creating an effective site are the same.

Before beginning your own site you should look at other sites, including those of major corporations and of small businesses. Look at the sites of your competitors. Look at hundreds of sites and click through them to see how they work—or do not work.

Site purpose. To know what to include on your site you must decide what its purpose will be. Do you want to take orders for your products or services, attract new employees, give away samples, or show off your company headquarters? You might want to do several of these things.

Site design. After looking at other sites you can see that there are numerous ways to design a site. It can be crowded or open and airy. It can have several windows (frames) open at once or just one. It can allow long scrolling or just click-throughs.

You will have to decide whether the site will have text only, text plus photographs and graphics, or text plus photos, graphics, and other design elements such as animation or Java script. Additionally, you will begin to make decisions about colors, fonts, and the basic graphic appearance of the site.

Site content. You must create the content for your site. For this, you can use your existing promotional materials, you can write new material just for the website, or you can use a combination of the two. Whatever you choose, remember that the written material should be concise, free of errors, and easy for your target audience to read. Any graphics, including photographs, and written materials not created by you require permission. You should obtain such permission from the lawful copyright holder in order to use any copyrighted material. Once you know your site's purpose, look, and content, you can begin to piece the site together.

Site structure. You must decide how the content (text plus photographs, graphics, animation, etc.) will be structured, what content will be on which page, and how a user will link from one part of the site to another. For example, your first page may have the business name and then choices to click on, such as "about us," "opportunities," "product catalog," etc. Have those choices connect to another page containing the detailed information so that a user will see the catalog when they click on "product catalog." Or your site could have a choice to click on a link to another website related to yours.

Site programming and setup. When you know nothing about setting up a website, it can seem like a daunting task that will require an expert. However, *programming* here means merely putting a site together. There are inexpensive computer programs available that make it very simple.

Commercial programs such as *Microsoft Frontpage, Dreamweaver, Pagemaker, Photoshop, MS Publisher,* and *GoLive* allow you to set up Web pages as easily as laying out a print publication. These programs will convert the text and graphics you create into HTML, the programming language of the Web. Before you choose Web design software and design your site, you should determine which Web hosting service you will use. Make sure that the design software you use is compatible with the host server's system. The Web host will be the provider who will give you space on their server and who may provide other services to you, such as secure order processing and analysis of your site to see who is visiting and linking to it.

If you have an America Online account, you can download design software and a tutorial for free. AOL has recently collaborated with a Web hosting service at **www.bigstep.com** and offers a number of different hosting packages for the consumer and e-business. You do not have to use AOL's design software in order to use this service. You are eligible to use this site whether you design your own pages, have someone else do the design work for you, or use AOL's templates. This service allows you to use your own domain name and choose the package that is appropriate for your business.

If you have used a page layout program, you can usually get a simple Web page up and running within a day or two. If you do not have much experience with a computer, you might consider hiring a college student to set up a Web page for you.

Site testing. Some of the website setup programs allow you to thoroughly check your new site to see if all the pictures are included and all the links are proper. There are also websites you can go to that will check out your site. Some even allow you to improve your site, such as by reducing the size of your graphics so they download faster.

Site publicity. Once you set up your website, you will want to get people to look at it. Publicity means getting your site noticed as much as possible by drawing people to it.

The first thing to do to get noticed is to be sure your site is registered with as many search engines as possible. These are pages that people use to find things on the Internet, such as Yahoo, Excite and Google. They do not automatically know about you just because you created a website. You must tell them about your site, and they must examine and catalog it.

For a fee, there are services that will register your site with numerous search engines. If you are starting out on a shoestring, you can easily do it yourself. While there are hundreds of search engines, most people use a dozen or so of the bigger ones. If your site is in a niche area, such as genealogy services, then you would want to be listed on any specific genealogy search engines. Most businesses should be mainly concerned with getting on the biggest ones. The biggest search engines at this time are:

www.altavista.com	www.infoseek.com
www.dejanews.com	www.lycos.com
www.excite.com	www.magellan.com
www.fastsearch	www.metacrawler.com
www.google.com	www.northernlight.com
www.goto.com	www.webcrawler.com
www.hotbot.com	www.yahoo.com

Most of these sites have a place to click to *add your site* to their system. There are sites that rate the search engines, help you list on the search engines, or check to see if you are listed. One site is:

www.searchiq.com

A *meta tag* is an invisible subject word added to your site that can be found by a search engine. For example, if you are a pest control company, you may want to list all of the scientific names of the pests you control and all of the treatments you have available, but you may not need them to be part of the visual design of your site. List these words as meta tags when you set up your page so people searching for those words will find your site.

Some companies thought that a clever way to get viewers would be to use commonly searched names, or names of major competitors, as meta tags to attract people looking for those big companies. For example, a small delivery service that has nothing to do with UPS or FedEx might use those company names as meta tags so people looking for them would find the smaller company. While it may sound like a good idea, it has been declared *illegal trademark infringement*. Today many companies have computer programs scanning the Internet for improper use of their trademarks.

Once you have made sure that your site is passively listed in all the search engines, you may want to actively promote your site. However, self-promotion is often seen as a bad thing on the Internet, especially if its purpose is to make money.

Newsgroups are places on the Internet where people interested in a specific topic can exchange information. For example, expectant mothers may have a group where they can trade advice and experiences. If you have a product that would be great for expectant mothers, that would be a good place for it to be discussed. However, if you log into the group and merely announce your product, suggesting people order it from your website, you will probably be *flamed* (sent a lot of hate mail).

If you join the group, however, and become a regular, and in answer to someone's problem, mention that you "saw this product that might help," your information will be better received. It may seem unethical to plug your product without disclosing your interest, but this is a procedure used by many large companies. They hire people to plug their product all over the Internet. So, perhaps it has become an acceptable marketing method and consumers know to take plugs with a grain of salt. Let your conscience be your guide.

Keep in mind that Internet publicity works both ways. If you have a great product and people love it, you will get a lot of business. If you sell a shoddy product, give poor service, and do not keep your customers happy, bad publicity on the Internet can kill your business. Besides being an equalizer between large and small companies, the Internet can be a filtering mechanism between good and bad products.

There is no worse breach of Internet etiquette (netiquette) than to send advertising by e-mail to strangers. It is called *spamming*, and doing it can have serious consequences. There is anti-spamming legislation currently pending at the federal level. Many states, including California, Colorado, Connecticut, Delaware, Idaho, Illinois, Iowa, Louisiana, Missouri, Nevada, North Carolina, Oklahoma, Pennsylvania, Rhode Island, Tennessee, Virginia, Washington, and West Virginia, have enacted anti-spamming legislation. This legislation sets specific requirements for unsolicited bulk e-mail and makes certain practices illegal. You should check with an attorney to see if your business practices fall within the legal limits of these laws. Additionally, many Internet Service Providers (ISPs) have restrictions on unsolicited bulk e-mail (spam). You should check with your ISP to make sure you do not violate its policies.

Advertising   *Banner ads* are the small rectangular ads on many Web pages that usually blink or move. Although most computer users seem to have become immune to them, there is still a big market in the sale and exchange of them.

If your site gets enough viewers, people may pay you to place their ads there. Another possibility is to trade ads with another site. In fact there are companies that broker ad trades among websites.

Legal Issues

Before you set up a Web page, you should consider the legal issues described below.

Jurisdiction   Jurisdiction is the power of a court in a particular location to decide a particular case. Usually you have to have been physically present in a jurisdiction or have done business there before you can be sued there. Since the Internet extends your business's ability to reach people in faraway places, there may be instances when you could be subject to legal jurisdiction far from your own state (or country). There are a number of cases that have been decided in this country regarding the Internet and jurisdiction, but very few cases have been decided on this issue outside of the United States.

In most instances, U.S. courts use the pre-Internet test—whether you have been present in another jurisdiction or have had enough contact with someone in the other jurisdiction. The fact that the Internet itself is not a *place* will not shield you from being sued in another state when you have shipped you company's product there, have entered into a contract with a resident of that state, or have defamed a foreign resident with content on your website.

According to the Court, there is a *spectrum of contact* required between you, your website, and consumers, or audiences. (*Zippo Manufacturing Co. v. Zippo Dot Corn, Inc.*, 952 F. Supp. 1119 (W.D. Pa 1997).) It is *clear* that the one end of the spectrum includes the shipping, contracting, and defamation mentioned above as sufficient to establish jurisdiction. The more interactive your site is with consumers, the more you target an audience for your goods in a particular location, and the farther you reach to send your goods out into the world, the more it becomes possible for someone to sue you outside of your own jurisdiction—possibly even in another country.

The law is not even remotely final on these issues. The American Bar Association, among other groups, is studying this topic in detail. At present, no final, global solution or agreement about jurisdictional issues exists.

One way to protect yourself from the possibility of being sued in a faraway jurisdiction would be to have a statement on your website stating that those using the site or doing business with you agree that "jurisdiction for any actions regarding this site" or your company will be in your home county.

For extra protection you can have a preliminary page that must be clicked before entering your website. However, this may be overkill for a small business with little risk of lawsuits. If you are in any business for which you could have serious liability, you should review some competitors' sites and see how they handle the liability issue. They often have a place to click for "legal notice" or "disclaimer" on their first page.

You may want to consult with an attorney to discuss the specific disclaimer you will use on your website, where it should appear, and whether you will have users of your site actively agree to this disclaimer or just passively read it. However, these disclaimers are not enforceable everywhere in the world. Until there is global agreement on jurisdictional issues, this may remain an area of uncertainty for some time to come.

Libel

Libel is any publication that injures the reputation of another. This can occur in print, writing, pictures, or signs. All that is required for *publication* is that you transmit the material to at least one other person. When putting together your website you must keep in mind that it is visible to millions of people all over the planet and that if you libel a person or company you may have to pay damages. Many countries do not have the freedom of speech that we do and a statement that is not libel in the United States may be libelous elsewhere.

Copyright Infringement

It is so easy to copy and *borrow* information on the Internet that it is easy to infringe copyrights without even knowing it. A *copyright* exists for a work as soon as the creator creates it. There is no need to register the copyright or to put a copyright notice on it. So, practically everything on the Internet belongs to someone. Some people freely give their works away. For example, many people have created web artwork (*gifs* and *animated gifs*) that they freely allow people to copy There are numerous sites that provide hundreds or thousands of free gifs that you can add to your Web pages. Some require you to acknowledge the source, some do not.

You should always be sure that the works are free for the taking before using them.

Linking and Framing

One way to violate copyright laws is to improperly link other sites to yours either directly or with framing. *Linking* is when you provide a place on your site to click that takes someone to another site. *Framing* occurs when you set up your site so that when you link to another site, your site is still viewable as a frame around the linked-to site.

While many sites are glad to be linked to others, some, especially providers of valuable information, object. Courts have ruled that linking and framing can be a copyright violation. One rule that has developed is that it is usually okay to link to the first page of a site, but not to link to some valuable information deeper within the site. The rationale for this is that the owner of the site wants visitors to go through the various levels of their site before getting the information. By linking to the information you are giving away their product without the ads.

The problem with linking to the first page of a site is that it may be a tedious or difficult task to find the needed page from there. Many sites are poorly designed and make it nearly impossible to find anything.

The best solution, if you wish to link to another page, is to ask permission. Email the *Webmaster* or other person in charge of the site, if one is given, and explain what you want to do. If they grant permission, be sure to print out a copy of their e-mail for your records.

Privacy   Since the Internet is such an easy way to share information, there are many concerns that it will cause a loss of individual privacy. The main concerns arise when you post information that others consider private, and when you gather information from customers and use it in a way that violates their privacy.

While public actions of politicians and celebrities are fair game, the law sometimes protects details about their private lives. Details about persons who are not *public figures* are often protected. The laws in each state are different, and what might be permitted in one state could be illegal in another. If your site will provide any personal information about individuals, you should discuss the possibility of liability with an attorney.

Several well-known companies have been in the news lately for violations of their customers' privacy. They either shared what the customer was buying or downloading, or looked for additional information on the customer's computer. To let customers know that you do not violate certain standards of privacy, you can subscribe to one of the privacy codes that have been promulgated for the Internet. These allow you to put a symbol on your site guaranteeing to your customers that you follow the code.

The websites of two organizations that offer this service, and their fees at the time of this publication, are:

        www.privacybot.com $100
        www.bbbonline.com $200 to $3000

Protecting Yourself   The easiest way to protect yourself personally from the various possible types of liability is to set up a corporation or limited liability company to own the website. This is not foolproof protection, since in some cases you could be sued personally as well, but it is one level of protection.

COPPA   If your website is aimed at children under the age of thirteen, or if it attracts children of that age, then you are governed by the federal *Children Online Privacy Protection Act of 1998 (COPPA)*. This law requires such websites to:

- ✪   give notice on the site of what information is being collected;

- ✪   obtain verifiable parental consent to collect the information;

- ✪   allow the parent to review the information collected;

- ✪   allow the parent to delete the child's information or to refuse to allow the use of the information;

- ✪   limit the information collected to only that necessary to participate on the site; and,

- ✪   protect the security and confidentiality of the information.

Financial Transactions

In the future, there will be easy ways to exchange money on the Internet. Some companies have already been started that promote their own kinds of electronic money. Whether any of these become universal is yet to be seen. A method gaining in popularity is Paypal (**www.paypal.com**). This service allows money to be deducted from a user's banking account or credit card and placed into another individual's paypal account. The money can then be deposited into the recipient's own banking account or kept online for other transactions. While many people find the convenience of this service when making purchases over the Internet very useful, be sure to read the service agreement of any online escrow or exchange service very carefully.

For now, the easiest way to exchange money on the Internet is through traditional credit cards. Because of concerns that email can be abducted in transit and read by others, most companies use a *secure* site in which customers are guaranteed that their card data is encrypted before being sent.

When setting up your website, you should ask the provider if you can be set up with a secure site for transmitting credit card data. If they cannot provide it, you will need to contract with another software provider. Use a major search engine to look for companies that provide credit card services to businesses on the web.

As a practical matter, there is very little to worry about when sending credit card data by email. If you do not have a secure site, another option is to allow purchasers to fax or phone in their credit card data. However, keep in mind that this extra step will lose some business unless your products are unique and your buyers are very motivated.

The least effective option is to provide an order form on the site, which can be printed out and mailed in with a check. Again, your customers must be really motivated or they will lose interest after finding out this extra work is involved.

FTC Rules

Because the Internet is an instrument of interstate commerce, it is a legitimate subject for federal regulation. The *Federal Trade Commission (FTC)* first said that all of its consumer protection rules applied to the Internet, but lately it has been adding specific rules and issuing publications. The following publications are available from the FTC website at **www.ftc.gov/bcp/menu-internet.htm** or by mail from the Consumer Response Center, Federal Trade Commission, 600 Pennsylvania, NW, Room H-130, Washington, DC 20580-0001.

- ✪ *Advertising and Marketing on the Internet: The Rules of the Road*
- ✪ *BBB-Online: Code of Online Business Practices*
- ✪ *Electronic Commerce: Selling Internationally. A Guide for Business Alert*
- ✪ *How to Comply With The Children's Online Privacy Protection Rule*
- ✪ *Internet Auctions: A Guide for Buyer and Sellers*
- ✪ *Selling on the Internet: Prompt Delivery Rules Alert*
- ✪ *Website Woes: Avoiding Web Service Scams Alert*

Fraud

Because the Internet is somewhat anonymous, it is a tempting place for those with fraudulent schemes to look for victims. As a business consumer, you should exercise caution when dealing with unknown or anonymous parties on the Internet.

Recently, the U.S. Department of Justice, the FBI, and the National White Collar Crime Center launched the *Internet Fraud Complaint Center (IFCC)*. If you suspect that you are the victim of fraud online, whether as a consumer or a business, you can report incidents to the IFCC on their website, **www.ifccfbi.gov**. The IFCC is staffed by FBI agents and representatives of the National White Collar Crime Center and will work with state and local law enforcement officials to prevent, investigate, and prosecute high-tech and economic crime online.

10 | HEALTH AND SAFETY LAWS

Health and safety laws at both the federal and state level must be followed. Depending on your particular business, specific regulations may apply to you. Below are some general laws of which all businesses should be aware.

Federal Laws

OSHA   The regulations from the *Occupational Safety and Health Administration (OSHA)*, part of the Department Of Labor (**www.dol.gov**), can be daunting for those unaccustomed to rigorous regulations. Fortunately for small businesses, the regulations are not as cumbersome as for larger enterprises. If you have ten or fewer employees or if you are in certain types of business, you do not have to keep a record of illnesses, injuries, and exposure to hazardous substances of employees. If you have eleven or more employees, you do have to keep this record, which is called *Log 200*.

Within forty-eight hours of an on-the-job death of an employee or injury of five or more employees on the job, the area director of OSHA must be contacted.

For more information, you should write or call your OSHA office:

Occupational Safety & Health Administration
200 Constitution Avenue, NW
Washington, DC 20210
800-321-OSHA (6742)

OSHA Baltimore/Washington Office
1099 Winterson Road, Suite 140
Linthicum, Maryland 21090
410-865-2055/2056
fax: 410-865-2068

OSHA Norfolk Area Office
Federal Office Building, Room 614
200 Granby Mall
Norfolk, Virginia 23510-1819
757-441-3820
fax: 757-441-3594

Programs available for employers within the District of Columbia, Maryland, or Virginia:

District of Columbia Consultation Office
DC Department of Employment Services
OSHA Consultation Services
64 New York Ave., N.E., 2nd Floor
Washington, D.C. 20002
202-671-1800
fax: (202) 671-3018

Maryland Consultation Office
MOSH Consultation Services
Montgomery Park Business Center
1800 Washington Blvd., Third Floor
Baltimore, MD 21230
410-537-4512
fax: 410-537-4518
www.dllr.state.md.us/labor/mosh.html

Virginia Consultation Office
Virginia Department of Labor & Industry
Occupational Safety & Health Training & Consultation
13 South Thirteenth Street
Richmond, Virginia 23219-4101
804-786-6613
fax: 804-786-8418
www.doli.state.va.us

Or, visit the OSHA website **www.osha.gov** and obtain copies of their publications, *OSHA Handbook for Small Business (OSHA 2209)*, and *OSHA Publications and Audiovisual Programs Catalog (OSHA 2019)*. They also have a poster that is required to be posted in the workplace. Find it at **www.osha.gov/Publications/poster.html.** Virginia also requires the *Job Safety and Health Protection Poster* be hung by all employers. It is available by clicking on "Info Center" at **www.dli.state.va.us**.

The *Hazard Communication Standard* requires that employees be made aware of the hazards in the workplace (Code of Federal Regulations (C.F.R.), Title 29, Section (Sec.) 1910.1200.)). It is especially applicable to those working with chemicals but this can even include offices that use copy machines. Businesses using hazardous chemicals must have a comprehensive program for informing employees of the hazards and for protecting them from contamination.

For more information, you can contact OSHA at the above addresses, phone numbers, or websites. They can supply a copy of the regulation and a booklet called *OSHA 3084*, which explains the law.

EPA The *Worker Protection Standard for Agricultural Pesticides* requires safety training, decontamination sites and posters. The Environmental Protection Agency will provide information on compliance with this law. They can be reached at:

Environmental Protection Agency
Ariel Ross Building
1200 Pennsylvania Ave. N.W.
Mail Code 3213A
Washington, DC 20460
800-490-9198
www.epa.gov

FDA   The *Pure Food and Drug Act of 1906* prohibits the misbranding or adulteration of food and drugs. It also created the *Food and Drug Administration (FDA)*, which has promulgated many regulations. The FDA must give permission before a new drug can be introduced into the market. If you will be dealing with any food or drugs you should keep abreast of their policies. Contact them at:

FDA, Central Region
US Customhouse
Second and Chestnut Street, Room 900
Philadelphia, PA 19106
215-597-2120 ext. 4003
fax: 215-597-5798
www.fda.gov
small business site: www.fda.gov/ora/fed_state/small_business/sb_guide

Hazardous Materials Transportation   There are regulations that control the shipping and packing of hazardous materials. For more information contact:

Office of Hazardous Materials Transportation
400 Seventh St., S.W
Washington, D.C. 20590
202-366-8553
http://hazmat.dot.gov

CPSC   The *Consumer Product Safety Commission* was mandated by Congress to protect the public against unreasonable risks of injuries and deaths associated with consumer products. The Commission feels that, because its rules cover products rather than people or companies, they apply to everyone producing and selling such products. However, federal laws do not apply to small businesses that do not affect *interstate commerce*. Whether a small business would fall under a CPSC rule would depend on the size and nature of the business, as well as on the products manufactured, imported, distributed, or sold. If you have questions about how the CPSC impacts your business, call the toll-free hotline at 800-638-2772 or contact the Small Buuusiness Ombudsman at:

Small Business Ombudsman, U.S. CPSC
Washington, D.C. 20207
800-638-2772, x 234

Additional
Regulations

Every day there are proposals for new laws and regulations. It would be impossible to include every conceivable one in this book. To be up to date on the laws that affect your type of business, you should belong to a trade association for your industry and subscribe to newsletters that cover your industry. Attending industry conventions is a good way to learn more and to discover new ways to increase your profits.

State and Local Laws on Smoking

Maryland

The *Maryland Occupational Safety and Health (MOSH) Act* covers every Maryland employer in a business, trade, commercial, or industrial activity, including state and local governments. It does not cover working conditions of federal employees as they are covered by OSHA.

In Maryland, it is illegal to sell tobacco to a minor less than 18 years of age. However, minors are allowed to handle tobacco products in the course of doing their jobs. Depending on the county, it may also be illegal to display tobacco products that are accessible by consumers without the assistance of a sales person.

It is illegal to smoke in most indoor workplaces unless confined to an enclosed and separately ventilated smoking room. This smoking room may not be a place where an employee other that a custodian or maintenance employee is required to work. No one is permitted to smoke in the room when maintenance or cleaning work is being done. Employers are required to post a no smoking sign.

Exclusions to this law are tobacconist shops, vehicles used in the course of business that are occupied by only one person, and smoking done in the course of scientific research.

Bars and clubs are permitted to allow smoking unless further restricted by county or local laws. Other establishments have the following restrictions.

✪ *Restaurants without a liquor license*—Smoking is permitted in a separate enclosed room, but is not to exceed 40% of the total area of the restaurant. The separate enclosed room in this case does not have to be separately ventilated.

✪ *Restaurants with a liquor license*—Smoking is permitted in a bar or bar area, a separate enclosed room not exceeding 40% of the restaurant, or a combination of a bar or bar area and a separate enclosed room not exceeding 40% of the total area of the restaurant including the bar or bar area. The separate enclosed room in this case does not have to be separately ventilated.

✪ *Hotels and Motels*—Smoking is permitted in up to 40% of the sleeping rooms in a hotel or motel.

✪ *Establishments with a liquor license for on-site consumption*—Smoking is permitted in a separate enclosed room of an establishment that has a liquor license that allows consumption of alcoholic beverages on the premises of the establishment (e.g., pool rooms, bowling alleys, etc). The separate enclosed room in this case does not have to be separately ventilated.

✪ *Other*—Smoking is permitted in up to 40% of the premises of a fraternal, religious, patriotic, or charitable organization or corporation or fire company or rescue squad (subject to occupational safety and health laws) during an event which is open to the public and held on its own property.

District of Columbia

Smoking in the District of Columbia is prohibited in the following:

✪ elevators;

✪ retail stores;

✪ public assembly or hearing rooms;

✪ government offices;

✪ educational facilities;

✪ District of Columbia government cars;

✪ health-care facilities, except where the management has provided a separate smoking room;

✪ public or private workplaces, except where a separate smoking section is provided with separate ventilation; and,

✪ restaurants or eating places. (Restaurants with a seating capacity of 50+ must designate 50%+ to a non-smoking area, and bar and lounge areas are not to be included in the total size. The smoking section must be separated by a physical barrier or be in a separate room. Smoking is prohibited in the no-smoking section even if food is no longer being served.)

NOTE: *"No Smoking" signs are to be posted. There is a fine for tampering with or removing signs.*

Smoking is permitted in the following situations: in tobacco shops, by actors on stage, in taverns or nightclubs, and in rooms or halls used for private parties.

Virginia   Smoking laws in Virginia are very similar to those in the District of Columbia, and perhaps more relaxed. There is a fine of not more than $25 for smoking in a no-smoking area, and any law enforcement officer can write tickets. All smoking and non-smoking areas should be marked with signs.

II EMPLOYMENT AND LABOR LAWS

Once your business needs employees other than yourself, employment and labor laws become another layer of compliance the business owner must follow.

Hiring and Firing Laws

For small businesses, there are not many rules regarding whom you may hire or fire. Fortunately, the ancient law that an employee can be fired at any time (or may quit at any time) still prevails for small businesses. But in certain situations, and as the business grows, you will come under a number of laws that affect your hiring and firing practices.

One of the most important things to consider when hiring someone is that, if you fire them, they may be entitled to unemployment compensation. If so, your unemployment compensation tax rate will go up and it can cost you a lot of money. Therefore, you should only hire people you are sure you will keep and you should avoid situations where your former employees can make claims against your company.

One way this can be done is by hiring only *part-time* employees. The drawback to this is that you may not be able to attract the best employees. When hiring dishwashers or busboys this may not be an issue, but if you are hiring someone to develop a software product, you do not want them to leave halfway through the development.

A better solution is to screen applicants, and only hire those who you feel certain will work out. Of course this is easier said than done. Some people interview well but then turn out to be incompetent at the job.

The best person to look for is someone who has stayed a long time at each of his or her previous jobs. Next best is someone who has not stayed as long (for good reasons) but has always been employed. The worst type of hire would be someone who is or has been collecting unemployment compensation. If an employee collects in the future, even if it is not your fault, your employment of them could make you chargeable for their claim.

For example, suppose you hire someone who has been on unemployment compensation and they work out well for a year, but then they quit to take another job and are fired after a few weeks. In this situation, you could be charged for most of their claim because their last five quarters of work are analyzed. Look for a steady job history.

The intelligence of an employee is often more important than his or her experience. An employee with years of typing experience may be fast, but unable to figure out how to use your new computer, whereas an intelligent employee can learn the equipment quickly and eventually gain speed. Of course, common sense is important in all situations.

The bottom line is that you cannot know if an employee will be able to fill your needs from a resume and interview. Once you have found someone who you think will work out, offer them a job with a ninety-day *probationary period*. If you are not completely satisfied with them after the ninety days, offer to extend the probationary period for ninety additional days rather than ending the relationship immediately. Of course, all of this should be in writing.

Background Checks

Checking references is important, but be aware that a former boss may be a good friend or even a relative. It has always been considered acceptable to exaggerate on resumes, but some applicants completely fabricate sections on their education and experience.

Polygraph Tests   Under the federal *Employee Polygraph Protection Act,* you cannot require an employee or prospective employee to take a polygraph test unless you are in the armored car, guard, or pharmaceutical business.

Drug Tests   Maryland has protected employers by enacting drug and alcohol testing laws that state that employers may require employees to be tested for the illegal use of alcohol and drugs for a *legitimate business purpose.* (Maryland Annotated Code, Health-General Article, Section 17-214.) Such tests should be conducted at the employer's expense. An employer who requires testing and receives a positive test result must provide the employee with a copy of the test results, a copy of the employer's written policies and a written notice of intent to take disciplinary action. This could amount to termination or the change of the conditions of employment. Employers may also be able to deny medical and indemnity benefits for failure to pass a test. Employees may request an independent test for verification of a positive test at their own expense.

Virginia does not have any employment drug and alcohol testing laws, but private employer programs have been upheld subject to a reasonableness test.

Firing

In most cases, unless you have a *contract* with an employee for a set time period, you can fire him or her at any time. This is only fair since the employee can quit at any time. The exceptions to this are:

✪   firing someone based on illegal discrimination (see pages 109–113);

✪   firing someone for filing some sort of health or safety complaint (see Chapter 10); or,

✪   firing someone for refusing sexual advances (see page 113).

You should check with local law to determine whether you have to pay any required severance such as two weeks wages.

New Hire Reporting

In order to track down parents who do not pay child support, a federal law was passed in 1996 that requires the reporting of new hires. The *Personal Responsibility and Work Opportunity Reconciliation Act of 1996 (PRWORA)* provides that employers must report such information to their state government.

Within twenty days of hiring a new employee, an employer must provide the state with information about the employee including the name, social security number and address. This information can be submitted in several ways including mail, fax, or over the Internet. There is a special form that can be used for this reporting; however, an employer can use the **EMPLOYEE'S WITHHOLDING ALLOWANCE CERTIFICATE (IRS FORM W-4)** for this purpose. (see form 14, p.262.) Since this form must be filled out for all employees anyway, it would be pointless to use a separate form for the new hire reporting. A copy of the IRS **FORM W-4** is included in Appendix B and this may be faxed or mailed to:

Maryland New Hire Registry
P.O. Box 1316
Baltimore, MD 21203-1316
410-281-6000 or 888-634-4737
www.mdnewhire.com

District of Columbia New Hire Reporting
DC New Hire Operations Center
P.O. Box 149291
Austin, TX 78714-9291
877-846-9523
dc@mail.newhire.org
www.new-hires.com/dc

Virginia New Hire Reporting Center
P.O. Box 25309
Richmond, VA 23260-5309
804-771-9733 or 800-979-9014
fax: 804-771-9709 or 800-688-2680
www.va-newhire.com

Employment Agreements

Generally speaking you should give employees an offering letter setting forth only their salary, benefits, and leave policy. You should reserve full-blown *employment agreements* for upper management. In the absence of an employment agreement, an individual is an *employee at will* and can be released at any time. In addition to an offer letter you may wish to have all new employees sign a new hire agreement that requires them to keep all company matters confidential (including company trade secrets), to assign all rights to inventions or other discoveries made while in the employ of the company and, in some instances, not to compete with the company's business for a specified time after they leave. The last stipulation is known as a *non-compete agreement*.

As your business grows larger, and to avoid misunderstanding with employees, you may wish to use an *employee handbook*. Such a handbook can spell out in detail the policies of your company and the rights of your employees. A handbook can protect your trade secrets and spell out clearly that either party can terminate employment at any time.

While it may be difficult or awkward to ask an existing employee to sign such an agreement, an applicant hoping you will hire them will usually sign whatever is necessary to obtain the job. However, because of the unequal bargaining position, you should not use an agreement that would make you look bad if the matter ever went to court.

If having an employee sign an agreement is awkward, you can usually obtain the same rights by putting the company policies in an *employee manual*. Each existing and new employee should be given a copy along with a letter stating that the rules apply to all employees and that by accepting or continuing employment at your company they agree to abide by the rules. Having an employee sign a receipt for the letter and manual is proof that they received it.

One danger of an employment agreement or handbook is that it may be interpreted to create an *employment contract*. To avoid this be sure that it is clearly stated in the agreement or handbook that the employment is *at will* and can be terminated at any time by either party. Some other things to consider in an employment agreement or handbook are:

✪   what the salary and other compensation will be;

- ✪ what the hours of employment will be;

- ✪ what the probationary period will be;

- ✪ that the employee cannot sign any contracts binding the employer; and,

- ✪ that the employee agrees to arbitration rather than filing a lawsuit.

Independent Contractors

One way to avoid problems with employees and avoid taxes at the same time is to have all of your work done through independent contractors. This can relieve you of most of the burdens of employment laws and the obligation to pay Social Security and Medicare taxes for the workers.

An independent contractor is, in effect, a separate business that you pay to do a job. You pay them just as you pay any company from which you buy products or services. At the end of the year, if the amount paid exceeds $600, you will issue a *1099 form* instead of the W-2 that you issue to employees.

This may seem too good to be true, and in some situations it is. The IRS does not like independent contractor arrangements because it is too easy for the independent contractors to cheat on their taxes. To limit the use of independent contractors, the IRS has strict regulations on who may nd may not be classified as an independent contractor. Also, companies who do not appear to pay enough in wages for their field of business are audited.

The independent contract jobs most likely to be regulated by the IRS are those that are not traditionally done by independent contractors. For example, you could not get away with hiring a secretary as an independent contractor. One of the most important factors considered in determining if a worker can be an independent contractor is the amount of *control* the company has over his or her work. If you need someone to paint your building and you agree to pay them a certain price to do it according to their own methods and schedule, you can pay them as an independent contractor. But if you tell them when to work and how to do the job, and provide them with the tools and materials, they will be classified as an employee.

If you just need some typing done and you take it to a typing service and pick it up when it is ready, you will be safe in treating them as independent contractors. But, if you need someone to come into your office to type on your machine at your schedule, you will probably be required to treat that person as an employee for tax purposes.

The IRS has a form you can use in determining if a person is an employee or an independent contractor called **DETERMINATION OF EMPLOYEE WORK STATUS (IRS FORM SS-8)**. It is included in Appendix B of this book along with instructions. (see form 13, page 257.)

In deciding whether to make use of independent contractors or employees, you should weigh the following advantages and disadvantages.

Advantages.

> ✪ *Lower taxes.* You do not have to pay Social Security, Medicare, unemployment, or other employee taxes.

> ✪ *Less paperwork.* You do not have to handle federal withholding deposits or the monthly employer returns to the state or federal government.

> ✪ *Less insurance.* You do not have to pay workers' compensation insurance, and since the workers are not your employees, you do not have to insure against their possible liabilities.

> ✪ *More flexibility.* You can use independent contractors when you need them and need not pay them when business is slow.

Disadvantages.

> ✪ The IRS and state tax offices are strict about when workers qualify as independent contractors. They will audit companies whose use of independent contractors does not appear to be legitimate.

> ✪ If your use of independent contractors is found to be improper, you may have to pay back taxes and penalties and have problems with your pension plan.

✪ While employees usually cannot sue you for their injuries (if you have covered them with workers' compensation), independent contractors can sue you if their injuries were your fault.

✪ If you are paying someone to produce a creative work (writing, photography, artwork) you receive fewer rights to the work of an independent contractor.

✪ You have less control over the work of independent contractor and less flexibility in terminating them if you are not satisfied that the job is being done the way you require.

✪ You have less loyalty from an independent contractor who works sporadically for you and possibly others, than from your own full time employees.

For some businesses, the advantages outweigh the disadvantages. For others they do not. Consider your business plans and the consequences from each type of arrangement. Keep in mind that it will be easier to start with independent contractors and switch to employees than to hire employees and have to fire them to hire independent contractors.

Temporary Workers

Another way to avoid the hassles of hiring employees is to get workers from a temporary agency. In this arrangement you may pay a higher amount per hour for the work, but the agency will take care of all of the tax and insurance requirements. Since these can be expensive and time-consuming, the extra cost may be well worth it.

Whether or not temporary workers will work for you will depend upon the type of business you are in and tasks you need performed. For such jobs as sales management, you would probably want someone who will stay with you long-term and develop relationships with the buyers, but for order fulfillment, temporary workers might work out well.

Another advantage of temporary workers is that you can easily stop using those who do not work out well for you, but if you find one who is ideal, you may be able to hire him or her on a full-time basis.

In recent years a new wrinkle has developed in the temporary worker area. Many large companies are beginning to use them because they are so much cheaper than paying the benefits demanded by full-time employees. For example, Microsoft Corp. has had as many as 6,000 temporary workers, some working there for years. Some of the temporary workers won a lawsuit declaring that they are really employees and are entitled to the same benefits as other employees (such as pension plans).

The law is not yet settled in this area as to what arrangements will result in a temporary worker being declared an employee. That will take several more court cases, some of which have already been filed. Following are a few things you can do to protect yourself.

- ✪ Be sure that all of your benefit plans make it clear that they do not apply to workers obtained through temporary agencies.

- ✪ Do not keep the same temporary workers for longer than a year.

- ✪ Do not list temporary workers in any employee directories or hold them out to the public as your employees.

- ✪ Do not allow them to use your business cards or stationery.

Federal Discrimination Laws

There are numerous federal laws forbidding discrimination based upon race, sex, pregnancy, color, religion, national origin, age, or disability. The laws apply to both hiring and firing, and to employment practices such as salaries, promotions and benefits. Most of these laws only apply to an employer who has fifteen or more employees for twenty weeks of a calendar year or has federal contracts or subcontracts. Therefore, you most likely will not be required to comply with the law immediately upon opening your business. However, there are similar state laws that may apply to your business. The *Equal Opportunity Employment*

Commission (EEOC) has a website for new businesses at **www.eeoc.gov /qs-employers.html**. You can get a copy of the *Guide to Disability Rights Laws* at **www.usdoj.gov/crt/ada/cguide.htm**.

One exception is the *Equal Pay Act*, which applies to employers with two or more employees and requires that women be paid the same as men in the same type of job. *Ten Steps to Equal Pay Self Audit for Employers*, a checklist from the Women's Bureau at the U.S. Department of Labor, is a simple private way for business owners to check equal pay compliance. You can find it at:

www.dol.gov/wb/10step71.htm

Employers with 100 or more employees are required to file an annual report with the EEOC. Employers with fifteen or more employees are required to display a poster regarding discrimination. This poster is available from:

Equal Employment Opportunity Commission
1801 L Street, N.W.
Washington, D.C. 20507
202-663-4900 or 800-669-3362
fax: 513-489-8692
www.eeog.gov

When hiring employees, some questions are illegal or inadvisable to ask. The following questions should not be included on your employment application or in your interviews unless the information is somehow directly tied to the duties of the job.

- ✪ Do not ask about an applicant's citizenship or place of birth. Know that, after hiring an employee you must ask about his or her right to work in this country.

- ✪ Do not ask a female applicant her maiden name. You can ask if she has been known by any other name in order to do a background check.

- ✪ Do not ask if applicants have children, plan to have them, or have child-care. You can ask if an applicant will be able to work the required hours.

✪ Do not ask if the applicant has religious objections for working Saturday or Sunday. You can mention if the job requires such hours and ask whether the applicant can meet this job requirement.

✪ Do not ask an applicant's age. You can ask if an applicant is eighteen or over, or for a liquor-related job, if they are twenty-one or over.

✪ Do not ask an applicant's weight.

✪ Do not ask if an applicant has AIDS or is HIV positive.

✪ Do not ask if the applicant has filed a workers' compensation claim.

✪ Do not ask about the applicant's previous health problems.

✪ Do not ask if the applicant is married or whether their spouse would object to the job, hours, or duties.

✪ Do not ask if the applicant owns a home, furniture, or a car, as these questions are considered racially discriminatory.

✪ Do not ask if the applicant was ever arrested. You can ask if the applicant was ever convicted of a crime.

ADA   The *Americans with Disabilities Act (ADA)* of 1990 is a federal civil rights law that prohibits the exclusion of people with disabilities from participating in everyday activities—shopping, watching movies, eating in a restaurant, or other activities. If you are planning to start a business that will serve the public, it is a good idea to call the ADA hotline at 800-514-0301 or go to their website at **www.ada.gov**. There are some guidelines for small businesses as well as information about tax credits and deductions that can help with the costs of compliance. The *ADA Guide for Small Businesses* is available at **www.usdoj.gov/crt/ada/smbusgd.pdf**. The *ADA Standards of Accessible Design* is available on the web at **www.usdoj.gov/crt/ada/adastd94.pdf**.

There are more strict penalties for employers who do not make *reasonable accommodations* for disabled employees. They could face fines of up to $100,000, as well as other civil penalties and civil damage awards. To find out how this law affects your business, you might want to send for the free

CDROM of the *ADA Technical Assistance Manual.* You can order it from their website page at **www.usdoj.gov/crt/ada/cdrequestform.htm.**

The ADA currently applies to employers with fifteen or more employees. Employers who need more than fifteen employees might want to consider contracting with independent contractors to avoid problems with this law, particularly if the number of employees is only slightly larger than fifteen.

Tax benefits. There are three types of tax credits to help small business with the burden of these laws.

- ✪ Businesses can deduct up to $15,000 a year for making their premises accessible to the disabled, and can depreciate the rest of the expense. (Internal Revenue Code (IRC), Sec. 190.)

- ✪ Small businesses (under $1,000,000 in revenue and under thirty employees) can get a tax credit each year for 50% of the cost of making their premises accessible to the disabled, but this only applies to the amount between $250 and $10,500.

- ✪ Small businesses can get a credit of up to 40% of the first $6,000 of wages paid to certain new employees who qualify through the **PRE-SCREENING NOTICE AND CERTIFICATION REQUEST (IRS FORM 8850)**. The form and instructions are in Appendix B. (see form 10, p.242.)

Records   To protect against potential claims of discrimination, all employers should keep detailed records showing reasons for hiring or not hiring applicants and for firing employees.

State Discrimination Laws

Both federal law and Maryland Law (Article 49B) prohibit employers with fifteen or more employees from discriminating in any employment practice or with regard to compensation, benefits, privileges, or conditions of employment among job applicants or employees on any of the following bases: race, color, national origin, sex (including pregnancy-related conditions), religion and age (40+ under the federal *Age Discrimination in Employment Act of 1967*).

Maryland law also prohibits employment discrimination on the basis of marital status or physical or mental handicap. Claims will be investigated by the Maryland Commission on Human Relations and will be mediated before allowing the claimant to file suit.

The *Virginia Human Rights Act* safeguards all individuals within the Commonwealth from unlawful discrimination because of race, color, religion, national origin, sex, pregnancy, childbirth or related medical conditions, age, marital status, or disability. Its purpose is to preserve the public safety, health and general welfare; and further the interests, rights and privileges of individuals within the Commonwealth. It also protects citizens against unfounded charges of unlawful discrimination.

Sexual Harassment

Federal Law   In the 1980s, the Equal Employment Opportunity Commission interpreted Title VII of the *Civil Rights Act of 1964* to forbid sexual harassment. After that, the courts took over and reviewed all types of conduct in the workplace. The numerous lawsuits that followed began a trend toward expanding the definition of sexual harassment and favoring employees.

The EEOC has held the following in sexual harassment cases.

- ✪   The victim as well as the harasser may be a woman or a man.

- ✪   The victim does not have to be of the opposite sex.

- ✪   The harasser can be the victim's supervisor, an agent of the employer, a supervisor in another area, a co-worker, or a non-employee.

- ✪   The victim does not have to be the person harassed but could be anyone affected by the offensive conduct.

- ✪   Unlawful sexual harassment may occur without economic injury to or discharge of the victim.

- ✪   The harasser's conduct must be unwelcome.

Some of the actions that have been considered harassment are:

- ✪ displaying sexually explicit posters in the workplace;

- ✪ requiring female employees to wear revealing uniforms;

- ✪ rating of sexual attractiveness of female employees as they passed male employees' desks;

- ✪ continued sexual jokes and innuendos;

- ✪ demands for sexual favors from subordinates;

- ✪ unwelcome sexual propositions or flirtation;

- ✪ unwelcome physical contact; and,

- ✪ whistling or leering at members of the opposite sex.

Employers can be liable for the harassment of an employee by a supervisor, even if the employer is unaware of the supervisor's conduct, if the employer does not have a system in place to allow complaints against harassment. This area of law is still developing, and to avoid a possible lawsuit you should be aware of the things that could potentially cause liability. Some things a business can do to protect against claims of sexual harassment are:

- ✪ distribute a written policy against all kinds of sexual harassment to all employees;

- ✪ encourage employees to report all incidents of sexual harassment;

- ✪ insure there is no retaliation against those who complain;

- ✪ make clear that your policy is *zero tolerance*;

- ✪ explain that sexual harassment includes both requests for sexual favors and a work environment that some employees may consider hostile;

✪ allow employees to report harassment to someone other than their immediate supervisor in case that person is involved in the harassment; and,

✪ promise as much confidentiality as possible to complainants.

Common Law   Although both the federal and state civil rights laws only apply to businesses with fifteen or more employees, it is possible for an employee to sue for sexual harassment in civil court. However, this is difficult and expensive, and would only be worthwhile if there were substantial damages.

Wage and Hour Laws

The *Fair Labor Standards Act (FLSA)* applies to all employers who are engaged in *interstate commerce* or in the production of goods for interstate commerce (anything which will cross the state line) and all employees of hospitals, schools, residential facilities for the disabled or aged, or public agencies. It also applies to all employees of enterprises that gross $500,000 or more per year.

While many small businesses might not think they are engaged in interstate commerce, the laws have been interpreted so broadly that nearly any use of mail, interstate telephone services, or other interstate services, however minor, is enough to bring a business under the law.

Minimum Wage   The federal wage and hour laws are contained in the FLSA. Since September 1, 1997, the minimum wage has been $5.15 an hour.

In certain circumstances a wage of $3.62 may be paid to employees under twenty years of age for a ninety-day training period.

For employees who regularly receive more than $30 a month in tips, the minimum wage is $2.13 per hour. But if the employee's tips do not bring him or her up to the full $5.15 minimum wage, then the employer must make up the difference.

Overtime   Workers who work over forty hours in a week must be paid *time-and-a-half* for the time worked over forty hours. What comes as a shock to many is that the practice of giving *comp time* instead of overtime pay is illegal in most situations.

Exempt While nearly all businesses are covered, certain employees are *exempt* from
Employees FLSA. Exempt employees include employees that are considered executives,
administrative and managerial, professionals, computer professionals, and outside salespeople.

Whether or not one of these exceptions applies to a particular employee is a
complicated legal question. Thousands of court cases have been decided on this
issue but they have given no clear answers. In one case a person could be determined to be exempt because of his or her duties, but in another, a person with
the same duties could be found not exempt.

One thing that is clear is that the determination is made on the employee's func-
tion, and not just the job title. You cannot make a secretary exempt by giving
the title of *manager* if most of the job duties are clerical. For more information,
contact the Wage and Hour Division at 866-4USWAGE or visit their website at:

www.dol.gov/esa/whd

On the Internet you can obtain information on the Department of Labor's
Employment Law Guide at:

www.dol.gov/asp/programs/guide.htm

Pension and Benefit Laws

There are no laws requiring small businesses to provide any types of special benefits to employees. Such benefits are given to attract and keep good employees.
With pension plans the main concern is, if you do start one, it must comply
with federal tax laws.

Holidays There are no federal or state laws that require that employees be given holidays.
You can require them to work Thanksgiving and Christmas and dock their pay
or fire them for failing to show up. Of course, you will not have much luck
keeping employees with such a policy.

Most companies give full time employees a certain number of paid holidays,
such as: New Year's Day (January 1), Memorial Day (last Monday in May),
Fourth of July, Labor Day (first Monday in September), Thanksgiving (fourth

Thursday in November) and Christmas (December 25). Some, but not many, employers include other holidays such as Martin Luther King, Jr.'s birthday (January 15), President's Day, and Columbus Day. If one of the holidays falls on a Saturday or Sunday, many employers give a holiday on the preceding Friday or following Monday.

Sick Days

There is no federal or state law mandating that an employee be paid for time that he or she is home sick. The situation seems to be that, the larger the company, the more paid sick leave is allowed. Part-time workers rarely are allowed sick leave, and sick leave for small businesses is usually limited because they cannot afford to pay for time that employees do not work.

Some small companies have an official policy of no paid sick leave, but when an important employee misses a day because he or she is clearly sick, it may be paid.

Breaks

There are no federal or state laws requiring coffee breaks or lunch breaks. However, it is common sense that employees will be more productive if they have reasonable breaks for nourishment or to use the toilet facilities.

Pension Plans and Retirement Accounts

Few small new businesses can afford to provide pension plans for their employees. The first concern of a small business is usually how the owner can shelter income in a pension plan without having to set up a pension plan for an employee. Under most pension plans this is not allowed.

IRA. Anyone with $3,000 of earnings can put up to that amount in an *Individual Retirement Account (IRA)*. Unless the person or his or her spouse are covered by a company pension plan and have income over a certain amount, the amount put into the account is fully tax deductible.

ROTH IRA. Contributions to a *Roth IRA* are not tax deductible, but the money is not taxable when taken out. People who expect to still have taxable income when they withdraw from their IRA can benefit from these.

SEP IRA, SAR-SEP IRA, SIMPLE IRA. With these types of retirement accounts, a person can put a much greater amount into a retirement plan and deduct it from their taxable income. Employees must also be covered by such plans, but certain employees are exempt, so it is sometimes possible to use these for the owners alone. The best source for more information is a mutual fund company (such as Vanguard, Fidelity, Dreyfus, etc.) or a local bank, which can set up the plan and provide you with all of the rules.

These have an advantage over qualified plans (discussed below) since they do not have the high annual fees. *IRS Publication 590: Individual Retirement Arrangements* discusses everything you need to know about IRAs:

www.irs.gov/pub/irs-pdf/p590.pdf

Qualified retirement plans. Qualified retirement plans are 401(k) plans, Keogh plans, and corporate retirement plans. These are covered by *ERISA, the Employee Retirement Income Security Act*, which is a complicated law meant to protect employee pension plans. Congress did not want employees who contributed to pension plans all their lives ending up with nothing when the plan goes bankrupt. The law is complicated and the penalties severe. Many banks and mutual funds have created *canned plans* that can be used instead of drafting one from scratch. Still the fees for administering them are steep. Check with a bank or mutual fund for details. Or, you can check out the ERISA Handbook at:

www.dol.gov/ebsa/publications/protect-your-pension.html

Family and Medical Leave Law

Federal Law   To assist business owners in deciding what type of leave to offer their employees, Congress passed the *Family and Medical Leave Act of 1993 (FMLA)*. This law requires an employee to be given up to twelve weeks of unpaid leave when:

✪   the employee or employee's spouse has a child;

✪   the employee adopts a child or takes in a foster child;

✪   the employee needs to care for an ill spouse, child, or parent; or,

✪   the employee becomes seriously ill.

The law only applies to employers with fifty or more employees. Also, the top ten percent of an employer's salaried employees can be denied this leave because of the disruption in business their loss could cause.

Federal Child Labor Laws

The federal *Fair Labor Standards Act* also contains rules regarding the hiring of children. The basic rules are that children under sixteen years old may not be hired at all except in a few jobs, such as acting and newspaper delivery, and those under eighteen may not be hired for dangerous jobs. Children may not work more than three hours a day and eighteen hours a week in a school week, or more than eight hours a day and forty hours a week in a non-school week. If you plan to hire children, you should check the Act, which is in United States Code (U.S.C.), Title 29 and also the related regulations, which are in Code of Federal Regulations (C.F.R.), Title 29. The Department of Labor supplies a *FLSA Advisor* to help answer questions about wage, hour and child labor regulations. It can be found at:

www.dol.gov/elaws/flsa.htm

State Child Labor Laws

Maryland   Maryland imposes the following restrictions on using children as employees.

✪   A minor under the age of 14 may not be employed or permitted to work unless the child is a model, performer, or entertainer with a special permit.

✪   Minors 14 through 17 years of age may only work with a work permit.

✪   These types of work do not require a work permit provided that the work does not include mining or hazardous occupations and takes place outside the school day: Farm work on a family farm, housework in the home, work performed in a family business, unpaid volunteer labor, caddying on a golf course, work done with written parental permission, newspaper delivery, charitable work, counseling or instruction at a certified youth camp, sailboat instruction, and unpaid volunteers of a volunteer fire department who have completed training courses and who are over 16.

✪   Children 14 and 15 can work no more than four hours on a school day, eight hours on a non-school day, twenty-three hours per week during school, and forty hours during school breaks. They may not work before 7am or after 8pm (they may work until 9pm in the summer). They must have a thirty-minute break after every five consecutive hours of work.

✪ Children 16 and 17 may spend no more than twelve hours in a combination of school hours and work hours each day, must have at least eight consecutive free hours each day, and also must have a thirty minute break every five hours.

The State of Maryland has adopted the list of hazardous occupations from the U.S. Department of Labor. The *Employment of Minors Fact Sheet* can be obtained by contacting the Division of Labor and Industry at:

Division of Labor and Industry
Employment Standards Service
1100 N. Eutaw St. Room 606
Baltimore, MD 21201
410-767-2239
fax: 410-767-2220

Virginia Virginia imposes the following restrictions with children in employment.

✪ With few exceptions, employment of minors is prohibited under the age of 14, and work permits must be issued for all minors under the age of 16.

✪ Restrictions are established for minors under 16; employers are required to keep records to verify hours worked and breaks given to minors under 16.

✪ The law also specifies types of employment that are prohibited or limited for minors under the age of 18.

✪ No minor under the age of 18 may be employed in a hazardous occupation.

✪ No minor under the age of 16 may be employed on a construction site or in a hazardous occupation on a farm, garden, orchard, or in other hazardous occupation. These hazardous occupations set forth by regulations of the Virginia Commissioner of Labor and Industry cover the following activities:

- operating a tractor of over 20 hp, or connecting or disconnecting an implement or any of its parts to or from such a tractor;

- operating or assisting to operate (including starting, stopping, adjusting, feeding, or any other activity involving physical contact associated with the operation) any of the following machines:

  - corn picker, cotton picker, grain combine, hay mower, forage harvester, hay baler, potato digger, or mobile pea viner;

  - feed grinder, crop dryer, forage blower, auger conveyor, or the unloading mechanism of a nongravity-type self-unloading wagon or trailer; or,

  - power post-hole digger, power post driver, or nonwalking type rotary tiller;

- operating or assisting to operate (including starting, stopping, adjusting, feeding, or any other activity involving physical contact associated with the operation) any of the following machines:

  - earthmoving equipment,

  - fork lift,

  - potato combine, or

  - chain saw;

- working on a farm in a yard, pen, or stall occupied by:

  - a bull, boar, or stud horse maintained for breeding purposes, or

  - a sow with suckling pigs, or cow with newborn calf (with umbilical cord present);

- working from a ladder at a height of over 20 feet for purposes such as pruning trees, picking fruit, etc.;

- driving a bus, truck, or automobile when transporting passengers or riding on a tractor as a passenger or helper;

- working inside:

  - a fruit, forage, or grain storage designed to retain an oxygen-deficient or toxic atmosphere;

  - an upright silo within two weeks after silage has been added or when a top unloading device is in operating position;

  - a manure pit; or,

  - a horizontal silo while operating a tractor for packing purposes;

- handling or applying (including cleaning or decontaminating equipment, disposal or return of empty containers, or serving as a flagman for aircraft applying) agricultural chemicals classified under the federal *Insecticide, Fungicide, and Rodenticide Act* (7 U.S.C. beginning with Sec.135) as *Category I* of toxicity, identified by the word *poison* and the *skull and crossbones* on the label; or *Category II* of toxicity, identified by the word *warning* on the label;

- handling or using a blasting agent including, but not limited to, dynamite, black powder, sensitized ammonium nitrate, blasting caps, and primer cord; or,

- transporting, transferring, or applying anhydrous ammonia.

A penalty of up to $1000 may be assessed for each violation. An employer may be fined for each minor who is employed the if code's requirements are not met for each individual. For more information, contact:

Virginia Department of Labor and Industry
Northern Virginia Regional Office
10515 Battlefield Parkway
Manassas, Virginia 20109
703-392-0900
fax: 703-392-0308

Immigration Laws

Documentation Requirement

In 1986, Congress passed a law that imposes strict penalties on any business that hires aliens who are not eligible to work. Under this law you must verify both the identity and the employment eligibility of anyone you hire by using the **EMPLOYMENT ELIGIBILITY VERIFICATION (FORM I-9)**. (see form 11, p.246.) This form is also available online at **www.immigration.gov/graphics/formsfee /forms/files/I-9.pdf**. Both you and the employee must fill out the form and you must check an employee's identification cards or papers. Fines for hiring illegal aliens range from $250 to $2,000 for the first offense and up to $10,000 for the third offense. Failure to maintain the proper paperwork may result in a fine of up to $1,000. The law does not apply to independent contractors with whom you may contract, and it does not penalize you if the employee used fake identification.

There are also penalties that apply to employers of four or more persons for discriminating against eligible applicants because they appear foreign or because of their national origin or citizenship status.

In Appendix A there is a sample filled-in **FORM I-9**. Appendix B has a list of acceptable documentation, a blank form, and instructions. (see form 11, p.246.)

For more information call 800-357-2099. The *Handbook for Employers and Instructions for Completing Form 1-9 (M-274)*, is available at **www.immigration.gov/graphics/lawsregs/handbook/hand_emp.pdf** or write to the following address:

Bureau of Citizen and Immigration Services
425 I Street, N.W.
Washington, DC 20536

Foreign Employees

If you wish to hire employees who are foreign citizens and are not able to provide the documentation explained above, they must first obtain a work visa. Work visas for foreigners are not easy to get. Millions of people around the globe would like to come to the U.S. to work and the laws are designed to keep most of them out to protect the jobs of American citizens.

Whether or not a person can get a work visa depends on whether there is a shortage of U.S. workers available to fill the job. For jobs requiring few or no skills, it is practically impossible to get a visa. For highly skilled jobs, such as nurses and physical therapists, and for those of exceptional ability, such as Nobel Prize winners and Olympic medallists, obtaining a visa is fairly easy.

There are several types of visas and different rules for different countries. For example, NAFTA has made it easier for some types of workers to enter the U.S. from Canada and Mexico. For some positions, a shortage of workers is assumed. For others, a business must first advertise a position available in the U.S. Only after no qualified persons apply, can it hire someone from another country.

The visa system is complicated and subject to regular change. In late 2000 a new law expanded the number of certain worker visas from 115,000 to 195,000. If you wish to hire a foreign worker you should consult with an immigration specialist or a book on the subject.

Hiring Off-the-Books

Because of the taxes, insurance, and red tape involved with hiring employees, some new businesses hire people *off-the-book*s. They pay them in cash and never admit they are employees. While the cash paid in wages would not be deductible, they consider this a smaller cost than compliance. Some even use off the books receipts to cover it.

Except when your spouse or child is giving you some temporary help, hiring off the books is a terrible idea. Hiring people off the books can result in civil fines, loss of insurance coverage, and even criminal penalties. When engaged in dangerous work like roofing or using power tools, you are risking millions of dollars in potential liability if a worker is killed or seriously injured.

It may be more costly and time consuming to comply with the employment laws, but if you are concerned with long-term growth with less risk, it is the wiser way to go.

Federal Contracts

Companies that do work for the federal government are subject to several laws.

The *Davis-Bacon Act* requires contractors engaged in U.S. government construction projects to pay wages and benefits that are equal to or better than the prevailing wages in the area. The government requires the posting of a notice at job sites. It is available from the Department of Labor online at:

www.dol.gov/osbp/sbrefa/poster/main.htm

The *McNamara-O'Hara Service Contract Act* sets wages and other labor standards for contractors furnishing services to agencies of the U.S. government.

The *Walsh-Healey Public Contracts Act* requires the Department of Labor to settle disputes regarding manufacturers supplying products to the U.S. government.

Miscellaneous Laws

Affirmative Action

In most cases, the federal government does not yet tell employers who they must hire. This would be especially true for new small businesses. The only situation where a small business would need to comply with affirmative action requirements would be if it accepted federal contracts or subcontracts. These requirements could include the hiring of minorities or of Vietnam veterans.

Layoffs

Companies with one hundred or more full-time employees at one location are subject to the *Worker Adjustment and Retraining Notification Act*. This law requires a sixty-day notification prior to certain lay-offs and has other strict provisions.

Unions

The *National Labor Relations Act of 1935* gives employees the right to organize a union or to join one. (29 U.S.C, beginning with Sec. 151.) There are things employers can do to protect themselves, but you should consult a labor attorney or a book on the subject before taking action that might be illegal and result in fines.

Poster Laws   Certain posters must be displayed to inform employees of their rights. Not all businesses are required to display all posters, but the following list should be of help.

> ✪   All employers must display the wage and hour poster available from

U. S. Department of Labor
200 Constitution Ave., NW
Washington, DC 20210

> ✪   Employers with fifteen or more employees for twenty weeks of the year must display the sex, race, religion, and ethnic discrimination poster and the age discrimination poster available from:

EEOC
2401 E Street NW
Washington, DC 20506

> ✪   Employers with federal contracts or subcontracts of $10,000 or more must display the sex, race, etc. discrimination poster mentioned earlier, plus a poster regarding Vietnam Era Veterans available from the local federal contracting office.

> ✪   Employers with government contracts subject to the *Service Contract Act* or the *Public Contracts Act* must display a notice to employees working on government contracts available from:

Employment Standards Division
U. S. Department of Labor
200 Constitution Ave.
NW, Washington, DC 20210

All of the above posters are available online at:

www.dol.gov/osbp/sbrefa/poster/main.htm

12 ADVERTISING AND PROMOTION LAWS

Laws and rules about advertising and promoting your products or services exist at both the federal and state level. In some areas, such as with labeling, the rules are very specific and strict. In other areas, more subjective standards will apply. Familiarize yourself with these rules to avoid potential violations.

Federal Laws

The federal government regulates advertising through the *Federal Trade Commission (FTC)*. The rules are contained in the *Code of Federal Regulations (C.F.R.)*. You can find these rules in most law libraries and many public libraries. If you plan any advertising that you think may be questionable, you might want to check the rules. As you read the rules below, you will probably think of many violations you see every day.

Federal rules do not apply to every business, and small businesses that operate only within the state and do not use the postal service may be exempt. However, many of the federal rules have been adopted into law by the states. Therefore, your state rather than the federal government could prosecute a violation.

Some of the important rules are summarized below. If you wish to learn more details about the rules you should obtain copies from your library. You can also receive guidance on these rules from the FTC on their website at:

www.ftc.gov/bcp/guides/guides.htm

Deceptive Pricing

When prices are being compared, it is required that actual and not inflated prices are used. For example, if an object would usually be sold for $7, you should not first offer it for $10 and then start offering it at 30% off. It is considered misleading to suggest that a discount from list price is a bargain if the item is seldom actually sold at list price. If most surrounding stores sell an item for $7 it is considered misleading to say it has a retail value of $ 10 even if there are some stores elsewhere selling it at that price. (See 16 C.F.R. Ch.1, Part 233.)

Bait Advertising

Bait advertising is placing an ad when you do not really want the respondents to buy the product offered, but want them to switch to another item. The factors used to determine if there was a violation are similar to those used by the states, as explained later in this chapter.(See. 16, C.F.R. Ch. I, Part 238.)

Free Items

Use of *free, half-off, 1¢ sale*, and the like must not be misleading. This means that the *regular price* must not include a mark-up to cover the *free* item. The seller must expect to sell the product without the free item at some time in the future. (See 16 C.F.R., Ch. I, Part 251.)

Substantiation of Claims

The FTC requires that advertisers be able to substantiate their claims. (See 48 Federal Regulations p. 10471.)

Endorsements

This rule forbids endorsements that are misleading. An example is a quote from a film review that is used in such a way as to change the substance of the review. It is not necessary to use the exact words of the person endorsing the product as long as the opinion is not distorted. If a product is changed, an endorsement that does not apply to the new version cannot be used. For some items, such as drugs, claims cannot be used without scientific proof. Endorsements by organizations cannot be used unless one is sure that the membership holds the same opinion. (See 16 C.F.R. Ch. 1 Part 255.)

Unfairness

The FTC forbids any advertising practices that can be deemed to be unfair. (See 15 U.S.C. 45.)

Negative Option Plans

When a seller uses a sales system in which the buyer must notify the seller if he does not want the goods, the seller must provide the buyer with a form to decline the sale and at least ten days in which to decline. Bonus merchandise must be shipped promptly and the seller must promptly terminate any who so request after completion of the contract. (See 16 C.F.R. Ch. 1, Part 425.)

Laser Eye Surgery

Under the laws governing deceptive advertising, the FTC and the FDA are regulating the advertising of laser eye surgery. Anyone involved in this area should obtain a copy of these rules. (See 15 U.S.C. Secs. 45, 52-57.)

Food and Dietary Supplements

Under the *Nutritional Labeling Education Act of 1990*, the FTC and the FDA regulate the packaging and advertising of food and dietary products. Anyone involved in this area should obtain a copy of these rules. (See 21 U.S.C. Sec. 343.)

Jewelry and Precious Metals

The FTC has numerous rules governing the sale and advertising of jewelry and precious metals. Anyone in this business should obtain a copy of these rules. (See 61 Federal Regulations p. 27212.)

State Laws

Maryland, Virginia, and the District of Columbia all have *Consumer Protection Acts* that govern advertising standards. Detailed information is available from the Maryland Attorney General, the District of Columbia Office of Corporation Counsel, and the Virginia Department of Agriculture and Consumer Services.

Misleading Advertising

In Maryland, the District of Columbia, and Virginia, it is illegal to use advertising that is *misleading*, or to use words like *wholesale* or *below cost* unless the goods are actually at or below the retailer's net cost. Retailers may not advertise items at a special price unless they have reasonable quantities or state in the ad the quantity available (unless they give rain checks). A customer may sue a business under this law and receive payment for attorney's fees, court costs, actual and punitive damages.

Under state law, it is generally forbidden to make any misrepresentations of goods or services to the public including any of the following:

- ✪ misrepresenting the owner, manufacturer, distributor, source or geographical origin of goods (sellers may use their own brand names on goods);

- ✪ misrepresenting the age, model, grade, style or standard of goods;

- ✪ misrepresenting the sponsorship, endorsement, approval, or certification of goods or services;

- ✪ misrepresenting the affiliation, connection, or association of any goods or services;

- ✪ misrepresenting the nature, characteristics, standard ingredients, uses, benefits, warranties, guarantees, quantities or qualities of goods or services;

- ✪ misrepresenting used, altered, deteriorated or repossessed goods as new; however, goods returned to a seller undamaged may be sold as new;

- ✪ disparaging goods, services, or business of another by false or misleading representation; or,

- ✪ advertising goods or services with intent not to sell them as advertised.

For detailed information on prohibited practices in advertising, see Maryland Commercial Law Code Sections 13-301, D.C. Code Sections 28-3904 and Virginia Code Sections 59.1-200.

Internet Sales Laws

There are not yet specific laws governing Internet transactions different from laws governing other transactions. The FTC feels that its current rules regarding deceptive advertising, substantiation, disclaimers, refunds, and related matters must be followed by Internet businesses and that consumers are adequately protected by them. See the first three pages of this chapter and Chapter 9 for that information.

For some specific guidelines on Internet advertising, see the FTC's site at:

www.ftc.gov/bcp/conline/pubs/buspubs/ruleroad.htm

Home Solicitation Laws

Federal Law   The Federal Trade Commission has rules governing door-to-door sales. In any such sale, it is a *deceptive trade practice* to fail to furnish a receipt explaining the sale (in the language of the presentation) and giving notice that there is a right to back out of the contract within three days, known as a *right of rescission*. The notice must be supplied in duplicate, must be in at least 10-point type, and must be captioned either "Notice of Right to Cancel" or "Notice of Cancellation." The notice must be worded as follows:

NOTICE OF CANCELLATION

Date _____

YOU MAY CANCEL THIS TRANSACTION, WITHOUT ANY PENALTY OR OBLIGATION, WITHIN THREE BUSINESS DAYS FROM THE ABOVE DATE.

IF YOU CANCEL, ANY PROPERTY TRADED IN, ANY PAYMENTS MADE BY YOU UNDER THE CONTRACT OR SALE, AND ANY NEGOTIABLE INSTRUMENT EXECUTED BY YOU WILL BE RETURNED TO YOU WITHIN 10 BUSINESS DAYS FOLLOWING RECEIPT BY THE SELLER OF YOUR CANCELLATION NOTICE, AND ANY SECURITY INTEREST ARISING OUT OF THE TRANSACTION WILL BE CANCELLED.

IF YOU CANCEL, YOU MUST MAKE AVAILABLE TO THE SELLER AT YOUR RESIDENCE, IN SUBSTANTIALLY AS GOOD CONDITION AS WHEN RECEIVED, ANY GOODS DELIVERED TO YOU UNDER THIS CONTRACT OR SALE; OR YOU MAY IF YOU WISH, COMPLY WITH THE INSTRUCTIONS OF THE SELLER REGARDING THE RETURN SHIPMENT OF THE GOODS AT THE SELLER'S EXPENSE AND RISK.

(continued)

IF YOU DO MAKE THE GOODS AVAILABLE TO THE SELLER AND THE SELLER DOES NOT PICK THEM UP WITHIN 20 DAYS OF THE DATE OF YOUR NOTICE OF CANCELLATION, YOU MAY RETAIN OR DISPOSE OF THE GOODS WITHOUT ANY FURTHER OBLIGATION. IF YOU FAIL TO MAKE THE GOODS AVAILABLE TO THE SELLER, OR IF YOU AGREE TO RETURN THE GOODS AND FAIL TO DO SO, THEN YOU REMAIN LIABLE FOR PERFORMANCE OF ALL OBLIGATIONS UNDER THE CONTRACT.

TO CANCEL THIS TRANSACTION, MAIL OR DELIVER A SIGNED AND DATED COPY OF THIS CANCELLATION NOTICE OR ANY OTHER WRITTEN NOTICE, OR SEND A TELEGRAM, TO [name of seller], AT [address of seller's place of business] NOT LATER THAN MIDNIGHT OF _____ (date).

I HEREBY CANCEL THIS TRANSACTION.

_____   _____
[Buyer's signature)   (Date)

The seller must complete the notice and orally inform the buyer of the right to cancel. The seller cannot misrepresent the right to cancel, assign the contract until the fifth business day, nor include a confession of judgment in the contract. For further information on federal consumer protection issues, visit the FTC website at:

www.ftc.gov/ftc/consumer.htm

State Law   Maryland, Virginia, and the District of Columbia all have laws governing home solicitation. (See Md. Commercial Law Code Sec. 14, D.C. Code Sec. 28-3811 and Va. Code Sec. 59.1.) There are many similarities among these consumer protection laws, including the following:

Right to cancel. Any such sale described above may be cancelled by the buyer by written notice, in any form, postmarked any time before midnight of the *third business day* after the sales day. Business days do not include Sunday, New Year's Day, Washington's Birthday, Memorial Day, Independence Day, Labor Day, Columbus Day, Veterans Day, Thanksgiving Day, and Christmas Day.

Written agreement. Every such sale must be in writing, contain the buyer's signature and the date the buyer signed, and must contain the following notice:

BUYER'S RIGHT TO CANCEL

THIS IS A HOME SOLICITATION SALE, AND IF YOU DO NOT WANT THE GOODS OR SERVICES, YOU MAY CANCEL THIS AGREEMENT BY PROVIDING WRITTEN NOTICE TO THE SELLER IN PERSON, BY TELEGRAM, OR BY MAIL. THIS NOTICE MUST INDICATE THAT YOU DO NOT WANT THE GOODS OR SERVICES AND MUST BE DELIVERED OR POSTMARKED BEFORE MIDNIGHT OF THE THIRD BUSINESS DAY AFTER YOU SIGN THIS AGREEMENT. IF YOU CANCEL THIS AGREEMENT, THE SELLER MAY NOT KEEP ALL OR PART OF ANY CASH DOWN PAYMENT.

Refund. The refund must be made to the Buyer within ten days. If it is not, the seller may be subject to criminal and civil penalties.

Buyer's duty. Within a reasonable time after cancellation and demand by seller, a buyer must return any goods received under the contract unless the seller fails to refund the buyer's deposit as required. If the seller has not made demand within forty days, the buyer may keep the goods. If the seller does not refund the buyer's deposit, the buyer may retain possession of the goods and has a lien on them for the amount due him. The buyer must take reasonable care of the goods in his possession but does not have to deliver them to the seller at any place other than the buyer's residence.

Seller's duty. All businesses conducting solicitation sales must:

✪   ensure that all employees have the required permits;

✪   provide identification to salesmen for face to face sales, which includes the seller's name, description, and signature: the name, address, and phone number of the company; and the name, address, and signature of seller's supervisor; and,

✪   direct sales agents to leave a business card, contract, or receipt with the buyer including the following information: name, address, and phone number of the company, and of the sales agent, and the buyer's Right to Cancel Notice described above.

In telephone solicitations, the name, address, and phone number of the company must be clearly disclosed on sales materials and contracts sent to the buyer.

Prohibitions. In conducting *home solicitations*, no person shall:

- misrepresent terms of the sale;

- misrepresent seller's affiliation with the company;

- misrepresent reasons for solicitation (such as contests, handicaps, etc. which are not true);

- imply the contract is non-cancelable; or,

- misrepresent anything else.

Telephone Solicitation Laws

Federal Laws Telephone solicitations are governed by the *Telemarketing and Consumer Fraud and Abuse Prevention* (15 U.S.C. Sec. 6101) and such rules as the *Telemarketing Sales Rule* (16 C.F.R. Part 310). For further guidance, go to the FTC website at **www.ftc.gov/bcp/rulemaking/tsr/index.html**. Anyone who violates the rules is subject to civil penalties of up to $10,000 per violation. In addition, violators may be subject to nation-wide injunctions that prohibit certain conduct, and may be required to pay redress to injured consumers. Some of the requirements under the law are as follows.

- Calls can only be made between 8 a.m. and 9 p.m.

- Solicitors must keep a *do not call* list and honor requests not to call.

- There must be a written policy that the parties called are told the name of the caller, the name and phone number or address of the caller's business, that the call is a sales call, and the nature of the goods or services.

- Personnel must be trained in the policies.

- Recorded messages cannot be used to call residences.

State Law   State telephone solicitation laws apply to any transaction involving real or personal property normally used primarily for personal, family, or household purposes. There are severe civil penalties for violations of these laws, so check with an attorney before soliciting sales over the phone. These laws generally contain provisions on identification and enforcablitily.

Identification. Any person who makes a telephone solicitation call must identify himself or herself by true first and last name and the name of the business represented immediately upon making contact.

Enforceability. A contract agreed to after a telephone solicitation is not enforceable until the seller obtains a signed contract from the buyer. The contract must accurately describe the goods and contain the name, address and phone number of the seller. It also must contain in bold conspicuous type the following clause:

> *"You are not obligated to pay any money unless you sign this contract and return it to the seller."*

The contract must also state that it includes all oral representations made by the seller and complies with "all applicable laws and rules."

Pricing, Weights, and Labeling

Federal Law   *Food products.* Beginning in 1994, all food products were required to have labels with information on the product's nutritional values such as calories, fat, and protein. For most products, the label must be in the required format so that consumers can easily compare products. For more information about food labeling requirements, see the FDA website at:

www.cfsan.fda.gov/label.html

Metric measures. Also in 1994, federal rules requiring metric measurement of products took effect. Some federal agencies, such as the federal highway department, indefinitely postponed implementation of the rules, but the Federal Trade Commission (FTC) and the Food and Drug Administration (FDA) intend to enforce the rules against businesses.

Under these rules, metric measures do not have to be the first measurement on the container, but they must be included. Food items that are packaged as they are sold (such as delicatessen items), do not have to contain metric labels.

Fortunately, there are numerous private companies that can help your business with labels for your products. They can help you with everything from product name and formulation development, label content analysis, assistance with regulatory interpretation, generic label approval evaluation, computerized nutritional analysis, USDA label approval, and nutrition facts panel development.

State Law
All states have laws against deceptive or misleading labeling that generally fall into the following categories—

Misrepresenting quantity. Misrepresenting the quantity of goods offered for sale or goods purchased.

Misrepresenting price. Misrepresenting the price of any commodity, or representing the price in any manner calculated to confuse. When a price includes a fraction of a cent, all elements of the fraction must be prominently displayed.

Method of sale. Generally, commodities in liquid form must be sold by liquid measure or weight, and those not sold in liquid form, sold only by weight, area or volume, or by count, as long as the method of sale provides accurate quantity information.

Bulk sale. Bulk sales of over a certain amount must be accompanied by a delivery ticket containing the following information:

- ✪ the name and address of the seller and buyer;

- ✪ date delivered;

- ✪ net quantity delivered and net quantity for basis of price if this differs from quantity delivered;

- ✪ identity of the commodity in commercially practicable terms, including representations made in connection with the sale; and,

✪ the count of individually wrapped packages, if there are more than one of such packages.

Information required on packages. Generally, all packages of commodities for sale must bear a conspicuous statement of:

✪ identity of commodity unless it can be identified through wrapper;

✪ net quantity of contents in terms of weight, measure or count; and,

✪ for goods sold other than where they are packed, the name and place of business of the manufacturer, packer, or distributor.

Declarations of unit price on random packages. In addition to the bulk sales requirements above, when goods are offered in packages of different weights with the price stated on them, the price per single unit of weight must also be stated.

Advertising packages for sale. When a packaged commodity is advertised for sale with a price stated, the quantity must also be conspicuously stated.

Refunds

Under state Consumer Protection laws, if a retail establishment has a policy of no refunds or exchanges, a notice of such policy must be posted at the point of sale. If no notice is posted, a seller must grant a refund to purchasers requesting one within seven days of purchase and producing proof of purchase. However, the merchandise must be unused and in the original packaging. These rules generally do not apply to food that cannot be resold by a merchant because of a law or regulation, perishables, goods that are custom-made or altered, or goods that cannot be resold.

13 | PAYMENT AND COLLECTION

Depending on the business you are in, you may be paid by cash, checks, credit cards, or some sort of financing arrangement such as a store account or a promissory note. Both state and federal laws affect the type of payments you collect, and failure to follow the laws can cost you considerably.

Cash

Cash is probably the easiest form of payment and it is subject to few restrictions. The most important one is that you keep an accurate account of your cash transactions and that you report all cash income on your tax return. Efforts to stop the drug trade have resulted in some serious penalties for failing to report cash transactions and for money laundering. The laws are so sweeping that even if you deal in cash in an ordinary business, like a restaurant, you may violate the law and face huge fines and imprisonment.

The most important law to be concerned with is the one requiring the filing of the **REPORT OF CASH PAYMENTS OVER $10,000 (IRS FORM 8300)**. (see form 15, p.264.) A transaction does not have to happen in one day. If a person brings you smaller amounts of cash that add up to $10,000 and the government can construe them as one transaction, then the form must be filed. Under this law, *cash* also includes travelers' checks, and money orders, but not cashier's checks or bank checks.

Checks

It is important to accept checks in your business. While a small percentage of these checks will be bad, most will be good, and you will be able to accommodate more customers. To avoid having problems with checks, you should adhere to the following rules.

Bad Checks

All of the states have their own laws regarding bad check collection and can vary from county to county. Maryland, the District of Columbia, and Virginia have fairly effective bad check collection processes. If you follow the rules you will probably be able to collect on a bad check. Some counties even have special divisions of the sheriff's department that actively help you collect on bad checks.

The first rule is that you must *identify* the person who gave you the check. To do this you should require identification and write down the sources of identification on the face of the check. Another rule is that you cannot accept *post-dated checks*. Also, you must send a *demand letter* to the person by certified mail that they must pay the amount of the check. Contact your local authorities for guidance regarding penalties.

Refunds after Cashing Check

A popular scam is for a person to purchase something by using a check and then come back the next day demanding a refund. After making the refund the business discovers the initial payment check bounced. Do not make refunds until checks clear.

Credit Cards

In our buy-now, pay-later society, charge cards can add greatly to your sales potential, especially with large, discretionary purchases. The more typical cards are MasterCard, Visa, Discover, and American Express. Fees for these cards, chargeable to you, the merchant, vary from 2% to 5%. American Express may have larger fees than the other credit cards. To establish a credit card facility you need a *merchant account* that can normally be supplied by your bank. Taking credit cards on the Internet requires a different type of merchant account. Rates for merchant accounts vary and you should negotiate with the provider bank to obtain the lowest fees and then renegotiate after you have established an account history with the bank.

With your merchant account in place your provider will transfer money from credit card sales electronically into your bank account on a daily basis. Under your merchant agreement you will undoubtedly be liable for some *charge-backs* by consumers, which will reduce your revenues.

For mail order businesses, especially those operating out of the home, it is much harder to get merchant status. This is because of the number of scams in which large amounts are charged, no products are shipped, and the company folds. At one point, even a business offering to post a large cash bond and let the bank hold the charges for six months was refused.

Today things are a little better. Some companies are even soliciting merchants. But beware of those that charge exorbitant fees (such as $5 or $10 per order for *processing*). One good thing about American Express is that they will accept mail order companies operating out of the home. However, not as many people have their cards as others.

You might be tempted to try to run your charges through another business. This may be effective if you actually sell your products through them, but if you run your business charges through their account the other business may lose its merchant status. People who bought a book by mail from you and then have a charge on their statement from a florist shop will probably call the credit card company saying that they never bought anything from the florist shop. If you have too many of these, your account will be closed.

A new money-making scheme by the credit card companies is to offer *business credit cards* that the merchants are charged a higher fee for accepting. To make these more profitable the credit card companies are telling customers they are not allowed to use their personal credit cards for business purposes. To keep your processing fees down, you can tell your customers you prefer personal, not business credit cards.

Financing Laws

Some businesses can more easily make sales if they finance the purchases themselves. If the business has enough capital to do this, it can earn extra profits on the financing terms. Nonetheless, because of abuses, both the federal and state governments have passed many consumer protection laws.

Federal Law Two important federal laws regarding financing are called the *Truth in Lending Act* and the *Fair Credit Billing Act*. These are implemented by what is called *Regulation Z (Reg. Z)*, issued by the Board of Governors of the Federal Reserve System. It is contained in Volume 12 of the Code of Federal Regulations, page 226. (1 C.F.R., Vol. 12, p. 226.) This is a very complicated law and some have said that no business can be sure to be in compliance with it.

Reg. Z. The regulation covers all transactions in which the following four conditions are met:

1. Credit is offered.

2. The offering of credit is regularly done.

3. There is a finance charge for the credit or there is a written agreement with more than four payments.

4. The credit is for personal, family, or household purposes.

It also covers credit card transactions where only the first two conditions are met. It applies to leases if the consumer ends up paying the full value and keeping the item leased. It does not apply to the following:

✪ transactions with businesses for agricultural purposes;

✪ transactions with organizations such as corporations or the government;

✪ transactions of over $25,000 that are not secured by the consumer's dwelling;

✪ credit involving public utilities;

✪   credit involving securities or commodities; and,

✪   home fuel budget plans.

The way for a small business to avoid Reg. Z violations is to avoid transactions that meet the conditions or to make sure all transactions fall under the exceptions. For many businesses this is easy. Instead of extending credit to customers, accept credit cards and let the credit card company extend the credit. However, if your customers usually do not have credit cards or if you are in a business, such as used car sales, which often extends credit, you should consult a lawyer knowledgeable about Reg. Z or get a copy for yourself at:

www.cardreport.com/laws/tila/tila.html

State Law   States also have laws regarding financing arrangements. Anyone engaged in retail installment selling must be licensed in Maryland by the Commissioner of Financial Regulation; in the District of Columbia, by the Department of Banking and Financial Institutions; and, in Virginia, by the State Corporation Commission Bureau of Financial Institutions. The law specifies what size type must be used in printed contracts, what notices must be included in them and many other details.

State laws also forbid discrimination based upon sex, marital status, or race in the areas of loaning money, granting credit, or providing equal pay for equal services performed. Discrimination is forbidden in the financing of residential real estate based upon race, color, national origin, sex, handicap, familial status, or religion.

Usury

Usury is the charging of an illegally high rate of interest.

District of Columbia   In the District of Columbia, the legal rate of interest is 6% per annum if there is no contract and 24% if there is a contract. The usury laws do not apply to loans to corporations. Usurious interest paid in the District of Columbia can be recovered.

Maryland   In Maryland the legal rate is 6%. If there is a contract the maximum rate is 8%. Persons guilty of usury must forfeit three times the excess of interest and charges above the legal rate or $500 whichever is greater.

Virginia   In Virginia, the legal rate is 8% and the contract rate is 12% on agricultural loans. If the borrower successfully shows the interest charged is usurious, then it is forfeited. The usury laws in Virginia do not apply to corporations.

Collections

Federal Law   Laws to protect consumers from overreaching debt collection practices exist on both the federal and state level.

The *Fair Debt Collection Practices Act of 1977* bans the use of deception, harassment, and other unreasonable acts in the collection of debts. It has strict requirements whenever someone is collecting a debt for someone else. If you are in the collection business, you must get a copy of this law.

The Federal Trade Commission has issued some rules that prohibit deceptive representations such as pretending to be in the motion picture industry, the government, or a credit bureau and/or using questionnaires that do not say they are for the purpose of collecting a debt. (16 C.F.R. Sec. 237.)

State Law   Consumer Collection Practice laws apply to debts owed by persons (not corporations) for transactions that were for personal, family, or household purposes. The law forbids:

- ✪   simulating a law enforcement officer or government agency;

- ✪   using or threatening force or violence;

- ✪   threatening to disclose the debt to others without explaining that the fact that there is a dispute over the debt will also be disclosed;

- ✪   contacting or threatening to contact a debtor's employer prior to obtaining a final judgment, unless the debtor has given permission in writing or unless the debtor has agreed in writing as to the debt, after the debt goes to collection;

✪ disclosing information affecting the debtor's reputation to persons outside the debtor's family who do not have a legitimate business need for the information;

✪ disclosing information affecting the debtor's reputation, knowing the information to be false;

✪ disclosing information about a disputed debt without disclosing the dispute;

✪ willfully harassing the debtor or the debtor's family;

✪ using profane, obscene, vulgar, or willfully abusive language with the debtor or the debtor's family;

✪ attempting to collect a debt that is not legitimate;

✪ claiming a legal right knowing that this right does not exist;

✪ using communication that looks like it is from a court, government, or attorney if it is not;

✪ pretending to be an attorney by using attorney's stationery or forms;

✪ orally pretending to be an attorney or associated with an attorney;

✪ advertising or threatening to advertise sale of a claim unless under court order or as assignee;

✪ publishing or posting a *deadbeat* list;

✪ refusing to identify one's self or employer when requested by a debtor;

✪ mailing any communication to a debtor that contains embarrassing words on the outside of the envelope; and,

✪ communicating with a debtor between 9 p.m. and 8 a.m. without prior consent of the debtor.

A debtor who is a victim of any of the above violations may sue the creditor for actual damages or $500 (whichever is greater), costs, and attorney fees, and in some cases *punitive* damages. (If a debtor wrongly brings a suit, he or she may have to pay the creditor's attorney's fees and court costs.)

14 | BUSINESS RELATIONS LAWS

Uniform laws, anti-trust regulations, and intellectual property rules are all things a business owner must be aware o to some degree.

The Uniform Commercial Code

The *Uniform Commercial Code (UCC)* is a set of laws regulating numerous aspects of doing business. A national group drafted this set of uniform laws to avoid having a patchwork of different laws around the fifty states. Although some states modified some sections of the laws, the code is basically the same in most of the states. In the District of Columbia, the UCC is contained in Title 28, Chapter 1 of the DC Code; in Virginia, in Title 8.1, Chapter 1 of the Va. Code Ann; and, in Maryland, in Chapter 1 of the Md. Commercial Law Code Ann. Each chapter is concerned with a different aspect of commercial relations such as sales, warranties, bank deposits, commercial paper, and bulk transfers.

Businesses that wish to know their rights in all types of transactions should obtain a copy of the UCC and become familiar with it. It is especially useful in transactions between merchants. However, the meaning is not always clear from a reading of the statutes. In law school, students usually spend a full semester studying each chapter of this law.

Commercial Discrimination

Discriminating between different purchasers of your product is generally prohibited.

Federal Law

The *Robinson-Patman Act of 1936* prohibits businesses from injuring competition by offering the same goods at different prices to different buyers. This means that the large chain stores should not be getting a better price than your small shop. It also requires that promotional allowances must be made on proportionally the same terms to all buyers.

As a small business, you may be a victim of Robinson-Patman Act violations. A good place to look for information on the Act is the following websites:

www.lawmall.com/rpa

www.newrules.org/retail/index.html

State Law

Maryland and Virginia law prohibits any person who is engaged in commerce to directly or indirectly discriminate in price between purchasers of commodities or services of like grade and quality, if the effects of the discrimination may substantially lessen competition, tend to create a monopoly in any line of trade or commerce, or injure, destroy, or prevent competition with any person who grants or knowingly receives the benefit of the discrimination or with customers of either of them. The District of Columbia has similar anti-trust laws.

Restraining Trade

If y our business provides a unique product or service, you may have a monopoly for that product or service. There is generally nothing illegal about that so long as your monopoly does not prohibit others from competing with you. When your monopoly does restrain trade, federal and state laws exist to correct the situation.

Federal Law   One of the earliest federal laws affecting business is the *Sherman Antitrust Act of 1890*. The purpose of the law was to protect competition in the marketplace by prohibiting monopolies. For example, one large company might buy out all of its competitors and then raise prices to astronomical levels. It was this law that was used to break up AT&T.

Examples of some things that are prohibited are:

- ✪ agreements between competitors to sell at the same prices;

- ✪ agreements between competitors on how much will be sold or produced;

- ✪ agreements between competitors to divide up a market;

- ✪ refusing to sell one product without a second product; or,

- ✪ exchanging information among competitors that results in similarity of prices.

As a new business you probably will not be in a position to violate the act, but you should be aware of it in case a larger competitor tries to put you out of business. A good place to find information on the act is the following Internet site:

www.lawmall.com/sherman.act/index.html

State Law   Generally, each state has laws against the restraint of trade. In most states, it is unlawful to have any contract, combination, or conspiracy to restrain trade or to monopolize, attempt to monopolize, or combine or conspire with any other person to monopolize any part of trade or commerce. Typical relief for violations include:

- ✪ a penalty for any violation up to $100,000 and

- ✪ a person whose business is hurt by a violation can seek an injunction to prohibit violations and may collect triple his damages in a suit against a violator, along with costs and attorney's fees.

Intellectual Property Protection

As a business owner you should know enough about intellectual property law to protect your own creations and to keep from violating the rights of others. *Intellectual property* is that which is the product of human creativity, such as writings, designs, inventions, melodies, and processes. They are things that can be stolen without being physically taken. For example, if you write a book, someone can steal the words from your book without stealing a physical copy of it.

As the Internet grows, intellectual property is becoming more valuable. Business owners should take the action necessary to protect their company's intellectual property. Additionally, business owners should know intellectual property law to be sure that they do not violate the rights of others. Even an unknowing violation of the law can result in stiff fines and penalties.

The following are the types of intellectual property and the ways to protect them.

Patent   A *patent* is protection given to new and useful inventions, discoveries, and designs. To be entitled to a patent, a work must be completely new and *unobvious*. A patent is granted to the first inventor who files for the patent. Once an invention is patented, no one else can make use of that invention, even if they discover it independently after a lifetime of research. A patent protects an invention for 17 years; for designs it is 3-1/2, 7, or 14 years. Patents cannot be renewed. The patent application must clearly explain how to make the invention so that when the patent expires, others will be able to freely make and use the invention. Patents are registered with the *United States Patent and Trademark Office (PTO)*. Examples of things that would be patentable would be mechanical devices or new drug formulas. In recent years, the patent office has issued patents on *business methods* opening up a new area for the creative entrepreneurial mind to explore.

Patent law is a legal specialty and you would be well advised to seek competent patent counsel if you wish to file a patent application.

Copyright   A *copyright* is protection given to *original works of authorship*, such as written works, musical works, visual works, performance works, or computer software programs. A copyright exists from the moment of creation, but one cannot register a copyright until it has been fixed in tangible form. Also, one cannot copyright titles, names, or slogans. A copyright currently gives the author and his or her heirs exclusive right to the work for the life of the author plus seventy years.

Copyrights first registered before 1978 last for 95 years. (This was previously 75 years but was extended 20 years to match the European system.) Copyrights are registered with the Register of Copyrights at the Library of Congress. Examples of works that would be copyrightable are books, paintings, songs, poems, plays, drawings, and films.

Copyright information on the Web may be obtained from **www.loc.gov/copy.**

Trademark
A *trademark* is protection given to a name or symbol that is used to distinguish one person's goods or services from those of others. It can consist of letters, numerals, packaging, labeling, musical notes, colors, or a combination of these. If a trademark is used on services as opposed to goods, it is called a *service mark.*

A trademark lasts indefinitely if it is used continuously and renewed properly. Trademarks are registered with the United States Patent and Trademark Office (PTO) and with individual states (see Chapter 3). Examples of trademarks are the *Chrysler* name on automobiles, the *red border* on TIME magazine, and the *shape* of the Coca-Cola bottle.

You can obtain a substantial amount of information on patents and trademarks on the PTO website. The web site is **www.uspto.gov**. You can perform a trademark search on the PTO website. In deciding whether to file a trademark application at the state or federal level, it is generally advisable to do the federal filing for a broader range of protection.

Trade Secrets
A *trade secret* is some information or process that provides a *commercial advantage* that is protected by keeping it a secret. Examples of trade secrets may be a list of successful distributors, the formula for Coca-Cola, or some unique source code in a computer program. Trade secrets are not registered anywhere, they are protected by the fact that they are not disclosed. They are protected only for as long as they are kept secret. If you independently discover the formula for Coca-Cola tomorrow, you can freely market it. (But you cannot use the trademark *Coca-Cola* on your product to market it.)

Maryland, Virginia and the District of Columbia have passed the *Uniform Trade Secrets Act*, which protects trade secrets from appropriation by other businesses. It provides for injunctions, damages, and attorney's fees for violation of the act.

Nonprotectable Creations

Some things are just not protectable. Such things as ideas, systems and discoveries are not allowed any protection under any law. If you have a great idea, such as selling packets of hangover medicine in bars, you cannot stop others from doing the same thing. If you invent a new medicine, you can patent it. If you pick a distinctive name for it, you can register it as a trademark. If you create a unique picture or instructions for the package, you can copyright them. But you cannot stop others from using your basic business idea of marketing hangover medicine in bars.

Notice the subtle differences between the protective systems available. If you invent something two days after someone else does, you cannot even use it yourself if the other person has patented it. But if you write the same poem as someone else and neither of you copied the other, both of you can copyright the poem. If you patent something, you can have the exclusive rights to it for the term of the patent, but you must disclose how others can make it after the patent expires. However, if you keep it a trade secret, you have exclusive rights as long as no one learns the secret.

We are in a time of transition of the law of intellectual property. Every year new changes are made in the laws and new forms of creativity win protection. For more information, you should consult a new edition of a book on these types of property. Some are listed at the end of this book.

15 | ENDLESS LAWS

Maryland, Virginia, the District of Columbia, and the federal government have numerous laws and rules that apply to every aspect of every type of business. There are laws governing even such things as fence posts, hosiery, rabbit raising, refund policies, frozen desserts, and advertising. Every business is affected by one or another of these laws.

Some activities are covered by both state and federal laws. In such cases, you must obey the stricter of the rules. In addition, more than one agency of the state or federal government may have rules governing your business. Each of these may have the power to investigate violations and impose fines or other penalties.

Penalties for violations of these laws can range from a warning to a criminal fine and even jail time. In some cases, employees can sue for damages. Recently, employees have been given awards of millions of dollars from employers who violated the law. Since ignorance of the law is no excuse, it is your duty to learn which laws apply to your business, or to risk these penalties.

Very few people in business know the laws that apply to their businesses. If you take the time to learn them, you can become an expert in your field and avoid problems with regulators. You can also fight back if one of your competitors uses some illegal method to compete with you.

The laws and rules that affect the most businesses are explained in this section. Following that is a list of more specialized laws. You should read through this list and see which ones may apply to your business. Then go to your public library or law library and read them. Some may not apply to your phase of the business, but if any of them do apply, you should make copies to keep on hand.

No one could possibly know all the rules that affect business, much less comply with them all. (The Interstate Commerce Commission alone has 40 trillion (that is 40 million million or 40,000,000,000,000) rates on its books telling the transportation industry what it should charge!) But if you keep up with the important rules you will stay out of trouble and have more chance of success.

Federal Laws

The federal laws that are most likely to affect small businesses are rules of the *Federal Trade Commission (FTC)*. The FTC has some rules that affect many businesses such as the rules about labeling, warranties, and mail order sales. Other rules affect only certain industries.

If you sell goods by mail you should send for their booklet, *A Business Guide to the Federal Trade Commission's Mail or Telephone Order Merchandise Rule*. If you are going to be involved in a certain industry such as those listed below, or using warranties or your own labeling, you should ask for their latest information on the subject. The address is:

Federal Trade Commission
CRC-240
Washington, DC 20580

The rules of the FTC are contained in the Code of Federal Regulations (C.F.R.) in Chapter 16. Some of the industries covered are:

Industry	Part
Adhesive Compositions	235
Aerosol Products Used for Frosting Cocktail Glasses	417
Automobiles (New car fuel economy advertising)	259

Television Sets	410
Textile Wearing Apparel	423
Textiles	236
Tires	228
Used Automobile Parts	20
Used Lubricating Oil	406
Used Motor Vehicles	455
Waist Belts	405
Watches	245
Wigs and Hairpieces	252

Some other federal laws that affect businesses are as follows:

Alcohol Administration Act
Child Protection and Toy Safety Act
Clean Water Act
Comprehensive Smokeless Tobacco Health Education Act
Consumer Credit Protection Act
Consumer Product Safety Act
Energy Policy and Conservation Act
Environmental Pesticide Control Act
Fair Credit Reporting Act
Fair Packaging and Labeling Act
Flammable Fabrics Act
Food, Drug, and Cosmetic Act
Fur Products Labeling Act
Hazardous Substances Act
Hobby Protection Act
Insecticide, Fungicide, and Rodenticide Act
Magnuson-Moss Warranty Act
Poison Prevention Packaging Act
Solid Waste Disposal Act
Textile Fiber Products Identification Act
Toxic Substance Control Act
Wool Products Labeling Act
Nutrition Labeling and Education Act
Food Safety Enforcement Enhancement Act

State Laws

Maryland, Virginia, and the District of Columbia have numerous laws regulating specific types of businesses or certain activities of businesses. The following is a list of those types of businesses and activities that are most likely to be regulated by the states.

Accountants
Animal Agriculture
Appraisers
Architects
Asbestos
Auctioneers
Audiology & Speech
Language Pathology
Barbers
Boxing and Wrestling
Branch Pilots
Campgrounds (Membership)
Cemeteries
Certified Interior Designers
Charitable Solicitations
Child Day Care
Contractors
Cosmetology
Counseling
Credit Services Businesses
Dentistry
Engineer in Training
Extended Service Contracts
Farm: Dairy
Farm: Meat and Poultry
Food Processing
Funeral Directors and Embalmers
Geology

Health Spas
Hearing Aid Specialists
Land Surveyors
Landscape Architects
Medicine
Nursing
Nursing Home Administrators
Opticians
Pesticide Services
Plant and Pest Services
Professional Soil Scientists
Pharmacy
Physical Therapy
Plant and Pest Services
Polygraph Examiners
Private Security Services
Professional Engineers
Professional Soil Scientist
Property Registration
Psychology
Real Estate
Social Work
Tradesman Licensure
Travel Clubs
Veterinary Medicine
Waste Management Facility Operator
Waste Water Treatment Works

If you are running a type of business that is mentioned here, or using some sales technique that could come under government regulation, you should check your state laws and regulations or reference your state's business regulatory website. In Maryland, visit the State Department Labor, Licensing, and Regulation at **www.dllr.state.md.us**. In the District of Columbia, visit the Department of Consumer and Regulatory Affairs at **www.dcra.dc.gov**. In Virginia, visit the Department of Business Assistance website at **www.dba.state.va.us**.

16 | BOOKKEEPING AND ACCOUNTING

It is beyond the scope of this book to explain all the intricacies of setting up a business's bookkeeping and accounting systems. But the important thing is to realize that if you do not set up an understandable bookkeeping system your business will undoubtedly fail.

Without accurate records of where your income is coming from and where it is going, you will be unable to increase your profits, lower your expenses, obtain needed financing, or make the right decisions in all areas of your business. The time to decide how you will handle your bookkeeping is when you open your business, not a year later when it is tax time.

Initial Bookkeeping

If you do not understand business taxation you should pick up a good book on the subject as well as the IRS tax guide for your type of business (proprietorship, partnership, corporation, or limited liability company).

The IRS tax book for small businesses is Publication 334, *Tax Guide for Small Businesses*. There are also instruction booklets for each type of business form:

Schedule C for proprietorships, Form 1120 or 1120S for C corporations and S corporations, and Form 1165 for partnerships and businesses that are taxed like partnerships (LLCs, LLPs). You can obtain copies of these forms and publications at:

www.irs.gov

Keep in mind that the IRS is not charged with the responsibility of being your tax advisor. For that you need a private tax guide or advisor. Most beginning businesses would be well advised to employ an accountant (CPA) early in its development and to coordinate business formation issues between your accountant and attorney.

The most important thing to do is to set up your bookkeeping so that you can easily fill out your monthly deposits, quarterly payroll tax, and annual income tax returns. There are several widely used software programs such as Quicken, Quickbooks and Peachtree that will provide you with the proper format for keeping track of your financial and payroll transactions. Certain of these products have helpful websites for start-up businesses, e.g., **www.quicken.com/small_business/start.**

The best way to set up your system is to get copies of the tax returns showing individual categories—not the totals that you will need to supply—and set up your bookkeeping system to group those totals.

For example, for a sole proprietorship you will use *Schedule C* to report business income and expenses to the IRS at the end of the year. Use the categories on that form to sort your expenses. To make your job especially easy, every time you pay a bill, put the category number on the check. Most of the accounting programs will allow you to categorize your income and expenditures to match the necessary tax reporting requirements.

Accountants

New businesses are often short on cash to hire professionals such as accountants or bookkeepers. Most accountants that specialize in small businesses will work with you to help set-up your books correctly from the start. If you cannot initially afford to hire a professional, set up the accounting records yourself. Doing the books yourself will force you to learn something about business accounting and taxation. The worst way to run a business is to know nothing about the tax laws and turn everything over to an accountant at the end of the year to find out what is due.

You should be familiar with the basics of tax law before making decisions, such as whether to buy or rent equipment or premises. You should understand enough accounting so you can time your financial and business affairs appropriately.

As your business becomes more complex it is very helpful to have an accountant to advise you and prepare your returns. The taxation of partnerships including LLCs and LLPs is exceedingly complex even for tax lawyers. Finally, if you have a payroll or when you have a payroll, you should find a reliable payroll tax service and turn the task over to them.

Tax Returns

If you decide not to use an accountant initially and do your own tax returns, there are several commercial software products which will allow you to prepare and file your own tax returns such as *TurboTax* (**www.turbotax.com**) and *Tax Cut* (**www.taxcut.com**), both of which will import information from Quicken, Quickbooks and Peachtree. Of course there are numerous tax preparation services that you can use to prepare your returns. Use of a tax preparation service may give you a more accurate return and help to maximize income tax deductions.

Tax Tips

Here are a few tax tips for small businesses that will help you save money.

✪   Usually when you buy equipment for a business, you must amortize the cost over several years. That is, you do not deduct it all when you buy it, you take, say, twenty-five percent of the cost off your taxes each year for four years. (The time is determined by the theoretical usefulness of the item.) However, small businesses are allowed to write off the entire cost of a limited amount of items under Internal Revenue Code (I.R.C.) Sec. 179. If you have income to shelter, use it.

✪ C corporations, partnerships, and limited liability company income is taxable to the maximum social security and unlimited Medicare amounts.

✪ Owners of S corporations do not have to pay social security or Medicare taxes on the part of their profits that is not considered salary. As long as you pay yourself a reasonable salary, other money you take out is not subject to these taxes.

✪ You must carefully track travel and entertainment expenses in accordance with the IRS rules. Entertainment expenses are only 50% deductible. You need to adopt an accountable expense reimbursement plan to maximize the tax savings.

✪ You should not neglect to deposit withholding taxes for your own salary or profits. Besides being a large sum to come up with at once in April, there are penalties that must be paid for failure to do so.

✪ Do not fail to keep track of and remit your employees' withholding taxes. You will be personally liable for them even if you are a corporation.

✪ If you keep track of the use of your car for business you can deduct 36¢ per mile (this may go up or down each year) if you own your car. If you use your car for business you may claim actual expenses including depreciation or lease payments, on the business portion of your business car usage. Keep a log book to substantiate your deductions.

✪ By setting up a retirement plan you can exempt up to twenty-five percent of your salary if your business is a corporation and twenty percent of net if a non-corporation, from income tax. (see Chapter 11.) But do not use money you might need later. There are penalties for taking it out of the retirement plan.

✪ When you buy things that will be resold or made into products that will be resold, you do not have to pay sales taxes on those purchases. (see Chapter 18.)

✪   If you are an employee of a corporation, then there are some other fringe tax benefits available such as a medical reimbursement plan.

✪   Check out the IRS web site for small business tax information:

www.irs.gov/businesses/small

I7 PAYING FEDERAL TAXES

Taxes are part of life and part of every business venture. Even in situations where the business owes no tax, it may be required to file records with the various taxing bodies. Knowing what types of taxes affect your business and the manner in which each type of business pays taxes is crucial.

Income Tax

Proprietorship
A proprietor reports profits and expenses on Schedule C attached to the usual *Form 1040* and pays tax on all of the net income of the business. Each quarter *Form ES-1040* must be filed along with payment of one-quarter of the amount of income tax and social security taxes estimated to be due for the year.

Partnerships
Partnerships and Limited Liability Companies file a return (federal *Form 1065*) showing the income and expenses but pay no tax. Each partner or member is given a form showing their share of the profits or losses and reports these on *Schedule E* of Form 1040. Each quarter, Form ES-1040 must be filed by each partner/member along with a payment of one-quarter of the amount of income tax and social security taxes estimated to be due for the year.

Limited Liability Companies

A Limited Liability Company is generally taxed the same as a partnership. If you are a single member LLC you will be taxed as a proprietorship and will file a schedule C. If you wish to be taxed as an unincorporated association (i.e., like a corporation), then you must file Form 8832, *Entity Classification Election* with the IRS. (Maryland, Virginia, and the District of Columbia all allow for a single member LLC.)

C Corporation

A regular corporation is treated as a separate taxpayer, and pays tax on its profits after deducting all expenses, including officers' salaries. If dividends are distributed, they are paid out of after-tax dollars, and the shareholders pay tax a second time when they receive the dividends. If a corporation needs to accumulate money for investment, it may be able to do so at lower tax rates than the shareholders. Generally, a start-up corporation does not have available funds to pay dividends or needs to retain extra funds for growth so the double taxation issue does not arise. A corporation is a C corporation by default without further action by the shareholders and files a *Form 1120* tax return.

S Corporation

A small corporation has the option of being taxed like a partnership. That type of corporation is known as an S corporation or S corp. In order to be treated as an S corporation, an election on *Form 2553* must be filed by the corporation and accepted by the Internal Revenue Service. Generally, the election must be filed within 75 days of the initial incorporation or when the corporation commences business or within 75 days of the beginning of the calendar year (March 15). If you file the Form 2553 during the year (other than the initial filing dates discussed above), the election will be effective for the next tax year, not the current one. The tax year of the S corp. must be a calendar tax year. The S corporation will only file an informational return (*Form 1120-S*) listing profits and expenses. Each shareholder will be taxed on a proportional share of the profits (or be able to deduct a proportional share of the losses if they have a basis in trier stock and actively participate in the business). If they do not actively participate in the business, then their losses are *passive losses* and can only be used to offset passive income.

Unless a corporation will make a large profit that will not be distributed, S-status is usually best in the beginning. An S corporation files Form 1120S and distributes *Form K-1* to each shareholder. If any money is taken out by a shareholder that is not listed as wages subject to withholding, then the shareholder will usually have to file form ES-1040 each quarter along with payment of the estimated withholding on the withdrawals.

There are limitations on the S Corp. that must be observed. For instance, there can only be one class of stock, no more than 75 shareholders, no foreign shareholders, and all shareholders must be individuals with one limited exception for a special type of trust.

Tax Booklets and Other Information

The IRS website, **www.irs.gov**, contains every tax form you are likely to ever need. The site also contains the yearly publications of the IRS on a variety of topics covering both personal and business tax issues. All of the forms and the publications are downloadable and printable from the site. Forms and publications are also available in printed form at the offices of the District Director of the IRS for your state.

Publication 334 is a Tax Guide for Small Businesses for Individuals who use Schedule C (i.e., proprietorships). *Publication 509* is the tax calendar for the year. *Publication 535* is Business Expenses and the like.

The IRS holds workshops at various locations within Maryland, Virginia, and the District of Columbia to assist with tax preparation issues.

Withholding, Social Security, and Medicare Taxes

If you need basic information on business tax returns, consult *Publication 334*. If you have any questions, look up their toll-free number in the phone book under United States Government/Internal Revenue Service. If you want more creative answers and tax saving information, you should find a good local accountant. But to get started you will need the following.

Employer Identification Number

If you are a sole proprietor with no employees, you can use your social security number for your business but you can also get a separate tax identification number for the proprietorship if you wish. If you are a corporation, a partnership, or a proprietorship with employees, you must obtain an Employer Identification Number. This is done by filing the **APPLICATION FOR EMPLOYER IDENTIFICATION NUMBER (IRS FORM SS-4)**. (see form 12, p.249.) In some states, you can fill out the information on the SS-4 and call or fax the information to get the number quickly. Instructions for the telephone submission are in the instructions If you mail the form, it usually takes a week or two to receive. You can also apply online through the IRS website at **www.irs.gov**. You will need this number to open bank accounts for the business, so you should file this form as soon as you decide to go into business. A sample filled-in form is in Appendix A, and the blank form with instructions is in Appendix B. The form can also be downloaded from the IRS website.

Employee's Withholding Allowance Certificate

You must have each employee fill out an **EMPLOYEE'S WITHHOLDING ALLOWANCE CERTIFICATE (IRS FORM W-4)** to calculate the amount of federal taxes to be deducted and to obtain their social security numbers. (see form 14, p.262.) (The number of allowances on this form is used with IRS Circular E, Publication 15, to figure out the exact deductions.) A sample filled-in form is in Appendix A.

Federal Tax Deposit Coupons

After taking withholdings from employees' wages, you must deposit them at a bank that is authorized to accept such funds. If at the end of any month you have over $1000 in withheld taxes (including your contribution to FICA), you must make a deposit prior to the 15th of the following month. If on the 3rd, 7th, 11th, 15th, 19th, 22nd, or 25th of any month you have over $3,000 in withheld taxes, you must make a deposit within three banking days.

Electronic Filing

The IRS is constantly seeking to have more and more material and taxes electronically filed. Check with the IRS to see if your business is required to file any of its taxes or returns electronically.

Estimated Tax Payment Voucher

Sole proprietors and partners usually take draws from their businesses without the formality of withholding. However, they are still required to make deposits of income and FICA taxes each quarter. If more than $500 is due in April on a person's 1040 form, then not enough money was withheld each quarter and a penalty is assessed unless the person falls into an exception. The quarterly withholding is submitted on *Form 1040-ES* on April 15th, June 15th, September 15th, and January 15th each year. If these days fall on a weekend then the due date is the following Monday. The worksheet with Form 1040-ES can be used to determine the amount to pay. A sample filled-in Form 1040-ES is in Appendix A on page 208.

NOTE: *One of the exceptions to the rule is that if you withhold the same amount as last year's tax bill, then you do not have to pay a penalty. This is usually a lot easier than filling out the 1040-ES worksheet.*

**Employer's
Quarterly Tax
Return**

Each quarter you must file *Form 941* reporting your federal withholding and FICA taxes. If you owe more than $1000 at the end of a quarter, you are required to make a deposit at the end of any month that you have $1000 in withholding. The deposits are made to the Federal Reserve Bank or an authorized financial institution on *Form 501*. Most banks are authorized to accept deposits. If you owe more than $3,000 for any month, you must make a deposit at any point in the month in which you owe $3,000. After you file Form SS-4, the 941 forms will be sent to you automatically if you checked the box saying that you expect to have employees.

**Wage and Tax
Statement**

At the end of each year, you are required to issue a W-2 Form to each employee. This form shows the amount of wages paid to the employee during the year as well as the amounts withheld for taxes, social security, Medicare, and other purposes. A sample filled-in W-2 is in Appendix A on page 209.

Miscellaneous

If you pay at least $600 to a person other than an employee (such as independent contractors) you are required to file a *Form 1099* for that person. Along with the 1099s, you must file a *Form 1096*, which is a summary sheet.

Many people are not aware of this law and fail to file these forms, but they are required for such things as services, royalties, rents, awards, and prizes that you pay to individuals (but not corporations). The rules for this are quite complicated so you should either obtain *Package 1099* from the IRS or consult your accountant. Sample filled-in forms 1099 and 1096 are in Appendix A on pages 210 and 211.

**Earned Income
Credit**

Persons who are not liable to pay income tax may have the right to a check from the government because of the *Earned Income Credit*. You are required to notify your employees of this. You can satisfy this requirement with one of the following:

- ✪ a W-2 Form with the notice on the back;

- ✪ a substitute for the W-2 Form with the notice on it;

- ✪ a copy of Notice 797; or,

- ✪ a written statement with the wording from Notice 797.

A Notice 797 can be obtained by calling 800-829-3676 or by going to the IRS website at **www.irs.gov**.

Excise Taxes

Excise taxes are taxes on certain activities or items. Most federal excise taxes have been eliminated since World War II, but a few remain.

Some of the things that are subject to federal excise taxes are tobacco and alcohol, gasoline, tires and inner tubes, some trucks and trailers, firearms, ammunition, bows, arrows, fishing equipment, the use of highway vehicles of over 55,000 pounds, aircraft, wagering, telephone and teletype services, coal, hazardous wastes, and vaccines. If you are involved with any of these, you should obtain from the IRS Publication 510, *Information on Excise Taxes*.

Unemployment Compensation Tax

You must pay federal unemployment taxes if you paid wages of $1,500 in any quarter, or if you had at least one employee for twenty calendar weeks. The federal tax amount is 0.8% of the first $7,000 of wages paid each employee. If more than $100 is due by the end of any quarter (if you paid $12,500 in wages for the quarter), then *Form 508* must be filed with an authorized financial institution or the Federal Reserve Bank in your area. You will receive Form 508 when you obtain your employer identification number.

For more information on unemployment compensation in the various states, see Chapter 18.

At the end of each year, you must file *Form 940* or *Form 940EZ*. This is your annual report of federal unemployment taxes. You will receive an original form from the IRS.

Payroll Tax Services

All small to medium-sized businesses should consider hiring a payroll tax service to take care of all of their payroll matters. These services issue all payroll checks, withhold the correct amount of taxes, file all payroll tax forms, federal and state, and issue all W-2s. The costs for these services are nominal and they will save you substantial headaches. If you do not use a payroll tax service, never fall into the habit of paying *net wages* and not making the required tax deposits. The section of the IRS that deals with payroll taxes is aggressive and unforgiving.

18 | PAYING STATE TAXES

It might be redundant, but the importance of hiring a payroll tax service cannot be stressed enough. Navigating through the labyrinth of state tax laws is confusing at best, especially for a young entrepreneur. To begin your search for a payroll tax service, you can start with the bank where you opened your corporate checking account or you can search on the Internet.

This chapter is intended to give you a broad overview of state taxes. A large majority of the forms for the taxes covered in this chapter are generated by the state and sent directly to you as a result of your filing a registration for with your state's tax authority, so do not forget this all-important step. You can obtain these state registration forms by visiting your state taxing authority's website. You will need to have some basic information before filling out these state forms, such as:

✪   your federal *Employer Identification Number* (see Chapter 17) and/or your Social Security Number;

✪   your legal form of business (e.g. sole proprietor, partnership, limited liability company, corporation);

✪   your business address;

✪ the names, titles, home address and Social Security Number of the proprietor, partners or principal officers; and,

✪ the addresses for all locations of the business if you intend to collect sales taxes.

In Maryland, you must complete a **COMBINED REGISTRATION APPLICATION.** (see form 2, p.217.) You can use the form in Appendix B or complete the form online using the Comptroller of Maryland website at **www.comp.state.md.us**.

In Virginia, check with the Department of Taxation website at **www.tax.state.va.us** to obtain a **FORM R-1 BUSINESS REGISTRATION APPLICATION.** (see form 5, p.225.) The registration can either be completed online or the form can be downloaded and mailed.

In the District of Columbia, you must complete an **FR-500 COMBINED BUSINESS TAX REGISTRATION APPLICATION.** (see form 8, p.231.) You can use the form in Appendix B or visit the Office of Tax and Revenue at **www.cfo.dc.gov** to complete the form online.

Sales and Use Taxes

If you will be selling or renting goods or services at retail, you must collect sales and use taxes. Some services such as doctors and attorney's fees and newspaper advertising are not taxed, but most others are. If you have any doubt, check with your state tax authority. The sales tax rate is 5% in Maryland, 5.75% in the District of Columbia, and 4.5% in Virginia.

One reason to get a state tax number early is to exempt your purchases from tax. When you buy a product that you plan to resell or use as part of a product that you will sell, you are exempt from paying tax on it.

If you will only be selling items wholesale or out of state, you might think that you would not need a tax number or need to submit returns, but you will need to be registered to obtain the tax number to exempt your purchases.

If you have any sales before you get your sales and use tax return forms, you should calculate the tax anyway and submit the tax before the filing deadline.

Otherwise, you will be charged a penalty even if it was not your fault that they did not send you the forms.

Selling to Tax Exempt Purchasers

You are required to collect sales and use taxes for all sales you make unless you have documentation on file proving that a purchase was exempt from the tax. If you sell to someone who claims to be exempt from sales and use taxes, (for example, if they plan to resell merchandise they have purchased from you) then you must have them complete a resale certificate.

Unemployment Compensation Tax

You are liable to pay unemployment compensation taxes when you begin to pay wages to your first employee. To learn more about how and when to pay unemployment taxes, visit your state's employment commission website. In Maryland, visit the Department of Labor, Licensing and Regulation at **www.dllr.state.md.us**; in the District of Columbia, visit the Department of Employment Services at **www.does.ci.washington.dc.us**; and, in Virginia, visit the Virginia Employment Commission at **www.vec.state.va.us**.

To learn more about unemployment compensation in general visit:

District of Columbia:

Office of Tax and Revenue
Customer Service Center
941 North Capitol Street, NE
1st Floor
Washington, DC 20002
202-727-4TAX
www.dc.gov

Maryland:

Allegany and Garrett Counties
112 Baltimore St., 2nd floor
Cumberland, MD 21502
301-777-2165 or 301-334-8880

Anne Arundel County
80 Calvert Street
Annapolis, MD 21401
410-260-7980

Baltimore City
301 W. Preston Street, Room 206
Baltimore, MD 21201
410-767-1995

Baltimore County
300 E. Joppa Road, Plaza Level 1A
Towson, MD 21286
410-321-2306

Calvert and St. Mary's Counties
Room 1300, 200 Duke Street
Prince Frederick, MD 20678
410-535-8830 or 301-855-1317

Caroline, Kent, Queen Anne's, and
Talbot Counties
514 Washington Avenue, Suite 2
Chestertown, MD 21620
410-810-1615

Caroline, Somerset, Talbot, Wicomico,
and Worcester Counties
201 Baptist St., Room 2248
Salisbury, MD 21801
410-543-6800

Carroll County
532 Baltimore Blvd., Suite 306
Westminster, MD 21157
410-848-4699

Cecil County
Upper Chesapeake Corporate Center
103 Chesapeake Blvd, Suite D
Elkton, MD 21921
410-996-0580
www.comp.state.md.us

Charles and St. Mary's Counties
183 Smallwood Village Center
Waldorf, MD 20602
301-645-2226 or 301-843-0977

Harford County
2 S. Bond Street, 4th Floor
Bel Air, MD 21014
410-836-4890

Howard County
7275B Waterloo Road
Jessup, MD 20794
410-799-4009

Maryland County
11510 Georgia Avenue, Suite 190
Wheaton, MD 20902
301-949-6030

Prince George's County
14735 Main Street, Room 083B
Upper Marlboro, MD 20772
301-952-2810

Prince George's County
8181 Professional Place, Suite 101
New Carrollton, MD 20785
301-459-9195

St. Frederick County
100 W. Patrick Street
Frederick, MD 21701
301-694-1982

Washington County
One South Potomac Street
Hagerstown, MD 21740
301-791-4776

Virginia:

Virginia Department of Taxation
Office of Customer Services
P.O. Box 1115
Richmond, VA 23218-1115
804-367-8037
www.tax.state.va.us

Income Tax

Maryland, the District of Columbia, and Virginia all have corporate income taxes. These only apply to C corporations and entities that elect to be taxed as corporations under federal law. Prior to 1998, limited liability companies were subject to the corporate income tax but now they can elect partnership taxation. In Maryland, the tax rate is 7%, in the District of Columbia is 9.975%, and in Virginia, the tax rate is 6%.

NOTE: *Professional service corporations that do not elect "S" status must pay the tax.*

Forms and instructions can be obtained from your local Department of Revenue office or from your state taxing authority website.

Excise Taxes

Some states impose excise taxes on particular goods. Check with your state taxing authority for a detailed list. Excise taxes generally apply to alcohol, tobacco and fuels, so if you intend to manufacture, transport or sell any of these items, make certain that you obtain the proper licenses and pay your excise taxes.

19 OUT-OF-STATE TAXES

In addition to the various tax liabilities a new business faces in its home state and to the federal government, other taxing bodies may try to impose a tax obligation on your business. This depends on the nature of your operation and the extent to which your business earns revenue out of state.

State Sales Taxes

In 1992, the United States Supreme Court sided with the rights of small businesses by ruling that state tax authorities cannot force them to collect sales taxes on interstate mail orders (*Quill Corporation v. North Dakota*).

However, the court left open the possibility that Congress could allow interstate taxation of mail order sales, and since then several bills have been introduced that would do so. At present, companies are only required to collect sales taxes for states in which they do business. Exactly what business is enough to result in taxation is a legal question and some states try to define it as broadly as possible.

If you have an office in a state, you are doing business there and any goods shipped to consumers in that state are subject to sales taxes. If you have a full time employee working in the state much of the year, many states will consider you doing business there. In some states, attending a two-day trade show is enough business to trigger taxation for the entire year for every order shipped to the state. One loophole that often works is to be represented at shows by persons who are not your employees.

Because the laws are different in each state you will have to do some research on a state-by-state basis to find out how much business you can do in a state without being subject to their taxation. You can request a state's rules from its department of revenue, but keep in mind that courts will not always rule on a law in the way a Department of Revenue would prefer. You should be especially careful if you are doing business in the surrounding jurisdictions of Maryland, Virginia and the District of Columbia since there is considerable sharing of information among the state agencies.

Business Taxes

Even worse than being subject to a state's sales taxes is to be subject to their income or other business taxes. For example, California charges every company doing business in the state a minimum $800 a year fee and charges income tax on a portion of the company's worldwide income. Doing a small amount of business in the state is clearly not worth getting mired in California taxation.

For this reason some trade shows have been moved from the state and this has resulted in a review of the tax policies and some *safe-harbor* guidelines to advise companies on what they can do without becoming subject to taxation. Write to the department of revenue or tax authority of any state with which you have business contacts to see what might trigger your taxation.

All corporations and LLCs **must** file an *annual return* with the state of their incorporation. This return is sometimes called a *franchise tax return*. Do not forget to file this annual return. If you fail to file the annual return (usually for two years in a row), the state will revoke your corporate or company charter and will loose the limited liability protection of the entity. This will cause the entity to lose its ability to sue and the principals could, in some instances, be held personally liable. However, if you forget to file the return and even if your charter is revoked, you can *reinstate* it by filing the delinquent returns and paying penalties and interest.

Internet Taxes

State revenue departments are drooling at the prospect of taxing commerce on the Internet. Theories have already been proposed that websites available to state residents mean a company is doing business in a state.

Congress has passed a moratorium on taxation of Internet sales. However, it will probably take a tremendous outcry to keep the Internet tax-free in the future.

Canadian Taxes

The Canadian government expects American companies which sell goods by mail order to Canadians to collect taxes for and file returns with Revenue Canada, the Canadian tax department.

Those that receive an occasional unsolicited order are not expected to register, and Canadian customers who order things from the U.S. pay the tax plus a $5 fee upon receipt of the goods. But companies that solicit Canadian orders are expected to be registered if their worldwide income is $30,000 or more per year. In some cases, a company may be required to post a bond and to pay for the cost of a Canadian auditor visiting its premises and auditing its books. For these reasons you may notice that some companies decline to accept orders from Canada.

20 THE END...
AND THE BEGINNING

If you have read through this whole book, you know more about the rules and laws for operating a business in Maryland, Virginia, and the District of Columbia, than most people in business today. However, after learning about all the governmental regulations, you may become discouraged. You are probably wondering how you can keep track of all the laws and how you will have any time left to make money after complying with the laws. It is not that bad. People are starting businesses every day and they are making money, lots of money.

To be successful in business you must have great determination of purpose, a viable business concept, and a bit of luck. The more practical skills you acquire through this book, seminars, or in the actual workplace, the more you reduce your risk of failure and enhance your chances of success. Where you do not have expertise, hire it or partner with it. Where you need capital, earn it or raise it though investors or financial partners.

Now that you have decided to start a business, you could use some extra help and guidance from entrepreneurs like yourself and from organizations that are dedicated to helping young entrepreneurs.

There are some terrific resources available locally in the DC Metro area of which you should take advantage. Check out the *Face Time* column in the Business section of the *Washington Post* every Thursday for helpful, low cost, seminars that are aimed at helping new businesses. These might include sessions on "how to write a business plan," "preparing a winning proposal," and "structuring intellectual property agreements."

Another great local resource is the Netpreneur Calendar where you can stay informed about business related events and seminars in the National Capital Region. You can subscribe to their free weekly email broadcast featuring events and seminars at:

www.netpreneur.org

You may also want to check out the *Dingman Center for Entrepreneurship* out of the University of Maryland. The Dingman Center hosts events and seminars on various business topics. Their website is:

www.rhsmith.umd.edu/dingman

Another fabulous resource for entrepreneurs is *IBI Global*. You can check out their website at **www.IBIGlobal.com**. The IBI Free Enterprise Forum seeks to promote resources and networking among entrepreneurs to help develop capital and customer markets. IBI hosts weekly meetings across the nation for entrepreneurs to network and develop contacts, and also hosts a week-long advanced management training program.

Whatever your business, we encourage you to take advantage of the resources available to you to learn, grow, and network with people like yourself…that rare breed of cat…the entrepreneur!

GLOSSARY

A

acceptance. Agreeing to the terms of an offer and creating a contract.

affirmative action. Programs' and regulations' attempt to compensate for discriminatory practices that have in the past denied fair consideration to members of minority groups.

alien. A person who is not a citizen of the country.

articles of incorporation. The document filed with the state authorities that sets forth the organization of a corporation. Articles normally include the purpose of the corporation, its principal place of business, the names of its initial directors, and the amounts and types of stock it is authorized to issue.

B

bait advertising. Offering a product for sale with the intention of selling another product.

board of Directors. See *Director*.

bulk sales. Selling substantially all of a company's inventory.

bylaws. The rules that govern the internal affairs of a corporation, which are normally adopted by the shareholders.

C

C corporation. A corporation that pays taxes on its profits.

collections. The collection of money owed to a business.

common law. Laws that are determined in court cases rather than statutes.

consideration. The exchange of value or promises in a contract.

contract. An agreement between two or more parties.

copyright. Legal protection given to original works of authorship.

corporation. An artificial person which is set up to conduct a business owned by shareholders and run by officers and directors.

D

DBA/doing business as. See *Fictitious name*.

deceptive pricing. Pricing goods or services in a manner intended to deceive the customers.

director. A member of the governing board of a corporation typically elected at an annual meeting of the shareholders. Directors are responsible for making important business decisions

discrimination. The choosing among various options based on their characteristics.

domain name. The address of a website.

E

employee. Person who works for another under that person's control and direction.

endorsements. Positive statements about goods or services.

excise tax. A tax paid on the sale or consumption of goods or services.

express warranty. A specific guarantee of a product or service.

F

fictitious name. A name used by a business that is not its personal or legal name.

G

general partnership. A business that is owned by two or more persons.

goods. Items of personal property.

guarantee/guaranty. A promise of quality of a good or service.

I

implied warranty. A guarantee of a product or service that is not specifically made, but can be implied from the circumstances of the sale.

independent contractor. Person who works for another as a separate business, not as an employee.

intangible property. Personal property that does not have physical presence, such as the ownership interest in a corporation.

intellectual property. Legal rights to the products of the mind, such as writings, musical compositions, formulas and designs.

L

liability. The legal responsibility to pay for an injury.

Limited Liability Company. An entity recognized as a legal *person* that is set up to conduct a business owned and run by members.

Limited Liability Partnership. An entity recognized as a legal *person* that is set up to conduct a business owned and run by members that is set up for professionals such as attorneys or doctors.

Limited Partnership. A business that is owned by two or more persons of which one or more is liable for the debts of the business and one or more has no liability for the debts.

limited warranty. A guarantee covering certain aspects of a good or service.

M

merchant. A person who is in business.

merchant's firm offer. An offer by a business made under specific terms.

N

nonprofit corporation. An entity recognized as a legal *person* that is set up to run an operation in which none of the profits are distributed to controlling members.

O

occupational license. A government-issued permit to transact business.

offer. A proposal to enter into a contract.

overtime. Hours worked in excess of forty hours in one week, or eight hours in one day.

P

partnership. A business formed by two or more persons.

patent. Protection given to inventions, discoveries and designs.

personal property. Any type of property other than land and the structures attached to it.

pierce the corporate veil. When a court ignores the structure of a corporation and holds its owners responsible for its debts or liabilities.

professional association. An entity recognized as a legal *person* that is set up to conduct a business of professionals such as attorneys or doctors.

proprietorship. A business that is owned by one person.

R

real property. Land and the structures attached to it.

resident alien. A person who is not a citizen of the country but who may legally reside and work there.

S

S corporation. A corporation in which the profits are taxed to the shareholders.

sale on approval. Selling an item with the agreement that it may be brought back and the sale cancelled.

sale or return. An agreement whereby goods are to be purchased or returned to the vendor.

securities. Interests in a business such as stocks or bonds.

sexual harassment. Activity that causes an employee to feel or be sexually threatened.

shares. Units of stock in a corporation.

shareholder/stockholder. An owner of a corporation whose ownership interest is represented by shares of stock in the corporation. A shareholder has rights conferred by state law and the bylaws of the corporation.

statute of frauds. Law that requires certain contracts to be in writing.

stock. Ownership interests in a corporation.

sublease. An agreement to rent premises from an existing tenant.

T

tangible property. Physical personal property such as desks and tables.

trade secret. Commercially valuable information or process that is protected by being kept a secret.

trademark. A name or symbol used to identify the source of goods or services.

U

unemployment compensation. Payments to a former employee who was terminated from a job for a reason not based on his or her fault.

usury. Charging an interest rate higher than that allowed by law.

W

withholding. Money taken out of an employee's salary and remitted to the government.

workers compensation. Insurance program to cover injuries or deaths of employees.

FOR FURTHER REFERENCE

The following books will provide valuable information to those who are starting new businesses. Some are out of print, but they are classics that are worth tracking down.

For hints on what it takes to be successful:

Carnegie, Dale, *How to Win Friends and Influence People*. Pocket Books, 1994, 276 pages.

Franklin, Burke, *Business Black Belt*. Jian, 1998, 358 pages.

Gustafson, Joan, *A Woman Can Do That!* Leader Dynamics, 2001, 209 pages.

Kawasaki, Guy and Moreno, Michele, *Rules for Revolutionaries; the Capitalist Manifesto*. HarperCollins, 1999, 179 pages.

Pestrak, Debra, *Playing with the Big Boys; Success Secrets of the Most Powerful Women in Business*. Sun Publishing. 2002, 240 pages.

For advice on bookkeeping and organization:

Caplan, Suzanne, *Streetwise Finance and Accounting*. Adams Media Corporation, 2000, 337 pages.

Kamoroff, Bernard, *Small Time Operator* (27th Edition). Bell Springs Publishing, 2000, 200 pages.

For additional advice on starting a business:

Amis, David and Stevenson, Howard H., *Winning Angels: The 7 Fundamentals of Early Stage Investing*. Financial Times Prentice Hall, 2001, 304 pages.

Blechman, Bruce and Levinson, Jay, *Guerrilla Financing*. Mariner Books, 1992, 335 pages.

Gerber, Michael E., *The E-Myth Revisited: Why Most Small Businesses Don't Work and What to Do About It*. HarperBusiness, 1995, 288 pages.

Gladstone, David J., *Venture Capital Handbook*. Prentice Hall, 1988, 350 pages.

Gumpert, David E., *How to Really Start Your Own Business* (3rd Edition). Goldhirsh Group, 1996, 268 pages.

Harroch, Richard D., *Small Business Kit For Dummies*. IDG Books Worldwide, 1998, 369 pages.

Haynsworth, Harry, *The American Bar Association Legal Guide for Small Business*. Three Rivers Press, 2000, 498 pages.

Hupalo, Peter I., *Thinking Like an Entrepreneur: How to Make Intelligent Business Decisions That Will Lead to Success in Building & Growing Your Own Company*. 1999, 272 pages.

Tyson, Eric and Schell, Jim, *Small Business For Dummies*. IDG Books Worldwide, 2000, 408 pages.

For a very practical guide to investing:

Tobias, Andrew, *The Only Investment Guide You'll Ever Need.* Harvest Books, 2002, 256 pages.

For practical advice on money:

Barton, Paul and Spilchuk, Barry, *Let's Talk...about Money.* Let's Talk, 2001, 197 pages.

For practical advice on publicity:

Levinson, Jay, Frishman, Rick and Lublin, Jill, *Guerrilla Publicity.* Adams Media Corporation, 2002, 304 pages.

The following are other books published by Sphinx Publishing that may be helpful to your business:

Eckert, W. Kelsea, Sartorius, Arthur, III, & Warda, Mark, *How to Form Your Own Corporation.* 2003.

Haman, Edward A., *How to Form Your Own Partnership.* 2003.

Ray, James C, *The Most Valuable Business Legal Forms You 'll Ever Need.* 2001.

Ray, James C., *The Complete Book of Corporate Forms.* 2001.

Warda, Mark, *Incorporate in Delaware from Any State.* 2002.

Warda, Mark, *Incorporate in Nevada from Any State.* 2001.

Warda, Mark, *How to Form a Limited Liability Company.* 2003.

Warda, Mark, *How to Register Your Own Copyright.* 2002.

Warda, Mark, *How to Register Your Own Trademark.* 2000.

The following are books published by Sourcebooks, Inc. that may be helpful to your business:

Fleury, Robert E., *The Small Business Survival Guide*. 1995.

Gutman, Jean E., *Accounting Made Easy*. 1998.

Milling, Bryan E., *How to Get a Small Business Loan* (2nd Edition). 1998.

Mullis, Darrell and Orloff, Judith, *The Accounting Game*. 1998.

The following websites provide information that may be useful to you in starting your business:

Federal Trade Commission: **www.ftc.gov**

Internal Revenue Service: **www.irs.gov**

Patent and Trademark Office: **www.uspto.gov**

Securities and Exchange Commission: **www.sec.gov**

Small Business Administration: **www.sba.gov**

Social Security Administration: **www.ssa.gov**

U. S. Business Advisor: **www.business.gov**

The following state websites provide information that will be helpful in starting your business:

Maryland State Department of Assessments and Taxation: **www.dat.state.md.us**

Comptroller of Maryland: **www.comp.state.md.us**

District of Columbia Business Resource Center: **www.brc.dc.gov**

District of Columbia Department of Consumer and Regulatory Affairs: **www.dcra.dc.gov**

District of Columbia Office of the Chief Financial Officer: **www.cfo.dc.gov**

Virginia Department of Taxation: **www.tax.state.va.us**

Virginia State Corporation Commission: **www.state.va.us/scc**

Appendix A
Sample Filled-In Forms

The following forms are selected filled-in forms for demonstration purposes. Most have a corresponding blank form in Appendix B. The form numbers in this appendix correspond to the form numbers in Appendix B. If there is no blank for a particular form, it is because you must obtain it from a government agency. If you need instructions for these forms as you follow how they are filled out, they can be found in Appendix B or in those pages in the chapters that discuss those forms.

(Sample filled-in forms A–D do not have an accompanying blank form in this appendix because you must use the original forms provided by the IRS.)

U.S. Department of Justice
Immigration and Naturalization Service

OMB No. 1115-0136

Employment Eligibility Verification

Please read instructions carefully before completing this form. The instructions must be available during completion of this form. ANTI-DISCRIMINATION NOTICE: It is illegal to discriminate against work eligible individuals. Employers CANNOT specify which document(s) they will accept from an employee. The refusal to hire an individual because of a future expiration date may also constitute illegal discrimination.

Section 1. Employee Information and Verification. To be completed and signed by employee at the time employment begins.

Print Name: Last	First	Middle Initial	Maiden Name
REDDENBACHER	MARY	J.	HASSENFUSS

Address (Street Name and Number)	Apt. #	Date of Birth (month/day/year)
1234 LIBERTY LANE		1/26/69

City	State	Zip Code	Social Security #
Baltimore	MD	12345	123-45-6789

I am aware that federal law provides for imprisonment and/or fines for false statements or use of false documents in connection with the completion of this form.

I attest, under penalty of perjury, that I am (check one of the following):
[X] A citizen or national of the United States
[ ] A Lawful Permanent Resident (Alien # A
[ ] An alien authorized to work until ___/___/___
(Alien # or Admission #)

Employee's Signature *Mary Reddenbacher*	Date (month/day/year) 2/2/04

Preparer and/or Translator Certification.   *(To be completed and signed if Section 1 is prepared by a person other than the employee.) I attest, under penalty of perjury, that I have assisted in the completion of this form and that to the best of my knowledge the information is true and correct.*

Preparer's/Translator's Signature	Print Name
Address (Street Name and Number, City, State, Zip Code)	Date (month/day/year)

Section 2. Employer Review and Verification. To be completed and signed by employer. Examine one document from List A OR examine one document from List B and one from List C, as listed on the reverse of this form, and record the title, number and expiration date, if any, of the document(s)

List A	OR	List B	AND	List C
Document title: PASSPORT		_____		_____
Issuing authority: PASSPORT AGENCY TPA		_____		_____
Document #: 123456789		_____		_____
Expiration Date (if any): 10/5/2010		__/__/__		__/__/__
Document #: _____				
Expiration Date (if any): __/__/__				

CERTIFICATION - I attest, under penalty of perjury, that I have examined the document(s) presented by the above-named employee, that the above-listed document(s) appear to be genuine and to relate to the employee named, that the employee began employment on (month/day/year) 02/02/04 and that to the best of my knowledge the employee is eligible to work in the United States. (State employment agencies may omit the date the employee began employment.)

Signature of Employer or Authorized Representative *Darron Krebbs*	Print Name Darron Krebbs	Title owner
Business or Organization Name Krebbs Company	Address (Street Name and Number, City, State, Zip Code) 100 Maynard Dr., Baltimore, MD 54321	Date (month/day/year) 2/2/04

Section 3. Updating and Reverification. To be completed and signed by employer.

A. New Name (if applicable)	B. Date of rehire (month/day/year) (if applicable)

C. If employee's previous grant of work authorization has expired, provide the information below for the document that establishes current employment eligibility.

Document Title: _____   Document #: _____   Expiration Date (if any): ___/___/___

I attest, under penalty of perjury, that to the best of my knowledge, this employee is eligible to work in the United States, and if the employee presented document(s), the document(s) I have examined appear to be genuine and to relate to the individual.

Signature of Employer or Authorized Representative	Date (month/day/year)

Form **SS-4**	**Application for Employer Identification Number**	EIN	

Form **SS-4**

(Rev. December 2001)

Department of the Treasury
Internal Revenue Service

Application for Employer Identification Number

(For use by employers, corporations, partnerships, trusts, estates, churches, government agencies, Indian tribal entities, certain individuals, and others.)

· See separate instructions for each line. · Keep a copy for your records.

EIN

OMB No. 1545-0003

Type or print clearly.

1 Legal name of entity (or individual) for whom the EIN is being requested
John Doe and James Doe

2 Trade name of business (if different from name on line 1)
Doe Company

3 Executor, trustee, "care of" name

4a Mailing address (room, apt., suite no. and street, or P.O. box)
123 Main Street

5a Street address (if different) (Do not enter a P.O. box.)

4b City, state, and ZIP code
Baltimore, MD 98765

5b City, state, and ZIP code

6 County and state where principal business is located
Baltimore, MD

7a Name of principal officer, general partner, grantor, owner, or trustor
John Doe

7b SSN, ITIN, or EIN
123-45-6789

8a Type of entity (check only one box)
- [ ] Sole proprietor (SSN) _____
- [X] Partnership
- [ ] Corporation (enter form number to be filed) · _____
- [ ] Personal service corp.
- [ ] Church or church-controlled organization
- [ ] Other nonprofit organization (specify) · _____
- [ ] Other (specify) ·
- [ ] Estate (SSN of decedent) _____
- [ ] Plan administrator (SSN) _____
- [ ] Trust (SSN of grantor) _____
- [ ] National Guard   [ ] State/local government
- [ ] Farmers' cooperative   [ ] Federal government/military
- [ ] REMIC   [ ] Indian tribal governments/enterprises
- Group Exemption Number (GEN) · _____

8b If a corporation, name the state or foreign country (if applicable) where incorporated | State | Foreign country

9 Reason for applying (check only one box)
- [X] Started new business (specify type) · _____
  clothing manufacturer
- [ ] Hired employees (Check the box and see line 12.)
- [ ] Compliance with IRS withholding regulations
- [ ] Other (specify) ·
- [ ] Banking purpose (specify purpose) · _____
- [ ] Changed type of organization (specify new type) · _____
- [ ] Purchased going business
- [ ] Created a trust (specify type) · _____
- [ ] Created a pension plan (specify type) · _____

10 Date business started or acquired (month, day, year)
10-15-2004

11 Closing month of accounting year
December

12 First date wages or annuities were paid or will be paid (month, day, year). **Note:** *If applicant is a withholding agent, enter date income will first be paid to nonresident alien. (month, day, year)* . . . . · 10-22-2004

13 Highest number of employees expected in the next 12 months. **Note:** *If the applicant does not expect to have any employees during the period, enter "-0-."* . . . . ·

Agricultural	Household	Other

14 Check **one** box that best describes the principal activity of your business.
- [ ] Construction   [ ] Rental & leasing   [ ] Transportation & warehousing
- [ ] Real estate   [X] Manufacturing   [ ] Finance & insurance
- [ ] Health care & social assistance   [ ] Wholesale–agent/broker
- [ ] Accommodation & food service   [ ] Wholesale–other   [ ] Retail
- [ ] Other (specify)

15 Indicate principal line of merchandise sold; specific construction work done; products produced; or services provided.
clothing

16a Has the applicant ever applied for an employer identification number for this or any other business? . . . . . [ ] **Yes** [X] **No**
Note: *If "Yes," please complete lines 16b and 16c.*

16b If you checked "Yes" on line 16a, give applicant's legal name and trade name shown on prior application if different from line 1 or 2 above.
Legal name ·   Trade name ·

16c Approximate date when, and city and state where, the application was filed. Enter previous employer identification number if known.
Approximate date when filed (mo., day, year) | City and state where filed | Previous EIN

Third Party Designee

Complete this section **only** if you want to authorize the named individual to receive the entity's EIN and answer questions about the completion of this form.

Designee's name | Designee's telephone number (include area code) ( )

Address and ZIP code | Designee's fax number (include area code) ( )

Under penalties of perjury, I declare that I have examined this application, and to the best of my knowledge and belief, it is true, correct, and complete.

Name and title (type or print clearly) · John Doe, Partner

Applicant's telephone number (include area code) (123) 555-0000

Signature · *John Doe*   Date · 10/15/04

Applicant's fax number (include area code) ( )

For Privacy Act and Paperwork Reduction Act Notice, see separate instructions.   Cat. No. 16055N   Form **SS-4** (Rev. 12-2001)

Form SS-8
(Rev. January 2001)
Department of the Treasury
Internal Revenue Service

Determination of Worker Status
for Purposes of Federal Employment Taxes
and Income Tax Withholding

OMB No. 1545-0004

Name of firm (or person) for whom the worker performed services Doe Company	Worker's name Mary Reddenbacher

Firm's address (include street address, apt. or suite no., city, state, and ZIP code)
123 Main St
Baltimore, MD   98765

Worker's address (include street address, apt. or suite no., city, state, and ZIP code)   1234 Liberty Ln.
Baltimore, MD   12345

Trade name

Telephone number (include area code)
(410) 555-2000

Worker's social security number
123 : 45 : 6789

Telephone number (include area code)
(410) 555-0000

Firm's employer identification number
59 : 123   45678

Worker's employer identification number (if any)

Important Information Needed To Process Your Request

If this form is being completed by the worker, the IRS must have your permission to disclose your name to the firm. Do you object to disclosing your name and the information on this form to the firm? . . . . ☐ Yes ☐ No
If you answered "Yes" or did not check a box, stop here. The IRS cannot act on your request and a determination will not be issued.

You must answer ALL items OR mark them "Unknown" or "Does not apply." If you need more space, attach another sheet.

A This form is being completed by: ☒ Firm ☐ Worker; for services performed ___5/2/04___ to ___present___ .
(beginning date)   (ending date)

B Explain your reason(s) for filing this form (e.g., you received a bill from the IRS, you believe you received a Form 1099 or Form W-2 erroneously, you are unable to get worker's compensation benefits, you were audited or are being audited by the IRS).

C Total number of workers who performed or are performing the same or similar services _____ .

D How did the worker obtain the job? ☐ Application ☐ Bid ☐ Employment Agency ☐ Other (specify) _____

E Attach copies of all supporting documentation (contracts, invoices, memos, Forms W-2, Forms 1099, IRS closing agreements, IRS rulings, etc.). In addition, please inform us of any current or past litigation concerning the worker's status. If no income reporting forms (Form 1099-MISC or W-2) were furnished to the worker, enter the amount of income earned for the year(s) at issue $ _____ .

F Describe the firm's business. ...clothing manufacturer...

G Describe the work done by the worker and provide the worker's job title. ...personalized embroidering...

H Explain why you believe the worker is an employee or an independent contractor.

I Did the worker perform services for the firm before getting this position? . . . . ☐ Yes ☐ No ☐ N/A
If "Yes," what were the dates of the prior service?
If "Yes," explain the differences, if any, between the current and prior service.

J If the work is done under a written agreement between the firm and the worker, attach a copy (preferably signed by both parties). Describe the terms and conditions of the work arrangement.

204 ◆

Part I   Behavioral Control

1 What specific training and/or instruction is the worker given by the firm? ..... none

2 How does the worker receive work assignments? ....

3 Who determines the methods by which the assignments are performed? ....

4 Who is the worker required to contact if problems or complaints arise and who is responsible for their resolution? ....

5 What types of reports are required from the worker? Attach examples. ....

6 Describe the worker's daily routine (i.e., schedule, hours, etc.). ....

7 At what location(s) does the worker perform services (e.g., firm's premises, own shop or office, home, customer's location, etc.)? ....

8 Describe any meetings the worker is required to attend and any penalties for not attending (e.g., sales meetings, monthly meetings, staff meetings, etc.). ....

9 Is the worker required to provide the services personally? .... [X] **Yes** [ ] **No**

10 If substitutes or helpers are needed, who hires them? ..... the worker

11 If the worker hires the substitutes or helpers, is approval required? .... [ ] **Yes** [X] **No**
If "Yes," by whom? ....

12 Who pays the substitutes or helpers? ..... the worker

13 Is the worker reimbursed if the worker pays the substitutes or helpers? .... [ ] **Yes** [X] **No**
If "Yes," by whom? ....

Part II   Financial Control

1 List the supplies, equipment, materials, and property provided by each party:
The firm ... None
The worker Embroidery machine
Other party ....

2 Does the worker lease equipment? .... [ ] **Yes** [ ] **No**
If "Yes," what are the terms of the lease? (Attach a copy or explanatory statement.) ....

3 What expenses are incurred by the worker in the performance of services for the firm? .. Worker sometimes hires help

4 Specify which, if any, expenses are reimbursed by:
The firm ....
Other party ....

5 Type of pay the worker receives: [ ] Salary [ ] Commission [ ] Hourly Wage [X] Piece Work
[ ] Lump Sum [ ] Other (specify) ....
If type of pay is commission, and the firm guarantees a minimum amount of pay, specify amount $ ____ .

6 If the worker is paid by a firm other than the one listed on this form for these services, enter name, address, and employer identification number of the payer. ....

7 Is the worker allowed a drawing account for advances? .... [ ] **Yes** [X] **No**
If "Yes," how often? ....
Specify any restrictions. ....

8 Whom does the customer pay? .... [ ] Firm [ ] Worker
If worker, does the worker pay the total amount to the firm? [ ] **Yes** [ ] **No** If "No," explain. ....

9 Does the firm carry worker's compensation insurance on the worker? .... [ ] **Yes** [X] **No**

10 What economic loss or financial risk, if any, can the worker incur beyond the normal loss of salary (e.g., loss or damage of equipment, material, etc.)? ....

Part III   Relationship of the Worker and Firm

1 List the benefits available to the worker (e.g., paid vacations, sick pay, pensions, bonuses). ....

2 Can the relationship be terminated by either party without incurring liability or penalty? . . . . ☒ **Yes** ☐ **No**
If "No," explain your answer. ....

3 Does the worker perform similar services for others? . . . . ☐ **Yes** ☐ **No**
If "Yes," is the worker required to get approval from the firm? . . . . ☐ **Yes** ☐ **No**

4 Describe any agreements prohibiting competition between the worker and the firm while the worker is performing services or during any later period. Attach any available documentation. ....

5 Is the worker a member of a union? . . . . ☐ **Yes** ☐ **No**

6 What type of advertising, if any, does the worker do (e.g., a business listing in a directory, business cards, etc.)? Provide copies, if applicable. ....

7 If the worker assembles or processes a product at home, who provides the materials and instructions or pattern? ....

8 What does the worker do with the finished product (e.g., return it to the firm, provide it to another party, or sell it)? ....

9 How does the firm represent the worker to its customers (e.g., employee, partner, representative, or contractor)? ....

10 If the worker no longer performs services for the firm, how did the relationship end? ....

Part IV   For Service Providers or Salespersons- Complete this part if the worker provided a service directly to customers or is a salesperson.

1 What are the worker's responsibilities in soliciting new customers? ....

2 Who provides the worker with leads to prospective customers? ....
3 Describe any reporting requirements pertaining to the leads. ....

4 What terms and conditions of sale, if any, are required by the firm? ....
5 Are orders submitted to and subject to approval by the firm? . . . . ☐ **Yes** ☐ **No**
6 Who determines the worker's territory? ....
7 Did the worker pay for the privilege of serving customers on the route or in the territory? . . . . ☐ **Yes** ☐ **No**
If "Yes," whom did the worker pay? ....
If "Yes," how much did the worker pay? . . . . $ _____
8 Where does the worker sell the product (e.g., in a home, retail establishment, etc.)? ....

9 List the product and/or services distributed by the worker (e.g., meat, vegetables, fruit, bakery products, beverages, or laundry or dry cleaning services). If more than one type of product and/or service is distributed, specify the principal one. ....

10 Does the worker sell life insurance full time? . . . . ☐ **Yes** ☐ **No**
11 Does the worker sell other types of insurance for the firm? . . . . ☐ **Yes** ☐ **No**
If "Yes," enter the percentage of the worker's total working time spent in selling other types of insurance. . . . _____%
12 If the worker solicits orders from wholesalers, retailers, contractors, or operators of hotels, restaurants, or other similar establishments, enter the percentage of the worker's time spent in the solicitation. . . . . _____%
13 Is the merchandise purchased by the customers for resale or use in their business operations? . . . . ☐ **Yes** ☐ **No**
Describe the merchandise and state whether it is equipment installed on the customers' premises. ....

Part V   Signature (see page 4)

Under penalties of perjury, I declare that I have examined this request, including accompanying documents, and to the best of my knowledge and belief, the facts presented are true, correct, and complete.

Signature ▶ *John Doe* Title ▶ Partner Date ▶ *10/15/01*
(Type or print name below)

Form W-4 (2003)

Purpose. Complete Form W-4 so that your employer can withhold the correct Federal income tax from your pay. Because your tax situation may change, you may want to refigure your withholding each year.

Exemption from withholding. If you are exempt, complete only lines 1, 2, 3, 4, and 7 and sign the form to validate it. Your exemption for 2003 expires February 16, 2004. See **Pub. 505,** Tax Withholding and Estimated Tax.

Note: *You cannot claim exemption from withholding if: (a) your income exceeds $750 and includes more than $250 of unearned income (e.g., interest and dividends) and (b) another person can claim you as a dependent on their tax return.*

Basic instructions. If you are not exempt, complete the **Personal Allowances Worksheet** below. The worksheets on page 2 adjust your withholding allowances based on itemized deductions, certain credits, adjustments to income, or two-earner/two-job situations. Complete all worksheets that apply. **However, you may claim fewer (or zero) allowances.**

Head of household. Generally, you may claim head of household filing status on your tax return only if you are unmarried and pay more than 50% of the costs of keeping up a home for yourself and your dependent(s) or other qualifying individuals. See line **E** below.

Tax credits. You can take projected tax credits into account in figuring your allowable number of withholding allowances. Credits for child or dependent care expenses and the child tax credit may be claimed using the **Personal Allowances Worksheet** below. See **Pub. 919,** How Do I Adjust My Tax Withholding? for information on converting your other credits into withholding allowances.

Nonwage income. If you have a large amount of nonwage income, such as interest or dividends, consider making estimated tax payments using **Form 1040-ES,** Estimated Tax for Individuals. Otherwise, you may owe additional tax.

Two earners/two jobs. If you have a working spouse or more than one job, figure the total number of allowances you are entitled to claim on all jobs using worksheets from only one Form W-4. Your withholding usually will be most accurate when all allowances are claimed on the Form W-4 for the highest paying job and zero allowances are claimed on the others.

Nonresident alien. If you are a nonresident alien, see the **Instructions for Form 8233** before completing this Form W-4.

Check your withholding. After your Form W-4 takes effect, use Pub. 919 to see how the dollar amount you are having withheld compares to your projected total tax for 2003. See Pub. 919, especially if your earnings exceed $125,000 (Single) or $175,000 (Married).

Recent name change? If your name on line 1 differs from that shown on your social security card, call 1-800-772-1213 for a new social security card.

Personal Allowances Worksheet (Keep for your records.)

A Enter "1" for **yourself** if no one else can claim you as a dependent . . . . **A** _____

B Enter "1" if:
- You are single and have only one job; or
- You are married, have only one job, and your spouse does not work; or
- Your wages from a second job or your spouse's wages (or the total of both) are $1,000 or less.

B __1__

C Enter "1" for your **spouse.** But, you may choose to enter "-0-" if you are married and have either a working spouse or more than one job. (Entering "-0-" may help you avoid having too little tax withheld.) . . . . **C** _____

D Enter number of **dependents** (other than your spouse or yourself) you will claim on your tax return . . . . **D** _____

E Enter "1" if you will file as **head of household** on your tax return (see conditions under **Head of household** above) . **E** _____

F Enter "1" if you have at least $1,500 of **child or dependent care expenses** for which you plan to claim a credit . . **F** _____

(**Note:** *Do not include child support payments. See **Pub. 503,** Child and Dependent Care Expenses, for details.*)

G **Child Tax Credit** (including additional child tax credit):
- If your total income will be between $15,000 and $42,000 ($20,000 and $65,000 if married), enter "1" for each eligible child plus **1 additional** if you have three to five eligible children or **2 additional** if you have six or more eligible children.
- If your total income will be between $42,000 and $80,000 ($65,000 and $115,000 if married), enter "1" if you have one or two eligible children, "2" if you have three eligible children, "3" if you have four eligible children, or "4" if you have five or more eligible children.

G __1__

H Add lines A through G and enter total here. **Note:** *This may be different from the number of exemptions you claim on your tax return.* ▸ **H** _____

For accuracy, complete all worksheets that apply.
- If you plan to **itemize or claim adjustments to income** and want to reduce your withholding, see the **Deductions and Adjustments Worksheet** on page 2.
- If you have **more than one job** or are **married and you and your spouse both work** and the combined earnings from all jobs exceed $35,000, see the **Two-Earner/Two-Job Worksheet** on page 2 to avoid having too little tax withheld.
- If **neither** of the above situations applies, **stop here** and enter the number from line H on line 5 of Form W-4 below.

- - - - - - - - - - - - - **Cut here and give Form W-4 to your employer. Keep the top part for your records.** - - - - - - - - - - - - -

Form **W-4**	**Employee's Withholding Allowance Certificate**	OMB No. 1545-0010
Department of the Treasury Internal Revenue Service	• **For Privacy Act and Paperwork Reduction Act Notice, see page 2.**	2003

1 Type or print your first name and middle initial	Last name	**2** Your social security number
John A.	Smith	123 45 6789

Home address (number and street or rural route)	**3** ☒ Single ☐ Married ☐ Married, but withhold at higher Single rate.
567 Wharf Blvd.	**Note:** *If married, but legally separated, or spouse is a nonresident alien, check the "Single" box.*

City or town, state, and ZIP code	**4** If your last name differs from that shown on your social security card, check here. You must call 1-800-772-1213 for a new card. ▸ ☐
Baltimore, MD 54321	

		5	**1**
5	Total number of allowances you are claiming (from line **H** above **or** from the applicable worksheet on page 2)	**5**	1
6	Additional amount, if any, you want withheld from each paycheck	**6**	$ 0

7 I claim exemption from withholding for 2003, and I certify that I meet **both** of the following conditions for exemption:
- Last year I had a right to a refund of **all** Federal income tax withheld because I had **no** tax liability **and**
- This year I expect a refund of **all** Federal income tax withheld because I expect to have **no** tax liability.

If you meet both conditions, write "Exempt" here . . . . ▸ **7**

Under penalties of perjury, I certify that I am entitled to the number of withholding allowances claimed on this certificate, or I am entitled to claim exempt status.

Employee's signature
(Form is not valid unless you sign it.) ▸ *John A. Smith*

Date ▸ *June 6 2004*

8 Employer's name and address (Employer: Complete lines 8 and 10 only if sending to the IRS.)	**9** Office code (optional)	**10** Employer identification number

◆ 207

Deductions and Adjustments Worksheet

Note: *Use this worksheet only if you plan to itemize deductions, claim certain credits, or claim adjustments to income on your 2003 tax return.*

1 Enter an estimate of your 2003 itemized deductions. These include qualifying home mortgage interest, charitable contributions, state and local taxes, medical expenses in excess of 7.5% of your income, and miscellaneous deductions. (For 2003, you may have to reduce your itemized deductions if your income is over $139,500 ($69,750 if married filing separately). See **Worksheet 3** in Pub. 919 for details.) . . . **1** $ _____

2 Enter: { $7,950 if married filing jointly or qualifying widow(er)
$7,000 if head of household
$4,750 if single
$3,975 if married filing separately } . . . . **2** $ _____

3 **Subtract** line 2 from line 1. If line 2 is greater than line 1, enter "-0-" . . . . . . **3** $ _____
4 Enter an estimate of your 2003 adjustments to income, including alimony, deductible IRA contributions, and student loan interest **4** $ _____
5 **Add** lines 3 and 4 and enter the total. Include any amount for credits from **Worksheet 7** in Pub. 919 . **5** $ _____
6 Enter an estimate of your 2003 nonwage income (such as dividends or interest) . . . . . . **6** $ _____
7 **Subtract** line 6 from line 5. Enter the result, but not less than "-0-" . . . . . . **7** $ _____
8 **Divide** the amount on line 7 by $3,000 and enter the result here. Drop any fraction . . . . **8** _____
9 Enter the number from the **Personal Allowances Worksheet,** line H, page 1 . . . . . . **9** _____
10 **Add** lines 8 and 9 and enter the total here. If you plan to use the **Two-Earner/Two-Job Worksheet,** also enter this total on line 1 below. Otherwise, **stop here** and enter this total on Form W-4, line 5, page 1 . **10** _____

Two-Earner/Two-Job Worksheet

Note: *Use this worksheet only if the instructions under line H on page 1 direct you here.*

1 Enter the number from line H, page 1 (or from line 10 above if you used the **Deductions and Adjustments Worksheet**) **1** _____
2 Find the number in **Table 1** below that applies to the **lowest** paying job and enter it here . . . . **2** _____
3 If line 1 is **more than or equal to** line 2, subtract line 2 from line 1. Enter the result here (if zero, enter "-0-") and on Form W-4, line 5, page 1. **Do not** use the rest of this worksheet . . . . **3** _____

Note: *If line 1 is **less than** line 2, enter "-0-" on Form W-4, line 5, page 1. Complete lines 4-9 below to calculate the additional withholding amount necessary to avoid a year-end tax bill.*

4 Enter the number from line 2 of this worksheet . . . . **4** _____
5 Enter the number from line 1 of this worksheet . . . . **5** _____
6 **Subtract** line 5 from line 4 . . . . **6** _____
7 Find the amount in **Table 2** below that applies to the **highest** paying job and enter it here . . . . **7** $ _____
8 **Multiply** line 7 by line 6 and enter the result here. This is the additional annual withholding needed . . **8** $ _____
9 Divide line 8 by the number of pay periods remaining in 2003. For example, divide by 26 if you are paid every two weeks and you complete this form in December 2002. Enter the result here and on Form W-4, line 6, page 1. This is the additional amount to be withheld from each paycheck . . . . **9** $ _____

Table 1: Two-Earner/Two-Job Worksheet

Married Filing Jointly				All Others			
If wages from LOWEST paying job are-	Enter on line 2 above	If wages from LOWEST paying job are-	Enter on line 2 above	If wages from LOWEST paying job are-	Enter on line 2 above	If wages from LOWEST paying job are-	Enter on line 2 above
$0 - $4,000	0	44,001 - 50,000	8	$0 - $6,000	0	75,001 - 100,000	8
4,001 - 9,000	1	50,001 - 60,000	9	6,001 - 11,000	1	100,001 - 110,000	9
9,001 - 15,000	2	60,001 - 70,000	10	11,001 - 18,000	2	110,001 and over	10
15,001 - 20,000	3	70,001 - 90,000	11	18,001 - 25,000	3		
20,001 - 25,000	4	90,001 - 100,000	12	25,001 - 29,000	4		
25,001 - 33,000	5	100,001 - 115,000	13	29,001 - 40,000	5		
33,001 - 38,000	6	115,001 - 125,000	14	40,001 - 55,000	6		
38,001 - 44,000	7	125,001 and over	15	55,001 - 75,000	7		

Table 2: Two-Earner/Two-Job Worksheet

Married Filing Jointly		All Others	
If wages from HIGHEST paying job are-	Enter on line 7 above	If wages from HIGHEST paying job are-	Enter on line 7 above
$0 - $50,000	$450	$0 - $30,000	$450
50,001 - 100,000	800	30,001 - 70,000	800
100,001 - 150,000	900	70,001 - 140,000	900
150,001 - 270,000	1,050	140,001 - 300,000	1,050
270,001 and over	1,200	300,001 and over	1,200

Form **1040-ES**				
Department of the Treasury Internal Revenue Service	**2002**	**Payment Voucher 3**		OMB No. 1545-0087

File only if you are making a payment of estimated tax by check or money order. Mail this voucher with your check or money order payable to the **"United States Treasury."** Write your social security number and "2002 Form 1040-ES" on your check or money order. Do not send cash. Enclose, but do not staple or attach, your payment with this voucher.

Calendar year- Due Sept. 16, 2002

Amount of estimated tax you are paying by check or money order.

	Dollars	Cents

Your first name and initial Rocky	Your last name Frankenfurter	Your social security number 123-45-6789

If joint payment, complete for spouse

Spouse's first name and initial	Spouse's last name	Spouse's social security number

Address (number, street, and apt. no.)
1234 Bayshore Blvd.

City, state, and ZIP code (If a foreign address, enter city, province or state, postal code, and country.)
Baltimore, MD 12345

Type or print

For Privacy Act and Paperwork Reduction Act Notice, see instructions on page 5.

a Control number	.....	Void ☐	For Official Use Only · OMB No. 1545-0008		

b Employer identification number 33-4897044		**1** Wages, tips, other compensation $ 25,650.00	**2** Federal income tax withheld $ 5,050.00

c Employer's name, address, and ZIP code John Doe 123 Main Street Baltimore, MD 98765	**3** Social security wages $ 25,650.00	**4** Social security tax withheld $ 1,590.30
	5 Medicare wages and tips $ 25,650.00	**6** Medicare tax withheld $ 371.93
	7 Social security tips $ 0	**8** Allocated tips $ 0

d Employee's social security number 123-45-6789	**9** Advance EIC payment $ 0	**10** Dependent care benefits $ 0

e Employee's first name and initial	Last name	**11** Nonqualified plans $ 0	**12a** See instructions for box 12 Code $
Rocky	Frankenfurter		

13 Statutory employee ☐ Retirement plan ☐ Third-party sick pay ☐   **12b** Code $

1234 Bayshore Blvd.
Baltimore, MD 12345

14 Other   **12c** Code $

12d Code $

f Employee's address and ZIP code

15 State	Employer's state ID number	**16** State wages, tips, etc.	**17** State income tax	**18** Local wages, tips, etc.	**19** Local income tax	**20** Locality name
MD	4448778	$ 26,650.00	$ 565.00	$	$	
		$	$	$	$	

Form **W-2** **Wage and Tax Statement** (99)

Copy A **For Social Security Administration**—Send this entire page with Form W-3 to the Social Security Administration; photocopies are **not** acceptable.

(Rev. February 2002)

Cat. No. 10134D

Department of the Treasury—Internal Revenue Service

For Privacy Act and Paperwork Reduction Act Notice, see separate instructions.

Do Not Cut, Fold, or Staple Forms on This Page — Do Not Cut, Fold, or Staple Forms on This Page

9595 ☐ VOID ☐ CORRECTED

PAYER'S name, street address, city, state, ZIP code, and telephone no.		**1** Rents $	OMB No. 1545-0115	

Jeremy Michaels
XYZ Builders
123 Maple Avenue
Oaktown, VA 22000
703-123-4567

2 Royalties $

2002 Form **1099-MISC**

Miscellaneous Income

3 Other income $	**4** Federal income tax withheld $

Copy A
For Internal Revenue Service Center

PAYER'S Federal identification number	RECIPIENT'S identification number
10-9999999	123-45-6789

5 Fishing boat proceeds $

6 Medical and health care payments $

File with Form 1096.

RECIPIENT'S name

Zachary Austin
Rock Hill Drywall

7 Nonemployee compensation $ 5500.00

8 Substitute payments in lieu of dividends or interest $

For Privacy Act and Paperwork Reduction Act Notice, see the **2002 General Instructions for Forms 1099, 1098, 5498, and W-2G.**

Street address (including apt. no.)

456 Flower Lane

9 Payer made direct sales of $5,000 or more of consumer products to a buyer (recipient) for resale ▶ ☐

10 Crop insurance proceeds $

City, state, and ZIP code
Oaktown, VA 22000

11 //// **12** ////

Account number (optional) | 2nd TIN not. ☐

13 Excess golden parachute payments $

14 Gross proceeds paid to an attorney $

15

16 State tax withheld $ ---- $	**17** State/Payer's state no.	**18** State income $ ---- $

Form **1099-MISC**   Cat. No. 14425J   Department of the Treasury - Internal Revenue Service

Do Not Staple   6969

Form **1096**	Annual Summary and Transmittal of	OMB No. 1545-0108
Department of the Treasury Internal Revenue Service	U.S. Information Returns	20**02**

┌ FILER'S name

   Doe Company

Street address (including room or suite number)

   123 Main Street

City, state, and ZIP code
└ Baltimore, MD 98765

For Official Use Only

Name of person to contact	Telephone number
John Doe	(410) 555-0000

Fax number	E-mail address
(410) 555-0001	John@Doe.com

1 Employer identification number	**2** Social security number	**3** Total number of forms	**4** Federal income tax withheld	**5** Total amount reported with this Form 1096
59-123456	123-45-6789	3	$ 0	$ $63,000

Enter an "X" in only one box below to indicate the type of form being filed.   If this is your **final return**, enter an "X" here . . . ▶ ☒

W-2G 32	1098 81	1098-E 84	1098-T 83	1099-A 80	1099-B 79	1099-C 85	1099-DIV 91	1099-G 86	1099-INT 92	1099-LTC 93	1099-MISC 95	1099-MSA 94	1099-OID 96
☐	☐	☐	☐	☐	☐	☐	☐	☐	☐	☐	☐	☐	☐

1099-PATR 97	1099-Q 31	1099-R 98	1099-S 75	5498 28	5498-MSA 27
☐	☐	☐	☐	☐	☐

Please return this entire page to the Internal Revenue Service. Photocopies are not acceptable.

Under penalties of perjury, I declare that I have examined this return and accompanying documents, and, to the best of my knowledge and belief, they are true, correct, and complete.

Signature ▶   *John Doe*   Title ▶   Owner   Date ▶ 3-11-2003

APPENDIX B
BLANK FORMS

The following forms may be photocopied or removed from this book and used immediately. We recommend that you photocopy them and save the originals in case you make a mistake, or for future use. Some of the tax forms explained in this book are not included here because you should use the original documents provided by the taxing authority.

These forms are included on the following pages:

Maryland Forms

Virginia Forms

TRADE NAME APPLICATION

TRADE NAME: _____

_____

ADDRESS(ES) WHERE NAME IS USED: _____

_____

_____

_____

_____

FULL LEGAL NAME OF OWNER OF BUSINESS USING THE TRADE NAME: _____

_____

If the owner is an individual or general partnership, does it have a personal property account (an "L" number)?   YES   NO

If YES, what is that number?   L __ __ __ __ __ __ __ __
If NO, see instruction 7.

ADDRESS OF OWNER: _____

_____

_____ ZIP: _____

DESCRIPTION OF BUSINESS: _____

_____

_____

I AFFIRM AND ACKNOWLEDGE UNDER PENALTIES OF PERJURY THAT THE FOREGOING IS TRUE AND CORRECT TO THE BEST OF MY KNOWLEDGE.

_____   _____
SIGNATURE OF OWNER   SIGNATURE OF OWNER

_____   _____
SIGNATURE OF OWNER   SIGNATURE OF OWNER

Revised 7/00

TRADE NAME INSTRUCTIONS

1. Only one trade name may appear on each application. To file more than one trade name, complete a separate application for each and send separate checks.

2. The fee is $25.00; make checks payable to: DEPARTMENT OF ASSESSMENTS AND TAXATION

Filings brought into the office and filed on a while-you-wait basis as well as by fax are subject to an additional $50.00 surcharge for Expedited Service.

3. Mail the form and check to:

Department of Assessments and Taxation
301 W. Preston Street, Room 801
Baltimore, Maryland 21201

For Fax service: 410-333-7097

4. All blanks on the form must be typed with black ink, completed and legible and the signature must be original (no stamp, photocopy or carbon copy). Each person listed as an owner must sign. The ADDRESS(ES) WHERE NAME IS USED must be in Maryland and no post office box addresses may be used anywhere on the form.

5. If the name is found to be available and all items on the form are completed, the Department will accept the filing for record and an acknowledgment with the filing date will be sent to the "Address of Owner", ordinarily within four weeks of acceptance.

6. This filing is effective for five years from the day of acceptance by the Department. During the last six months of the period the filing may be renewed for an additional five years.

7. All unincorporated businesses that own or lease personal property (furniture, fixtures, tools, machinery, equipment, etc.) or anticipate owning or leasing personal property in the future, or need a business license must file an annual personal property return with this Department. Registration applications can be obtained by contacting your local assessment office or by calling (410)767-4991.

8. Walk-in hours are 8:30 a.m. to 5:00 p.m.

NOTICE: Acceptance of a trade name application does not confer on the owner any greater right to use the name than he otherwise already has. The Department checks the name only against other names filed with this Department. Federal trademarks, State service marks, records in other states and unfiled trade names are not checked. A name similar to yours in any of those places could cause problems with your use of the name. The purpose of this registration is let third parties who deal with this trade name know the identity of the legal person using the name. It is not meant to reserve the name for its owners, to act as a trademark filing or to confer on the owner any greater right to the name than he already possesses. For further information, contact your lawyer, accountant or financial advisor.

Combined Registration Application

 You can register online 24 hours a day at ***www.marylandtaxes.com***

Use this application to register for:

◆ **Admissions and amusement tax account**

◆ **Alcohol tax license**

◆ **Income tax withholding account**

◆ **Motor fuel tax account**

◆ **Sales and use tax license**

◆ **Use tax account**

◆ **Sales and use tax exemption certificate (for non-profit organizations)**

◆ **Tire recycling fee account**

◆ **Tobacco tax license**

◆ **Transient vendor license**

◆ **Unemployment insurance account**

Further registration is required for motor fuel, alcohol or tobacco taxes before engaging in business. The appropriate division of the Comptroller's Office will contact you and provide the necessary forms.

Other requirements

Depending on the nature of your business, you may be required to contact or register with some of the following agencies.

◆ **Local Licenses** may be required for corporations or individuals doing business in Maryland. Local licenses may be obtained from the Clerk of the Circuit Court for the jurisdiction in which the business is to be located.

◆ **Domestic and foreign corporations and limited liability companies** must register with the Department of Assessments and Taxation, Charter Division, at 301 West Preston Street, Baltimore, Maryland 21201-2395, 410-767-1340. Each entity must file an annual personal property return.

◆ **Individuals, sole proprietorships and partnerships** which possess personal property (furniture, fixtures, tools, machinery, equipment, etc.) or need a business license must register and file an annual personal property return with the Department of Assessments and Taxation, Unincorporated Personal Property Unit, 301 West Preston Street, Room 806, Baltimore, Maryland 21201-2395, 410-767-4991.

◆ **Every corporation and association** (domestic or foreign) having income allocable to Maryland must file a state income tax return.

◆ **All corporations** whose total Maryland income tax for the current taxable year can reasonably be expected to exceed $1,000 must file a declaration of estimated tax. 410-260-7980 or 1-800-MD TAXES.

◆ **To form a corporation,** contact the State Department of Assessments & Taxation, 301 West Preston Street, Baltimore, Maryland 21201-2315. 410-767-1340.

◆ **Worker's compensation insurance** coverage for employees is required of every employer in Maryland. This coverage may be obtained from a private carrier, the Injured Worker's Insurance Fund or by becoming self-insured. Contact the IWIF, 8722 Loch Raven Boulevard, Towson, Maryland 21204-6285. 410-494-2000 or 1-800-492-0197.

◆ **Unclaimed property.** The Maryland abandoned property law requires businesses to review their records each year to determine whether they are in possession of any unclaimed funds and securities due and owing Maryland residents that have remained unclaimed for more than five years, and to file an annual report. Contact the Comptroller of Maryland, Unclaimed Property Section, 301 W. Preston Street, Baltimore, Maryland 21201-2385. 410-767-1700 or 1-800-782-7383.

◆ **Charitable organizations** may be required to register with the secretary of state if they solicit the public for contributions. Contact the Secretary of State's Office, Annapolis, Maryland 21401. 410-974-5534.

◆ **Weights and measures.** If you buy or sell commodities on the basis of weight or measure, or use a weighing or measuring device commercially, your firm is subject to the Maryland Weights and Measures Law. To obtain information, call the Department of Agriculture, Weights and Measures Section at 410-841-5790.

◆ **Food businesses** are required to be licensed with the Department of Health and Mental Hygiene. Contact your local county health department or call DHMH at 410-767-8400.

COM/RAD-093 (Rev.9/00)

Instructions for page II

SECTION B. Complete this section if you are an employer registering for unemployment insurance.

PART 1. All industrial and commercial employers and many nonprofit charitable, educational and religious institutions in Maryland are covered by the state unemployment insurance law. There is no employee contribution. An employer must register upon establishing a new business in the state. If an employer is found liable to provide unemployment coverage, an account number and tax rate will be assigned. The employer must report and pay contributions on a report mailed to the employer each quarter by the Office of Unemployment Insurance.

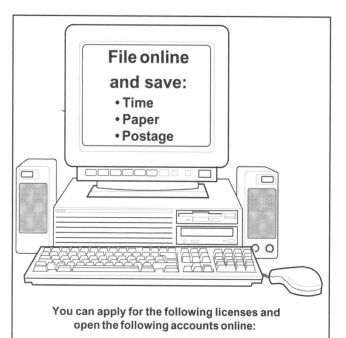

File online and save:
- **Time**
- **Paper**
- **Postage**

You can apply for the following licenses and open the following accounts online:

◆ Admissions and amusement tax account
◆ Income tax withholding account
◆ Sales and use tax license

◆ Use tax account
◆ Tire recycling fee account
◆ Transient vendor license
◆ Unemployment insurance account

www.marylandtaxes.com
24 hours a day

PART 2. Complete this part if you are a non-profit organization.

Item 1. Your exemption from the Internal Revenue Service should state if you are exempt from Federal Unemployment Taxes.

Item 2. Check the appropriate box and include a copy of the Internal Revenue Service exemption, if applicable.

Item 4. Indicate your option to finance unemployment insurance coverage:

Option (a) - Contributions.

The employer has the option to pay contributions. A rate assigned by the administration is applied to the first $8,500.00 of wages paid to each employee during a calendar year. Contributions are paid on a calendar quarter basis.

An employer who has not been subject to the Maryland Unemployment Insurance Law for a sufficient period of time to have its rates computed is required to pay at the new account rate, which is approximately 2.3%. Thereafter, the employer will be assigned a rate reflecting its own experience with layoffs. If the employer's former employees receive benefits regularly which result in benefit charges, the employer will have a higher tax rate. Employers which incur little or no benefit charges will have a lower tax rate.

Option (b) - Reimbursement Of Trust Fund.

The employer may elect to reimburse the Trust Fund. At the end of each calendar quarter, the employer is billed for unemployment benefits paid to its former employees during the quarter. A nonprofit organization that elects to reimburse must also provide collateral to protect the administration from default in reimbursement.

If (b) is checked, indicate which method of providing collateral you will use.

For more information on the financing options, call 410-767-2691. Toll Free 1-800-492-5524.

Executive order on privacy and state data system security notice

The information on this application will be used to determine if you are liable for certain taxes, to register you and, where appropriate, to issue a required license.

If you fail to provide required information, you will not be properly registered with state tax authorities, and necessary licenses may not be issued. If you operate a business without the appropriate registration and licenses, you may be subject to civil and criminal penalties, including confiscation in some instances.

If you are a sole proprietor, partner or officer in a corporation, you have the right to inspect any tax records for which you are responsible, and you may ask the tax authorities to correct any inaccurate or incomplete information on those records.

This application and the information you provide on it are generally not available for public inspection. This information will be shared with the state tax authorities with whom you should be registered.

Page IV

Instructions for completing the Maryland Combined Registration Application

 Register online at **www.marylandtaxes.com**

General instructions

NOTE: Incomplete applications cannot be processed and will be returned. To ensure that your application is processed without delay, be sure to provide all requested information. Please type or print clearly using a dark ink pen. Before mailing this application, be sure to:

1. Complete all of Section A.

2. Answer all questions in all the other sections that pertain to your business.

3. Sign the application in Section E.

4. Detach this instruction sheet from the application.

5. Mail the application to:
   Comptroller of Maryland
   Central Registration
   Revenue Administration Center
   Annapolis, MD 21411-0001

Instructions for page 1

Item 1 (a) A Federal Employer Identification Number (FEIN) is required by: all Corporations (Regular, Closed, or S), all Partnerships, all Non-Profit Organizations, and Sole Proprietorships who pay wages to one or more employees (a Sole Proprietorship with no employees, other than self, is not required to have a FEIN). If you don't have a FEIN at the time you submit this application, and one is required, leave this space blank and submit the number to Central Registration when you receive it from the Internal Revenue Service.

Item 1 (b) The social security number of the individual owner of the company or officer or agent of a corporation responsible for remitting the taxes is required. Also enter the name of the individual owner, officer or agent responsible for the taxes on the first line of Item 21.

Item 2. Enter the true name of the business, organization, corporation (John Smith, Inc.), partnership (Smith & Jones), individual proprietor or professional (Smith, John T.), or governmental agency.

Item 3. Enter the name by which your business is known to the public (Example: Smith's Ceramics).

Item 8 If you are already registered for any of the taxes listed, enter your registration number.

Item 8 (b) Sales and use tax exemption: Exemption certificates are issued to non-profit charitable, educational or religious organizations, volunteer fire or ambulance companies or volunteer rescue squads located in this state. Possession of an effective determination letter from the Internal Revenue Service stating that the organization qualifies under 501(c)(3) of the Internal Revenue Code may be treated as evidence that an organization qualifies for this exemption. You must enclose a non-returnable copy of the IRS determination letter, articles of incorporation, bylaws, and other organizational documents.

Item 8 (c) Tire recycling fee: You must register for a tire fee account if you will make any sales of tires to a retailer or you are a retailer who purchases tires from an out-of-state tire wholesaler or other person who does not show payment of Maryland's used tire recycling fees on invoices to you.

Item 8 (d) Admissions and amusement tax: Typical activities subject to the admissions and amusement tax include admissions to any place, including motion pictures, athletic events, races, shows and exhibits. Also subject to tax are receipts from athletic equipment rentals, bingo, coin-operated amusement devices, boat rides and excursions, amusement rides, golf greens fees, golf cart rentals, skating, bowling shoe rentals, lift tickets, riding academies, horse rentals, and merchandise, refreshments, or a service sold or served in connection with entertainment at a night club or room in a hotel, restaurant, hall, or other place where dancing privileges, music or other entertainment is provided.

Item 8 (j) Transient vendor license. If you make sales of property subject to the sales and use tax from either motor vehicles or from roadside or temporary locations, you must, in addition to any other license required by law, obtain and display a transient vendor license. Transient vendor licenses will be issued and reissued only to persons who have sales and use tax and trader's licenses and who are not delinquent in the payment of any state taxes.

Exhibitors at fairs, trade shows, flea markets and individuals who sell by catalogues, samples or brochures for future delivery do not need transient vendor licenses.

Other licenses you may need

In addition to a sales and use tax license, you may also need to obtain one or more of the licenses listed below from your local Clerk of the Court to operate your business in the state of Maryland:

Traders	Plumber & gas fitter	Junk dealer	Music box
Restaurant	Laundry	Auctioneer	Vending machine
Cigarette	Chain store	Hawkers & peddlers	Console machine
Special cigarette	Commercial garage	Billiard table	Wholesale dealer - farm
Construction firm	Storage warehouse	Pinball	machinery

These licenses are issued by the Clerk of the Circuit Court in the County (or Baltimore City) where the business is located. If your business falls into one or more of the above categories, please contact the Clerk of the Court in your county courthouse. Check the blue government pages of your local telephone directory for the street address and phone number. The clerk can also advise you on any local licensing requirements.

Register online

You can file your Combined Registration Application online at **www.marylandtaxes.com** 24 hours a day. You only view and complete the parts of the application that apply to your situation. It's fast and easy. You'll receive a confirmation number immediately and your account information will be in the mail quickly.

Get on the right 'TRAC'

The Taxpayer Registration Assistance Center (TRAC), located in Room 206, 301 West Preston Street, Baltimore, Maryland, offers on-the-spot help in completing this application. No appointment is necessary. Please contact us in advance if you need reasonable accommodation due to a disability.

Register by fax

You can file your Maryland Combined Registration Application by fax 24 hours a day. When applying by fax, be sure to complete Sections A and E of the application and any other sections that apply to your business. You *must* provide your federal employer ID number, if available, and Social Security number requested in Section A-1 and describe your business in Section A-18. Fax pages I and II of the application separately. Please *do not* fax a cover sheet or our instructions. The Central Registration fax number is 410-767-1571.

Add registrations by telephone

If you have (or recently had) a business tax registration with the Comptroller's Office, an account with the Unemployment Insurance Division or a business license issued by a clerk of the circuit court, we can open a sales and use tax, admissions and amusement tax or tire recycling fee account for you in just minutes by telephone. Telephone registration eliminates the need for you to fill out a Combined Registration Application. Just give us a call at: 410-767-1300 or 1-800-492-1751.

Questions?

☎ Call Central Registration at 410-767-1313 in Baltimore

☎ Toll free from elsewhere in Maryland 1-800-492-1751

For the hearing impaired: Maryland Relay Service 711 or 1-800-735-2258
Maryland tax forms and publications are available on our Forms-by-Fax System 410-974-FAXX (974-3299)
and on the World Wide Web www.marylandtaxes.com

Comptroller of Maryland
Central Registration
Revenue Administration Center
Annapolis, MD 21411-0001

Comptroller of Maryland
Combined Registration Application
See instructions on page IV

Office use only

SECTION A: All applicants must complete this section.

1a) Federal Employer Identification Number (See instructions)

☐☐–☐☐☐☐☐☐☐ **AND**

b) Social Security number of owner, officer or agent responsible for taxes (must be supplied)

☐☐☐–☐☐–☐☐☐☐

2. Legal name of dealer, employer, corporation, or owner

3. Trade name (if different from above)

4. Street address of business location (Post office box not acceptable)

City, County, and State   ZIP code (nine digits if known)

Telephone number   (__ __ __) __ __ __ - __ __ __ __

Fax number   (__ __ __) __ __ __ - __ __ __ __

5. Mailing address (post office box acceptable)

City, State   ZIP code (nine digits if known)

6. Reason for applying:
☐ New business   ☐ Additional location(s)
☐ Merger   ☐ Purchased going business
☐ Change of entity   ☐ Remit use tax on purchases
☐ Reorganization   ☐ Other (describe)

7. List previous owner's name and address:

---

8. Indicate registration sought: Number if registered:

a ☐ Sales and use tax   _____

b ☐ Sales and use tax exemption
     for non-profit organizations   _____

c ☐ Tire recycling fee   _____

d ☐ Admissions & amusement tax   _____

e ☐ Employer withholding tax   _____

f ☐ Unemployment insurance   _____

g ☐ Alcohol tax   _____

h ☐ Tobacco tax   _____

i ☐ Motor fuel tax   _____

j ☐ Transient vendor license   _____

9. Type of ownership: (Check appropriate box)
a ☐ Sole proprietorship   e ☐ Limited liability company
b ☐ Partnership   f ☐ Non-Maryland corporation
c ☐ Non-profit corporation j ☐ Governmental
d ☐ Maryland corporation   k ☐ Fiduciary l ☐ Business trust

10. Date first sales made in Maryland:	11. Date first wages paid in Maryland subject to withholding:

12. If you currently file a consolidated sales and use tax return, enter the number of your account:	13. If you have employees enter the number of your workers' compensation isurance policy or binder:

14. Date first wages paid to employees performing services in Maryland (Write N/A if no services performed in Maryland):	15. Number of employees:

16. Estimated gross wages paid in first quarter of operations:	17. Do you need a sales and use tax account only to remit taxes on untaxed purchases? ☐ Yes ☐ No

18. Describe business activity which generates revenue. Specify the product manufactured and/or sold, or the type of service performed.

19. Are you a non-profit organization applying for an exemption certificate? ☐ Yes ☐ No
If yes, enclose a non-returnable copy of IRS determination letter, articles of incorporation, bylaws, and other organization documents.

20. If the location described above is primarily engaged in providing support services to other units of the company, please indicate the nature of these activities. ☐ Administrative ☐ R&D ☐ Storage ☐ Other (specify) _____

21. Identify owners, partners, corporate officers, trustees, or members: (Please list person whose Social Security number is listed in Section A.1b first.)

Name and Social Security number	Title	Home address, city, state, ZIP code	Telephone number

Page II - See instructions on page III   FEIN or SSN ☐☐☐☐☐☐☐☐☐

SECTION B: Complete this section to register for an unemployment insurance account.

PART 1.

| 1. Will corporate officers receive compensation, salary or distribution of profits? ☐ Yes ☐ No | 2. Do you operate more than one location in Maryland? ☐ Yes ☐ No | 3. Did you acquire by sale or otherwise all or part of the assets, business, organization, or trade of another employee? ☐ Yes ☐ No |

4. If your answer to question 3 is "No", proceed to item 6 of this section. If your answer to question 3 is "Yes", provide the information below and answer question 5, if applicable:

   a. Percentage of common ownership between current business and former business: _____

   b. Percentage of assets acquired from former business: _____

   c. Date former business was acquired by current business: _____

   d. Unemployment insurance number of former business, if known: _____

5. If the percentage of common ownership, as shown in item 4(a), is 50% or less, choose the type of tax rate you desire from the following:

   ☐ rate based on former employer's experience with unemployment insurance claims and taxable payrolls.

   ☐ new employer rate (approximately 2.3%)

6. **For employers of domestic help only:**
   a) Have you or will you have as an individual or local college club, college fraternity or sorority a total payroll of $1,000 or more in the state of Maryland during any calendar quarter?
   ☐ Yes   ☐ No

   b) If yes, indicate the earliest quarter and calendar year.

7. **For agricultural operations only:**
   a) Have you had or will you have 10 or more workers for 20 weeks or more in any calendar year or have you paid or will you pay $20,000 or more in wages during any calendar quarter?
   ☐ Yes   ☐ No

   b) If yes, indicate the earliest quarter and calendar year.

PART 2. COMPLETE THIS PART IF YOU ARE A NON-PROFIT ORGANIZATION.

1. Are you covered by the Federal Unemployment Tax Act?
   ☐ Yes   ☐ No

2. If not, are you exempt under Section 3306(c)(8) of the Federal Unemployment Tax Act?   ☐ Yes   ☐ No

3. Are you a non-profit organization as described in Section 501(c)(3) of the United States Internal Revenue Code which is exempt from Income Tax under Section 501(a) of such code? If YES, attach a copy of your exemption from Internal Revenue Service.   ☐ Yes ☐ No

4. Elect option to finance unemployment insurance coverage. See instructions.
   a ☐ Contributions
   b ☐ Reimbursement of trust fund If b) is checked, indicate the total taxable payroll ($8,500 maximum per individual per calendar year)

   $ _____ for 20 _____   ☐ Letter of credit   ☐ Surety bond   ☐ Security deposit   ☐ Cash in escrow

SECTION C: Complete this section if you are applying for an alcohol or tobacco tax license.

| 1. Will you engage in any business activity pertaining to the manufacture, sale, distribution, or storage of alcoholic beverages?
☐ Yes   ☐ No | 2. Will you engage in any wholesale activity regarding the sale and/or distribution of cigarettes in Maryland?
☐ Yes   ☐ No |

SECTION D: Complete this section if you plan to sell, use or transport any fuels in Maryland.

| 1. Do you import any of the following fuels into Maryland?
☐ Gasoline (including av/gas)
☐ Special fuel (any fuel other than gasoline)
☐ Turbine fuel (jet fuel) | 2. Do you buy or manufacture any of the following fuels for resale or distribution?
☐ Gasoline (including av/gas)
☐ Special fuel (any fuel other than gasoline)
☐ Turbine fuel (jet fuel) | 3. Do you operate any motor vehicle which exceeds 26,000 lbs. (registered, operating, or in combination with another vehicle on a Maryland highway)?
☐ Yes   ☐ No |

| 4. Do you operate a retail service station?
☐ Yes ☐ No | 5. Do you transport petroleum in any transporting device exceeding 50 gallons? ☐ Yes ☐ No |

SECTION E: All applicants must complete this section.

I DECLARE UNDER THE PENALTY OF PERJURY THAT THIS APPLICATION HAS BEEN EXAMINED BY ME AND TO THE BEST OF MY KNOWLEDGE AND BELIEF IS TRUE, CORRECT, AND COMPLETE.

SIGN HERE ➤ _____ Title _____ Date _____

If the business is a corporation, an officer of the corporation authorized to sign on behalf of the corporation must sign; if a partnership, one partner must sign; if an unincorporated association, one member must sign; if a sole proprietorship, the proprietor must sign. (The signature of any other person will not be accepted.)

Suggested Blanket Resale Certificate

This is to certify that all tangible personal property or taxable services purchased from:

_____

_____

are intended for resale as tangible property or for use or incorporation as a material or part of other tangible personal property to be produced for sale.

This certificate shall be considered as a part of each order we shall give, provided that the order bears our Maryland sales and use tax registration number, and is to continue in force until revoked.

_____

Buyer's Name

_____   _____

Signature   Date

_____

_____

Buyer's Address

_____

Buyer's MD Sales and Use
Tax Registration No.

FOR CORPORATION ONLY

CERTIFICATE REQUIRED TO BE FILED BY A CORPORATION CONDUCTING BUSINESS IN THE STATE OF VIRGINIA UNDER AS ASSUMED OR FICTITIOUS NAME

      We hereby certify with the provisions of Section 59.1-69 of the 1960 Code of Virginia that we are conducting the business of _____,

at _____, Virginia,

the name of _____,

and that no other corporation or person has interest of any kind in said business and that we are the sole proprietors thereof and that our Post Office address is _____

_____ and it's Registered Agent's name

is _____, and his address

is _____.

      We further certify that we were authorized to do business in the State of Virginia on the _____ day

of _____, 20_____.

(Note: to be used only for foreign corporations).

      GIVEN Under my hand this _____ day of _____, 20_____.

_____

                                 CORPORATE NAME

BY: _____

Title: _____

Commonwealth of Virginia

County of Arlington, to-wit:

      I, the undersigned Notary Public in and for the Commonwealth and County aforesaid, do hereby certify that

_____, whose name is signed to the foregoing and hereunto annexed Certificate dated the _____ day of _____, 20_____.

_____

                                  NOTARY PUBLIC

      In the Clerk's Office of the Circuit Court of Arlington County, Virginia, _____,

20_____, at _____ o'clock _____M, this Certificate with the Certificate of Acknowledgement annexed, was recorded and filed and admitted to record.

              TESTE: _____

              By: _____

                                  DEPUTY CLERK

Register online at www.tax.state.va.us

FORM R-1 **VIRGINIA DEPARTMENT OF TAXATION**
BUSINESS REGISTRATION APPLICATION
PLEASE PRINT OR TYPE THIS APPLICATION
READ THE INSTRUCTIONS BEFORE COMPLETING THIS FORM

FOR OFFICE USE ONLY
Virginia Account Number

OPERATOR #	DATE PROCESSED

CHECK THE REASON(s) you are submitting this application. Retail Sales and Use Tax and Motor Vehicle Fuel Sales Tax applicants must complete a separate Form R-1 for each location that collects retail sales tax. For vending machine sales tax applicants, complete a separate Form R-1 for each city or county in which vending machines are located.

NEW BUSINESS-NEVER REGISTERED

☐ I want to **register a new business** that has never been registered for any Virginia business tax (never assigned a Virginia business account number).

    ☐ *Check this box if this* business is a new specialty dealer for flea markets, gun shows, arts/crafts shows, etc., making sales at locations throughout Virginia.

REOPEN A CLOSED BUSINESS ACCOUNT

☐ I want to **reopen a closed account** for a business that was previously registered with the VIRGINIA DEPARTMENT OF TAXATION. Enter name and account number below. If more space is needed, attach a separate sheet and check here. ☐

Business name_____

Virginia account number _____

EXISTING BUSINESS-ALREADY REGISTERED

☐ **Sales and Use Tax.** I want to register a new location to collect Virginia sales and use tax or tire tax. Complete one of the following if applicable.

    A. This new location is in the same city or county as my other location(s) and I want to file a combined return for these locations using the following existing account number:

    _____

    B. I want to pay taxes for this new location using my consolidated account number:

    _____

☐ **Other Taxes.** I want to register my business for other taxes. My current Virginia account number is:

_____

SECTION A: BUSINESS NAME, LOCATION AND ENTITY TYPE INFORMATION

1. Check the **TYPE OF ENTITY** below and enter the **FULL LEGAL NAME OF THE BUSINESS** as applicable. Complete only one.

	OFFICE USE ONLY

☐ **SOLE PROPRIETOR** - Individual's full name: .... _____   I

☐ **PARTNERSHIP** - Partnership name: .... _____   P

☐ **LIMITED LIABILITY COMPANY** - Company name: ..... _____   P

☐ **CORPORATION** - Corporation name: .... _____   1
    Also, check any of the following boxes that apply:
    ☐ Sub Chapter S Corporation;   7
    ☐ Multi-State Corporation; or   M
    ☐ Non-profit Corporation exempt under IRC Section 501(c).   N
        Also enter qualifying paragraph number: IRC 501(c)(___).

☐ **GOVERNMENT AGENCIES & UNITS** - Agency/Unit name: _____ —   F S G
    ☐ U.S.   ☐ State   ☐ Other Government

☐ **OTHER TYPE -**
    ☐ Enter entity type: _____ Enter entity's full name: _____

2. Enter the **"TRADING-AS" NAME OF THE BUSINESS** here *only*
if it is different from the legal name of the business on line 1 above: _____

3. Enter the business location's street address **(PHYSICAL LOCATION)**. Rural route addresses *must* include the route and box number. Post Office box numbers will **not** be accepted. See the instructions before continuing. Enter a daytime phone number so we can contact you if we need additional information.

    IMPORTANT ⟹ **The address entered on this line will be used to allocate local sales tax revenue to the city or county where the business is physically located. The mailing address should be entered on line 7, not here.**

_____

Physical Address: Number and Street Address

_____   (   ) _____

City or County   State   ZIP Code (9 digit)   Phone Number

4. Complete line 4a, 4b, 4c or 4d, whichever best identifies the business' **PHYSICAL LOCATION** (street address) entered on line 3. See the instructions for details on determining locality codes. **Enter the correct locality code. Local sales tax revenue is distributed using this information.** *** Locality codes are listed on page 2 of the instructions.** This business is located:

   `IMPORTANT!`

   4a. OUTSIDE Virginia in the state (or District) of _____.

   4b. INSIDE Virginia, ENTIRELY WITHIN the CITY or COUNTY OF _____. *Locality Code _____

   4c. INSIDE Virginia, but NOT ENTIRELY IN ONE LOCALITY:

       Partly in the CITY or COUNTY of_____. *Locality Code _____, and

       Partly in the CITY or COUNTY of_____. *Locality Code _____.

   4d. Are you a specialty dealer selling in flea markets, gun shows, arts/crafts shows, etc., at various locations in Virginia? ☐ **Yes**

5. Enter your Federal Employer Identification Number (FEIN) |__|__| - |__|__|__|__|__|__|__|

   If not required by the IRS to have a FEIN, enter your social security number |__|__|__| - |__|__| - |__|__|__|__|

6. Enter your four-digit Principal Business Activity Code from page 6 of the instructions |__|__|__|__|
   - AND - describe the products you SELL or the type of SERVICES you provide:
   _____
   _____

7. Complete this line *only if different* from line 3, *or*, if separate mailing addresses are desired for different taxes. If additional space is needed, attach a separate sheet showing the appropriate address for each tax. A list of tax types is on pages 3 and 4.

Tax Type	Mailing Name	Mailing Address
_____	_____	Address _____
		City or County / State / ZIP Code (9 digit)
_____	_____	Address _____
		City or County / State / ZIP Code (9 digit)

8. If you sell alcoholic beverages, enter your Virginia Alcoholic Beverage Control license number: _____

SECTION B: RESPONSIBLE OFFICER(S)

Section 58.1-1813 of the *Code of Virginia* provides that a corporate or partnership officer may be held personally liable for any of the taxes registered on this form if that person willfully fails to pay, collect or truthfully account for the tax, or willfully attempts in any way to evade, defeat or not pay the tax. Notify the Department of Taxation when there is a change of responsible officers. Notification must be in writing and include changes in names, addresses and telephone numbers.

9. Complete this line for each owner, partner, member, corporation officer or trustee. Attach additional pages, if needed. In the case of a limited partnership, complete this line for each general partner. See instructions.

Social Security Number _____ | Social Security Number _____
Name _____ | Name _____
Title _____ | Title _____
Home Address _____ | Home Address _____
City State ZIP Code (9 digit) Home Phone: (___) _____ | City State ZIP Code (9 digit) Home Phone: (___) _____

Social Security Number _____ | Social Security Number _____
Name _____ | Name _____
Title _____ | Title _____
Home Address _____ | Home Address _____
City State ZIP Code (9 digit) Home Phone: (___) _____ | City State ZIP Code (9 digit) Home Phone: (___) _____

SECTION C: TAX TYPES

10.   Check the box beside each tax for which you are registering. Also, enter the date you became liable or will become liable for that tax type. If the telephone number of the contact person for tax information is different than the number entered on line 3, complete the third column. **Please do not check taxes for which you are already registered.** See the instructions.

Tax Types	Date you will be liable for the tax	Contact person's phone number (if different from line 3)

◆SALES AND USE TAXES◆

Tax Types		Date you will be liable for the tax	Contact person's phone number (if different from line 3)
☐ **Retail Sales and Use Tax (In-State Dealers)**	(ST)	/ /	( )
☐ **Use Tax (Out-of-State Dealers)**	(UT)	/ /	( )
☐ **Consumer Use Tax**	(CU)	/ /	( )
☐ **Aircraft Dealers**	(AS)	/ /	( )

Enter your Virginia Commercial Fleet Aircraft
License Number:_____
Date Issued:____/____/____ Date Expires:____/____/____
Enter the number of aircraft owned during the
preceding calendar year _____.

		Date	Phone
☐ **Motor Vehicle Fuel Sales Tax**	(MF)	/ /	( )
☐ **Tire Tax**	(TR)	/ /	( )
☐ **Vending Machine Sales Tax**	(VM)	/ /	( )
☐ **Watercraft Sales and Use Tax**	(WC)	/ /	( )

Seasonal Businesses: If your business is SEASONAL (not operational the entire year) check the month(s) it will be active:

JAN	FEB	MAR	APR	MAY	JUN	JUL	AUG	SEP	OCT	NOV	DEC

◆INCOME TAXES◆

		Date	Phone
☐ **Employer Withholding Tax**	(WH)	/ /	( )

Check the box beside the TOTAL amount of Virginia Income Tax you expect to withhold from employee wages for each quarter:

☐ $300 or less per quarter (Quarterly Filer)
☐ More than $300 but less than $3,000 per quarter (Monthly Filer)
☐ $3,000 or more per quarter (Semi-Weekly Filer)

Seasonal Businesses: If your business is SEASONAL (not operational the entire year), check the month(s) it will be active:

JAN	FEB	MAR	APR	MAY	JUN	JUL	AUG	SEP	OCT	NOV	DEC

		Date	Phone
☐ **Corporation Income Tax**	(CP)	/ /	( )

Check Taxable or Fiscal Year (same as Federal purposes)
  ☐ Calendar Year - January 1 to December 31
  ☐ Fiscal Year - First month of your taxable year _____

Subsidiary/Affiliate: ☐ Check here if this business is a subsidiary or affiliate of another business and will be filing a combined or consolidated return with its affiliate(s). Enter the Virginia account number, FEIN and name of the parent or affiliated corporation(s).

Virginia Account Number _____

FEIN _____

Name_____

FOR OFFICE USE ONLY		
AK	NMAI	NPC
PBA	ET	BC
LC	LD	ELD

Tax Types		Date you will be liable for the tax:	Contact person's phone number (if different from line 3)
◆Miscellaneous Taxes◆			
☐ Corn Assessment	(CO)	/ /	( )
☐ Cotton Assessment	(CX)	/ /	( )
☐ Egg Excise Tax	(EG)	/ /	( )
☐ Forest Products Tax	(FP)	/ /	( )
☐ Litter Tax	(LT)	/ /	( )
☐ Peanut Excise Tax	(PN)	/ /	( )
☐ Sheep Assessment	(SH)	/ /	( )
☐ Small Grains Assessment	(SG)	/ /	( )
☐ Soft Drink Excise Tax	(SD)	/ /	( )
☐ Soybean Assessment	(SB)	/ /	( )

SECTION D: MULTIPLE PLACES OF BUSINESS (SALES TAX)

Complete this section if you have more than one location and are registering for Retail Sales And Use Tax, Tire Tax, Consumers Use Tax, Motor Vehicle Fuel Sales Tax, or Watercraft Sales And Use Tax. Also complete this section to register an additional VENDING MACHINE SALES TAX location in an additional locality. Attach a separate sheet if space is needed.

11.   Enter the Virginia account number of each location.

Account Number _____   Account Number _____

Account Number _____   Account Number _____

SECTION E: ELECTRONIC FUNDS TRANSFER (EFT)

Businesses with an average monthly Virginia employer withholding, sales and use, or corporation income tax liability exceeding $20,000 are required by law to pay that tax by Electronic Funds Transfer (EFT). This threshold applies to each tax separately. For consolidated sales tax accounts, the return tax liability for the account of the parent company reporting for its subsidiaries is used to determine if EFT is required. Check the box for each tax for which electronic funds transfer is required.

☐ **Sales and Use Tax (In-State-Dealers)**   ☐ **Use Tax (Out-Of-State Dealer)**
☐ **Corporation Income Tax**   ☐ **Employer Withholding Tax**

If you are not required to pay by EFT, but would like to use this payment method, check this box to receive an EFT guide. ☐

SECTION F: SIGNATURE

IMPORTANT - READ BEFORE SIGNING

Sections 58.1-1814 and 1815 of the *Code of Virginia* provide criminal penalties for a person who willfully fails to make a return, keep records or supply information required by law for the administration of state taxes, or who willfully fails to collect, account for and pay over any sales, use and withholding taxes.

This registration form and returns for the taxes registered on this form must be signed by an officer of the corporation, or member of the partnership, limited liability company or unincorporated association, who is authorized to sign on behalf of the organization. The proprietor must sign for a sole proprietorship. Signatures of accountants, certified public accountants or persons who are not authorized to sign on behalf of the organization are not acceptable.

I have read and understand the statements above, including those in SECTION B of this form, and I am authorized to sign this form on behalf of this organization.

Name (Print or type) _____   Title _____

Signature _____ Date _____ Daytime Telephone Number _____( )_____

MAIL FORM R-1 TO: OR **FAX TO:**
Registration Unit, Virginia Department of Taxation
P.O. BOX 1114   **Registration Unit**
Richmond, VA 23218-1114   **Virginia Department of Taxation**
                                         (804) 367-2603

Form ST-10

COMMONWEALTH OF VIRGINIA
SALES AND USE TAX CERTIFICATE OF EXEMPTION

**(For use by a Virginia dealer who purchases tangible personal property for resale,
or for lease or rental, or who purchases materials or containers
to package tangible personal property for sale)**

To: _____   Date _____ , _____
(Name of supplier)

_____   _____   _____   _____
(Number and street or rural route)   (City, town, or post office)   (State)   (ZIP Code)

The Virginia Retail Sales and Use Tax Act provides that the Virginia Sales and use tax shall not apply to tangible personal property purchased for resale; that such tax shall not apply to tangible personal property purchased for future use by a person for taxable lease or rental as an established business or part of an established business, or incidental or germane to such business, including a simultaneous purchase and taxable leaseback. The Act provides also that such tax shall not apply to packaging materials such as containers, labels, sacks, cans, boxes, drums or bags if the materials are marketed with a product being sold and become the property of the purchaser.

This Certificate of Exemption may not be used by a using or consuming construction contractor as defined in the Regulations.

The undersigned dealer hereby certifies that all tangible personal property purchased from the above named supplier on and after this date will be purchased for the purpose indicated below, unless otherwise specified on each order, and that this Certificate shall remain in effect until revoked in writing by the Department of Taxation. (Check proper box below.)

☐ 1. Tangible personal property for RESALE only.

☐ 2. Tangible personal property for future use by a person for taxable LEASE OR RENTAL as an established business, or part of an established business, or incidental or germane to such business, or a simultaneous purchase and taxable leaseback.

☐ 3. Packaging materials such as containers, labels, sacks, cans, boxes, drums or bags that are marketed with a product being sold and become the property of the purchaser.

Name of Dealer _____   **Certificate of Registration No.** _____

Trading as _____

Address _____   _____   _____   _____
(Number and street or rural route)   (City, town, or post office)   (State)   (ZIP Code)

Kind of business engaged in by dealer _____

I certify that I am authorized to sign this Certificate of Exemption and that, to the best of my knowledge and belief, it is true and correct, made in good faith, pursuant to the Virginia Retail Sales and Use Tax Act.

By _____   _____
(Signature)   (Title)

(If the dealer is a corporation, an officer of the corporation or other person authorized to sign on behalf of the corporation must sign; if a partnership, one partner must sign; if an unincorporated association, a member must sign; if a sole proprietorship, the proprietor must sign.)

Information for supplier—A supplier is required to have on file only one Certificate of Exemption properly executed by the dealer who buys tax exempt tangible personal property for the purpose indicated hereon.

Virginia Department of Taxation
(REV. 10/99)

ADD TO DOMESTIC FOR-PROFIT CORPORATION

Department of Consumer and Regulatory Affairs
Business & Professional Licensing Administration
Corporations Division
941 North Capitol Street, N.E.
Washington, D.C. 20002

[ ] Domestic Entity
[ ] Foreign Entity

APPLICATION FOR NAME RESERVATION

Pursuant to the provisions of the District of Columbia of Columbia statute. We, the undersigned hereby apply for reservation of name for the following entity for a period of sixty (60) days.

IF FOREIGN, WHAT STATE ORGANIZED IN:
_____?

1. The name of the entity: _____

   _____

2. Date: _____.

By   _____
        Signature Name

Title   _____
        (Type or print)

FILE IN DUPLICATE WITH ORIGINAL SIGNATURES ON EACH
Filing Fee: $35.00 for Business Entities and $65.00 for Nonprofit Entities.

FR-500 COMBINED BUSINESS TAX REGISTRATION APPLICATION

GOVERNMENT OF THE DISTRICT OF COLUMBIA
OFFICE OF TAX AND REVENUE

PART I — GENERAL INFORMATION

1(a). Federal Employer Identification Number ☐☐–☐☐☐☐☐☐☐   2. NAICS Business Code ☐☐☐☐☐☐

1(b). Social Security Number ☐☐☐–☐☐–☐☐☐☐

3. Reason for application: (please check)
❑ New business
❑ Additional location
❑ Purchased existing business
❑ Name change
   (if a corporation, attach corporation amendment)
❑ Legal form change
❑ Street vendor
❑ Employment of household/domestic help
❑ Address change
❑ Merger (attach merger agree.)
❑ Other (describe on an attachment)
❑ Heating oil company
❑ Utility company

4. Legal form of business (please check):
❑ Sole proprietor
❑ Limited Liability Company
❑ General partnership
❑ Limited liability partnership
❑ Corporation
❑ Limited partnership
❑ Government
❑ Joint venture
❑ Other (specify)
If Incorporated, enter state and date of Incorporation
State _____ Mo. _____ Day _____ Yr _____

5. Business Name (Individual, Partnership, Corporation)

6. Trade Name (if different from Line 5)

7. Business Address (P.O. Box is not acceptable unless located in a Rural Area)

8. Mailing Address

9. Local Business Phone No.   10. Main Office Phone No.   10(a). FAX No.   11. Date present business began in D.C. or date expected to begin
(   )   (   )   (   )   Mo. _____ Day _____ Year _____

12. If previously registered with the District of Columbia, please indicate:

Former Entity Name _____ Business Tax Registration Number _____

Former Trade Name _____ Name of Former Owners _____

13. NAME, TITLE, HOME ADDRESS, SOCIAL SECURITY NUMBER OF PROPRIETOR, PARTNERS OR PRINCIPAL OFFICERS

Name and Title	Home Address	Zip Code	Social Security Number
Name and Title	Home Address	Zip Code	Social Security Number
Name and Title	Home Address	Zip Code	Social Security Number

PART II — Franchise Tax Registration

14. Indicate your profession, principal business activity or service (for example, retail grocery, wholesale auto parts, barber shop, doctor, contractor, landscaper, etc.)

15. Do you or will you have an office, warehouse, or other place of business in the District of Columbia, or a representative with a D.C. location? ❑ Yes ❑ No

16. Do you or will you have merchandise stored in a public or private warehouse in D.C.? ❑ Yes ❑ No

17. Do you or will you perform in D.C. personal services (medical, accounting, consulting); or other services such as electrical, heating, construction, etc., or installations or repairs of any type? ❑ Yes ❑ No

18. Do you or will you generate any business related income from D.C. sources? ❑ Yes ❑ No

19. Do you or will you have rental property in D.C.? ❑ Yes ❑ No | 20. Date converted or expected to be converted to rental property ___/___/___

21. Date on which your taxable year ends: Month _____ Day _____ Year _____

22. Describe fully ALL your current or expected business activities and/or major type of services performed within D.C. (Attach separate sheet if necessary.)

— INCOMPLETE APPLICATIONS WILL BE RETURNED —

PART III — Employer's D.C. Withholding Tax Registration

23. Estimated total number of employees _____	24. Number of D.C. resident employees subject to D.C. Withholding Tax: _____
25. Date when you began to employ D.C. resident(s) ____-____-____ 　　　　　　　　　　　　　　　　　　　　　mo. day yr.	26. Estimate of amount of D.C. tax to be withheld monthly from D.C. resident employees:
Date when you began or date expected to begin to withhold D.C. tax from resident employees ____-____-____ 　　　　　　　　　　　　　　　　　　mo. day yr.	27. Will you have employee(s) working within D.C.? 　　❑ Yes ❑ No

PART IV — Sales and Use Tax Registration

28. Check applicable box(es) below 　❑ Reporting Sales Tax on retail sales or rentals. 　❑ Reporting Use Tax on items purchased tax free inside/outside D.C. 　❑ Purchasing in D.C. items for resale outside D.C. (Attach photocopy of state/county sales tax registration.) 　❑ Purchasing in D.C. cigarettes for resale outside D.C. (Attach photocopy of state/county cigarette/tobacco license.) 　❑ Making no taxable sales and tax is paid to vendors in all taxable purchases. 　❑ Making exempt sales where a Certificate of Resale is issued.	29. **Date when sales/use began in D.C.** ____-____-____ 　　**or date expected to begin**　　mo. day yr.

30. If you have more than one place of business where you collect taxes on sales in the District of Columbia, do you
wish to file a Combined Sales Tax Return for all locations?　　　　　　　　　　　❑ Yes　❑ No
Please attach a statement listing any additional places of business.

PART V1 — Personal Property Tax Registration

Describe the type of Personal Property at each location (ex. furniture, fixtures, machinery equipment and supplies), used for business purposes.

_____

_____

PART V2 — Miscellaneous Tax Registration

Check applicable block(s) below and the appropriate payment booklets/returns will be sent to you.
　❑ Alcoholic Beverage Wholesaler
　❑ Cable Television, Satellite Relay or Distribution of Video or Radio Transmission only
　❑ Cigarette Wholesaler
　❑ Commercial Mobile Service Tax
　❑ Gross Receipts Public Utility

　❑ Heating Oil
　❑ Interstate Bus
　❑ Motor Vehicle Fuel Tax
　❑ Natural or Artificial Gas by Non-Public Utility Person
　❑ Toll Telecommunication Service Tax

If you have questions please contact the Customer Service Administration at (202) 727-4829.

CERTIFICATION
I declare under penalties as provided by law that this application (including any accompanying schedules and statements) has been examined by me and to the best of my knowledge and belief it is true, correct and complete.

_____　　_____　　_____
　　　　　Signature　　　　　　　　　　　　**Title**　　　　　　　　　　　**Date**
COMPLETED APPLICATIONS MUST BE SIGNED BY EITHER THE OWNER, PARTNER OR PRINCIPAL OFFICER
OF THE CORPORATION. (Agents or Representatives must attach a *Power of Attorney*.)

OFFICIAL USE ONLY

Type Tax	Date Lia. began	Cycle	Method	Remarks
H				
J				
W				
S				
P				
Reviewer/Date				
Date Data Entered/Initials				

COMPLETE THIS PART IF ANY OF YOUR EMPLOYEES <u>WORK</u> IN THE DISTRICT OF COLUMBIA

PART VI — Unemployment Compensation Tax Registration

IMPORTANT: Although some information has already been requested in Part I, it is necessary that the Unemployment Compensation Tax Registration be completed by all applicants who have employees working in the District. Part VI will be processed separately from Parts I through V. For more information on this part call (202) 698-7550.

1. Federal Employer Identification Number ☐☐–☐☐☐☐☐☐☐

2. Previously assigned Unemployment Insurance Number *(if applicable)* ☐☐–☐☐☐☐

3. Type of ownership *(check one)*

☐ Sole Proprietor ☐ Household
☐ Partnership ☐ Limited liability company
☐ Joint Venture ☐ Limited liability partnership
☐ Corporation ☐ Other (specify) _____

If Incorporated, enter:
State _____ Date _____
Mo. Day Yr.

Reason for applying:

☐ New Business ☐ Additional location
☐ Merger (attach merger agreement) ☐ Purchased existing business
☐ Household/domestic ☐ Other (specify)
☐ Name Change _____
(if a corporation attach corporation amendment)
☐ Change of Entity
☐ Reorganization

4. Describe in *detail* your business activity and/or major source of sales that generate sales and use tax; specify the product manufactured and/or sold, or the type of service performed. *(Omission of this information may result in a delay of your status determination.)*

5. Entity Name

6. Trade Name *(if different from line 5)*

7. Street Address of D.C. Business or D.C. Worksite
(P.O. Box is not acceptable)

8. Mailing Address for ALL Returns

9. Electronic Means of Communication
(Leave blank if not applicable)

☐ Local Voice Number _____
☐ Local Fax Number _____
☐ Main Office Voice Number _____
☐ Main Office Fax Number _____
☐ E-mail Address _____
☐ Website Address _____

10. Owner, officer, or agent responsible for reporting and remitting unemployment taxes:

Name _____
Title _____
Voice No. _____
Fax No. _____

11. List Proprietor, Partners, or Principal Officers

Name and Title	Address	Social Security Number

— COMPLETE REVERSE SIDE —

12a. Date when the first wages were paid to employees performing services in D.C. *(write N/A if there were no services performed in D.C.)* **Month:** **Day:** **Year:**	**This space for official use only.** Account Number _____ Date _____
12b. **For employers of domestic help only.** Have you or will you have for an individual or local college club, college fraternity or sorority, a total payroll of $500 or more in D.C. during any calendar year: ❑ Yes ❑ No If yes, indicate earliest quarter and calendar year: **Quarter:** **Year:**	Signature _____
13. Number of workers employed in D.C. *(including officers)*	

14. List all places of business in D.C.

BUSINESS NAME	D.C. ADDRESS	ZIP CODE

15. If the reason for registering is due to the purchase of a going business, merger, reorganization, or change of legal entity, provide the following information including the percentage of assets acquired *(if needed, attach additional explanation of transaction).*

    Nature of transfer *(check appropriate box):*

❑ Purchase   ❑ Merger or consolidation   ❑ Foreclosure   ❑ Receivership

❑ Lease   ❑ Corporate Reorganization   ❑ Bankruptcy   ❑ Assignment

❑ Partnership reorganization *(admission or withdrawal of one or more partners).*

❑ Other *(specify in detail):* _____

Percent of assets acquired: _____ %   Date of transfer: Month: Day: Year:

Predecessor's Name   Predecessor's Account Number

Address

Trade name under which transferred business was operated

16. **COMPLETE THIS PART ONLY IF YOU ARE A NON-PROFIT ORGANIZATION**

16a. Are you covered by the Federal Unemployment Tax Act? ❑ Yes ❑ No If NO, are you exempt under §3306(c)(8) of the Federal Unemployment Tax Act? ❑ Yes ❑ No	16b. Are you a non-profit organization as described in §501(c)(3) of the United States Internal Revenue Code which is exempt from income tax under §501(a) of such code? ❑ Yes ❑ No *(If yes, please attach a copy of the §501(c)(3) exemption letter.)*

16c. Elect an option to finance unemployment insurance coverage *(see instructions)*   ❑ Contributions   ❑ Reimbursement of trust fund

CERTIFICATION. *I declare under penalties as provided by law that Part VI (including any accompanying schedules and statements) has been examined by me and to the best of my knowledge and belief it is true, correct and complete.*

Signature	*Title*	*Date*	*Telephone Number*

THE COMPLETED PART VI MUST BE SIGNED BY THE OWNER, PARTNER OR PRINCIPAL OFFICER OF THE CORPORATION, OR AGENT *(Power of Attorney must be attached if signed by an agent.)*

Part VI is to be mailed to: Department of Employment Services
                    609 H St., N.E., Room 362
                    Washington, D.C. 20002

FR-500

GOVERNMENT OF THE DISTRICT OF COLUMBIA
OFFICE OF TAX AND REVENUE

COMBINED BUSINESS TAX REGISTRATION APPLICATION

- Codes for Principal Business Activity (New)
- Instructions
- General Information (Part I)
- Franchise Tax Registration (Part II)
- Employer's D.C. Withholding Tax Registration (Part III)
- Sales and Use Tax Registration (Part IV)
- Personal Property Tax Registration (Part V-1)
- Gross Receipts Tax (Part V-2)
- Unemployment Compensation Tax Registration (Part VI)

OFFICE OF TAX AND REVENUE
CUSTOMER SERVICE ADMINISTRATION
941 North Capitol Street, N.E.
Washington, D.C. 20002

Telephone No. (202) 727-4TAX (4829)

CONTENTS:
- Listing of Business Activity Codes (New)
- Instructions
- Combined Business Tax Registration Application (Form FR-500)
- Unemployment Compensation Tax Registration Application

(Rev. 8/01)

Codes for Principal Business Activity

This list of principal business activities and their associated codes is designed to classify an enterprise by the type of activity in which it is engaged. These principal business activity codes are based on the North American Industry Classification System.

If the company purchases raw materials and supplies them to a subcontractor to produce the finished product, but retains title to the product, the company is considered a manufacturer and must use one of the manufacturing codes (311110-339900).

Agriculture, Forestry, Fishing and Hunting

Code

Crop Production
111100 Oilseed & Grain Farming
111210 Vegetable & Melon Farming (including potatoes & yams)
111300 Fruit & Tree Nut Farming
111400 Greenhouse Nursery, & Floriculture Production
111900 Other Crop Farming (including tobacco, cotton, sugarcane, hay, peanut, sugar beet & all other crop farming)

Animal Production
112111 Beef Cattle Ranching & Farming
112112 Cattle Feedlots
112120 Dairy Cattle & Milk Production
112210 Hog & Pig Farming
112300 Poultry & Egg Production
112400 Sheep & Goat Farming
112510 Animal Aquaculture (including shellfish & finfish farms & hatcheries)
112900 Other Animal Production

Forestry and Logging
113110 Timber Tract Operations
113210 Forest Nurseries & Gathering of Forest Products
113310 Logging

Fishing, Hunting and Trapping
114110 Fishing
114210 Hunting & Trapping

Support Activities for Agriculture and Forestry
115110 Support Activities for Crop Production (including cotton ginning, soil preparation, planting & cultivating)
115210 Support Activities for Animal Production
115310 Support Activities for Forestry

Mining
211110 Oil & Gas Extraction
212110 Coal Mining
212200 Metal Ore Mining
212310 Stone Mining & Quarrying
212320 Sand, Gravel, Clay, & Ceramic & Refractory Minerals Mining & Quarrying
212390 Other Nonmetallic Mineral Mining & Quarrying
213110 Support Activities for Mining

Utilities
221100 Electric Power Generation, Transmission & Distribution
221210 Natural Gas Distribution
221300 Water, Sewage & Other Systems

Construction

Building, Developing, and General Contracting
233110 Land Subdivision & Land Development

Code

233200 Residential Building Construction
233300 Nonresidential Building Construction

Heavy Construction
234100 Highway, Street, Bridge, & Tunnel Construction
234900 Other Heavy Construction

Special Trade Contractors
235110 Plumbing, Heating, & Air-Conditioning Contractors
235210 Painting & Wall Covering Contractors
235310 Electrical Contractors
235400 Masonry, Drywall, Insulation, & Tile Contractors
235500 Carpentry & Floor Contractors
235610 Roofing, Siding, & Sheet Metal Contractors
235710 Concrete Contractors
235810 Water Well Drilling Contractors
235900 Other Special Trade Contractors

Manufacturing

Food Manufacturing
311110 Animal Food Mfg
311200 Grain & Oilseed Milling
311300 Sugar & Confectionery Product Mfg
311400 Fruit & Vegetable Preserving & Specialty Food Mfg
311500 Dairy Product Mfg
311610 Animal Slaughtering and Processing
311710 Seafood Product Preparation & Packaging
311800 Bakeries & Tortilla Mfg
311900 Other Food Mfg (including coffee, tea, flavorings & seasonings)

Beverage and Tobacco Product Manufacturing
312110 Soft Drink & Ice Mfg
312120 Breweries
312130 Wineries
312140 Distilleries
312200 Tobacco Manufacturing

Textile Mills and Textile Product Mills
313000 Textile Mills
314000 Textile Product Mills

Apparel Manufacturing
315100 Apparel Knitting Mills
315210 Cut & Sew Apparel Contractors
315220 Men's & Boys' Cut & Sew Apparel Mfg
315230 Women's & Girls' Cut & Sew Apparel Mfg
315290 Other Cut & Sew Apparel mfg
315990 Apparel Accessories & Other Apparel Mfg

Leather and Allied Product Manufacturing
316110 Leather & Hide Tanning & Finishing
316210 Footwear Mfg (including rubber & plastics)
316990 Other Leather & Allied Product Mfg

Code

Wood Product Manufacturing
321110 Sawmills & Wood Preservation
321210 Veneer, Plywood, & Engineered Wood Product Mfg
321900 Other Wood Product Mfg

Paper Manufacturing
322100 Pulp, Paper & Paperboard Mills
322200 Converted Paper Product Mfg

Printing and Related Support Activities
323100 Printing & Related Support Activities

Petroleum and Coal Products Manufacturing
324100 Petroleum Refineries (including integrated)
324120 Asphalt Paving, Roofing, & Saturated Materials Mfg
324190 Other Petroleum & Coal Products Mfg

Chemical Manufacturing
325100 Basic Chemical Mfg
325200 Resin, Synthetic Rubber & Artificial & Synthetic Fibers & Filaments Mfg
325300 Pesticide, Fertilizer, & Other Agricultural Chemical Mfg
325410 Pharmaceutical & Medicine Mfg
325500 Paint Coating, & Adhesive Mfg
325600 Soap, Cleaning Compound, & Toilet Preparation Mfg
325900 Other Chemical Product & Preparation Mfg

Plastics and Rubber Products Manufacturing
326100 Plastics Product Mfg
326200 Rubber Product Mfg

Nonmetallic Mineral Product Manufacturing
327100 Clay Product & Refractory Mfg
327210 Glass & Glass product Mfg
327300 Cement & Concrete Product Mfg
327400 Lime & Gypsum Product Mfg
327900 Other Nonmetallic Mineral Product Mfg

Primary Metal Manufacturing
331110 Iron & Steel Mills & Ferroalloy Mfg
331200 Steel Product Mfg from Purchased Steel
331310 Alumina & Aluminum Production & Processing
331400 Nonferrous Metal (except Aluminum) Production & Processing
331500 Foundries

Fabricated Metal Product Manufacturing
332110 Forging & Stamping
332210 Cutlery & Handtool Mfg
332300 Architectural & Structural Metals Mfg
332400 Boiler, Tank, & Shipping Container Mfg
332510 Hardware Mfg
332610 Spring & Wire Product Mfg
332700 Machine Shops; Turned Product; & Screw, Nut, & Bolt Mfg
332810 Coating, Engraving, Heat Treating, & Allied Activities
332900 Other Fabricated Metal Product Mfg

Machinery Manufacturing
333100 Agriculture, Construction, & Mining Machinery Mfg
333200 Industrial Machinery Mfg
333310 Commercial & Service Industry Machinery Mfg
333410 Ventilation, Heating, Air-Conditioning, & Commercial Refrigeration Equipment Mfg
333510 Metalworking Machinery Mfg
333610 Engine, Turbine & Power Transmission Equipment Mfg

Code

333900 Other General Purpose Machinery Mfg

Computer and Electronic Product Manufacturing
334110 Computer & Peripheral Equipment Mfg
334200 Communications Equipment Mfg
334310 Audio & Video Equipment Mfg
334410 Semiconductor & Other Electronic Component Mfg
334500 Navigational, Measuring, Electromedical, & Control Instruments Mfg
334610 Manufacturing & Reproducing Magnetic & Optical Media

Electrical Equipment, Appliance, and Component Manufacturing
335100 Electric Lighting Equipment Mfg
335200 Household Appliance Mfg
335310 Electrical Equipment Mfg
335900 Other Electrical Equipment & Component Mfg

Transportation Equipment Manufacturing
336100 Motor Vehicle Mfg
336210 Motor Vehicle Body & Trailer Mfg
336300 Motor Vehicle Parts Mfg
336410 Aerospace Product & Parts Mfg
336510 Railroad Rolling Stock Mfg
336610 Ship & Boat Building
336990 Other Transportation Equipment Mfg

Furniture and Related Product Manufacturing
337000 Furniture & Related Product Manufacturing

Miscellaneous Manufacturing
339110 Medical Equipment & Supplies Mfg
339900 Other Miscellaneous Manufacturing

Wholesale Trade

Wholesale Trade, Durable Goods
421100 Motor Vehicle & Motor Vehicle Parts & Supplies Wholesalers
421200 Furniture & Home Furnishing Wholesalers
421300 Lumber & Other Construction Materials Wholesalers
421400 Professional & Commercial Equipment & Supplies Wholesalers
421500 Metal & Mineral (except Petroleum) Wholesalers
421600 Electrical Goods Wholesalers
421700 Hardware, & Plumbing & Heating Equipment & Supplies Wholesalers
421800 Machinery, Equipment, & Supplies Wholesalers
421910 Sporting & Recreational Goods & Supplies Wholesalers
421920 Toy & Hobby Goods & Supplies Wholesalers
421930 Recyclable Material Wholesalers
421940 Jewelry, Watch, Precious Stone, & Precious Metal Wholesalers
421990 Other Miscellaneous Durable Goods Wholesalers
422100 Paper & Paper Product Wholesalers
422210 Drugs & Druggists' Sundries Wholesalers
422300 Apparel, Piece Goods, & Notions Wholesalers
422400 Grocery & Related Product Wholesalers
422500 Farm Products Raw Material Wholesalers
422600 Chemical & Allied Products Wholesalers

Code

Wholesale Trade, Durable Goods
- 422700 Petroleum & Petroleum Products Wholesalers
- 422800 Beer, Wine, & Distilled Alcoholic Beverage Wholesalers
- 422910 Farm Supplies Wholesalers
- 422920 Books, Periodical, & Newspaper Wholesalers
- 422930 Flower, Nursery Stock & Florists' Supplies Wholesalers
- 422940 Tobacco & Tobacco Product Wholesalers
- 422950 Paint, Varnish, & Supplies Wholesalers
- 422990 Other Miscellaneous Nondurable Goods Wholesalers

Retail Trade

Motor Vehicle and Parts Dealers
- 441110 New Car Dealers
- 441120 Used Car Dealers
- 441210 Recreational Vehicle Dealers
- 441221 Motorcycle Dealers
- 441222 Boat Dealers
- 441229 All Other Motor Vehicle Dealers
- 441300 Automotive Parts, Accessories, & Tire Stores

Furniture and Home Furnishings Stores
- 442110 Furniture Stores
- 442210 Floor Covering Stores
- 442291 Window Treatment Stores
- 442299 All Other Home Furnishings Stores

Electronics and Appliance Stores
- 443111 Household Appliance Stores
- 443112 Radio, Television, & Other Electronics Stores
- 443120 Computer & Software Stores
- 443130 Camera & Photographic Supplies Stores

Building Material and Garden Equipment and Supplies Dealers
- 444110 Home Centers
- 444120 Paint & Wallpaper Stores
- 444130 Hardware Stores
- 444190 Other Building Material Dealers
- 444200 Lawn & Garden Equipment & Supplies Stores

Food and Beverage Stores
- 445110 Supermarkets and Other Grocery (except Convenience) Stores
- 445120 Convenience Stores
- 445210 Meat Markets
- 445220 Fish & Seafood Markets
- 445230 Fruit & Vegetable Markets
- 445291 Baked Goods Stores
- 445292 Confectionery & Nut Stores
- 445299 All Other Specialty Food Stores
- 445310 Beer, Wine, & Liquor Stores

Health and Personal Care Stores
- 446110 Pharmacies & Drug Stores
- 446120 Cosmetics, Beauty Supplies, & Perfume Stores
- 446130 Optical Goods Stores
- 446190 Other Health & Personal Care Stores

Gasoline Stations
- 447100 Gasoline Stations (including convenience stores with gas)

Clothing and Clothing Accessories Stores
- 448110 Men's Clothing Stores
- 448120 Women's Clothing Stores
- 448130 Children's & Infants' Clothing Stores
- 448140 Family Clothing Stores
- 448150 Clothing Accessories Stores
- 448190 Other Clothing Stores
- 448219 Shoe Stores
- 448310 Jewelry Stores
- 448320 Luggage & Leather Goods Stores

Code

Sporting Goods, Hobby, Book, and Music Stores
- 451110 Sporting Goods Stores
- 451120 Hobby, Toy, & Game Stores
- 451130 Sewing, Needlework, & Piece Goods Stores
- 451140 Musical Instrument & Supplies Stores
- 451211 Book Stores
- 451212 News Dealers & Newsstands
- 451220 Prerecorded Tape, Compact Disc, & Record Stores

General Merchandise Stores
- 452110 Department Stores
- 452900 Other General Merchandise Stores

Miscellaneous Store Retailers
- 453110 Florists
- 453210 Office Supplies & Stationery Stores
- 453220 Gift, Novelty, & Souvenir Stores
- 453310 Used Merchandise Stores
- 453910 Pet & Pet Supplies Stores
- 453920 Art Dealers
- 453930 Manufactured (Mobile) Home Dealers
- 453990 All Other Miscellaneous Store Retailers (including tobacco, candle, & trophy shops)

Nonstore Retailers
- 454110 Electronic Shopping & Mail-Order Houses
- 454210 Vending Machine Operators
- 454311 Heating Oil Dealers
- 454312 Liquefied Petroleum Gas (Bottled Gas) Dealers
- 454319 Other Fuel Dealers
- 454390 Other Direct Selling Establishments (including door-to-door retailing, frozen food plan providers, party plan merchandisers, & coffee-break service providers)

Transportation and Warehousing

Air, Rail, and Water Transportation
- 481000 Air Transportation
- 482110 Rail Transportation
- 483000 Water Transportation

Truck Transportation
- 484110 General Freight Trucking, Local
- 484120 General Freight Trucking, Long-distance
- 484200 Specialized Freight Trucking

Transit and Ground Passenger Transportation
- 485110 Urban Transit Systems
- 485210 Interurban & Rural Bus Transportation
- 485310 Taxi Service
- 485320 Limousine Service
- 485410 School & Employee Bus Transportation
- 485510 Charter Bus Industry
- 485990 Other Transit & Ground Passenger Transportation

Pipeline Transportation
- 486000 Pipeline Transportation

Scenic & Sightseeing Transportation
- 487000 Scenic & Sightseeing Transportation

Support Activities for Transportation
- 488100 Support Activities for Air Transportation
- 488210 Support Activities for Rail Transportation
- 488300 Support Activities for Water Transportation
- 488410 Motor Vehicle Towing
- 488490 Other Support Activities for Road Transportation
- 488510 Freight Transportation Arrangement

Code

- 488990 Other Support Activities for Transportation

Couriers and Messengers
- 492110 Couriers
- 492210 Local Messengers & Local Delivery

Warehousing And Storage
- 493100 Warehousing & Storage (except lessors of miniwarehouses & self-storage units)

Information

Publishing Industries
- 511110 Newspaper Publishers
- 511120 Periodical Publishers
- 511130 Book Publishers
- 511140 Database & Directory Publishers
- 511190 Other Publishers
- 511210 Software Publishers

Motion Picture and Sound Recording Industries
- 512100 Motion Picture & Video Industries (except video rental)
- 512200 Sound Recording Industries

Broadcasting and Telecommunications
- 513100 Radio & Television Broadcasting
- 513200 Cable Networks & Program Distribution
- 513300 Telecommunications (including paging, cellular, satellite, & other telecommunications)

Information Services and Data Processing Services
- 514100 Information Services (including news syndicates, libraries, & on-line information services)
- 514210 Data Processing Services

Finance and Insurance

Depository Credit Intermediation
- 522110 Commercial Banking
- 522120 Savings Institutions
- 522130 Credit Unions
- 522190 Other Depository Credit Intermediation

Nondepository Credit Intermediation
- 522210 Credit Card Issuing
- 522220 Sales Financing
- 522291 Consumer Lending
- 522292 Real Estate Credit (including mortgage bankers & originators)
- 522293 International Trade Financing
- 522294 Secondary Market Financing
- 522298 All Other Nondepository Credit Intermediation

Activities Related to Credit Intermediation
- 522300 Activities Related to Credit Intermediation (including loan brokers)

Securities, Commodity Contracts, and Other Financial Investments and Related Activities
- 523110 Investment Banking & Securities Dealing
- 523120 Securities Brokerage
- 523130 Commodity Contracts Dealing
- 523140 Commodity Contracts Brokerage
- 523210 Securities & Commodity Exchanges
- 523900 Other Financial Investment Activities (including portfolio management & investment advice)

Code

Insurance Carriers and Related Activities
- 524140 Direct Life, Health, & Medical Insurance & Reinsurance Carriers
- 524150 Direct Insurance & Reinsurance (except Life, Health & Medical) Carriers
- 524210 Insurance Agencies & Brokerages
- 524290 Other Insurance Related Activities

Funds, Trusts, and Other Financial Vehicles
- 525100 Insurance & Employee Benefit Funds
- 525910 Open-end Investment Funds
- 525920 Trusts, Estates, & Agency Accounts
- 525930 Real Estate Investment Trusts
- 525990 Other Financial Vehicles

"Offices of Bank Holding Companies" and "Offices of Other Holding Companies," are located under

Management of Companies (Holding Companies)

Real Estate and Rental and Leasing

Real Estate
- 531110 Lessors of Residential Buildings & Dwellings
- 531114 Cooperative Housing
- 531120 Lessors of Miniwarehouses & Self-Storage Units
- 531190 Lessors of Other Real Estate Property
- 531210 Offices of Real Estate Agents & Brokers
- 531310 Real Estate Property Managers
- 531320 Offices of Real Estate Appraisers
- 531390 Other Activities Related to Real Estate

Rental and Leasing Services
- 532100 Automotive Equipment Rental & Leasing
- 532210 Consumer Electronics & Appliances Rental
- 532220 Formal Wear & Costume Rental
- 532230 Video Tape & Disc Rental
- 532290 Other Consumer Goods Rental
- 532310 General Rental Centers
- 532400 Commercial & Industrial Machinery & Equipment Rental & Leasing

Lessors of Nonfinancial Intangible Assets (except copyrighted works)
- 533110 Lessors of Nonfinancial Intangible Assets (except copyrighted works)

Professional, Scientific, and Technical Services

Legal Services
- 541110 Offices of Lawyers
- 541190 Other Legal Services

Accounting, Tax Preparation, Bookkeeping, and Payroll Services
- 541211 Offices of Certified Public Accountants
- 541213 Tax Preparation Services
- 541214 Payroll Services
- 541219 Other Accounting Services

Architectural, Engineering, and Related Services
- 541310 Architectural Services
- 541320 Landscape Architecture Services
- 541330 Engineering Services
- 541340 Drafting Services

Architectural Engineering, and Related Services

Code	
541350	Building Inspection Services
541360	Geophysical Surveying & Mapping Services
541370	Surveying & Mapping (except Geophysical) Services
541380	Testing Laboratories

Specialized Design Services
Code	
541400	Specialized Design Services (including interior, industrial, graphic, & fashion design)

Computer Systems Design and Related Services
Code	
541511	Custom Computer Programming Services
541512	Computer Systems Design Services
541513	Computer Facilities Management Services
541519	Other Computer Related Services

Other Professional, Scientific, and Technical Services
Code	
541600	Management, Scientific, & Technical Consulting Services
541700	Scientific Research & Development Services
541800	Advertising & Related Services
541910	Marketing Research & Public Opinion Polling
541920	Photographic Services
541930	Translation & Interpretation Services
541940	Veterinary Services
541990	All Other Professional, Scientific, & Technical Services

Management of Companies (Holding Companies)
Code	
551111	Offices of Bank Holding Companies
551112	Offices of Other Holding Companies

Administrative and Support and Waste Management and Remediation Services

Administrative and Support Services
Code	
561110	Office Administrative Services
561210	Facilities Support Services
561300	Employment Services
561410	Document Preparation Services
561420	Telephone Call Centers
561430	Business Service Centers (including private mail centers & copy shops)
561440	Collection Agencies
561450	Credit Bureaus
561490	Other Business Support Services (including repossession services, court reporting, & stenotype services)

Code
Code	
561500	Travel Arrangement & Reservation Services
561600	Investigation & Security Services
561710	Exterminating & Pest Control Services
561720	Janitorial Services
561730	Landscaping Services
561740	Carpet & Upholstery Cleaning Services
561790	Other Services to Buildings & Dwellings
561900	Other Support Services (including packaging & labeling services, & convention & trade show organizers)

Waste Management and Remediation Services
Code	
562000	Waste Management & Remediation Services

Educational Services
Code	
611000	Educational Services (including schools, colleges, & universities)

Health Care and Social Assistance

Offices of Physicians and Dentists
Code	
621111	Offices of Physicians (except mental health specialists)
621112	Offices of Physicians, mental Health Specialists
621210	Office of Dentists

Offices of Other Health Practitioners
Code	
621310	Offices of Chiropractors
621320	Offices of Optometrists
621330	Offices of Mental Health Practitioners (except Physicians)
621340	Offices of Physical, Occupational & Speech Therapists, & Audiologists
621391	Offices of Podiatrists
621399	Offices of All Other Miscellaneous Health Practitioners

Outpatient Care Centers
Code	
621410	Family Planning Centers
621420	Outpatient Mental Health & Substance Abuse Centers
621491	HMO Medical Centers
621492	Kidney Dialysis Centers
621493	Freestanding Ambulatory Surgical & Emergency Centers
621498	All Other Outpatient Care Centers

Medical and Diagnostic Laboratories
Code	
621510	Medical & Diagnostic Laboratories

Home Health Care Services
Code	
621610	Home Health Care Services

Code

Other Ambulatory Health Care Services
Code	
621900	Other Ambulatory Health Care Services (including ambulance services & blood & organ banks)

Hospitals
Code	
622000	Hospitals

Nursing and Residential Care Facilities
Code	
623000	Nursing & Residential Care Facilities

Social Assistance
Code	
624100	Individual & Family Services
624200	Community Food & Housing, & Emergency & Other Relief Services
624310	Vocational Rehabilitation Services
624410	Child Day Care Services

Arts, Entertainment, and Recreation

Performing Arts, Spectator Sports, and Related Industries
Code	
711100	Performing Arts Companies
711210	Spectator Sports (including sports clubs & racetracks)
711300	Promoters of Performing Arts, Sports, & Similar Events
711410	Agents & Managers for Artists, Athletes, Entertainers & Other Public Figures
711510	Independent Artists, Writers, & Performers

Museums, Historical Sites, and Similar Institutions
Code	
712100	Museums, Historical Sites & Similar Institutions

Amusement, Gambling, and Recreation Industries
Code	
713100	Amusement Parks & Arcades
713200	Gambling Industries
713900	Other Amusement & Recreation Industries (including golf courses, skiing facilities, marinas, fitness centers, & bowling centers)

Accommodation and Food Services

Accommodation
Code	
721110	Hotels (except casino hotels) & Motels
721120	Casino Hotels
721191	Bed & Breakfast Inns
721199	All Other Traveler Accommodation
721210	RV (Recreational Vehicle) Parks & Recreational Camps
721310	Rooming & Boarding Houses

Code

Food Services and Drinking Places
Code	
722110	Full-Service Restaurants
722210	Limited-Service Eating Places
722300	Special Food Services (including food service contractors & caterers)
722410	Drinking Places (Alcoholic Beverages)

Other Services

Repair and Maintenance
Code	
811110	Automotive Mechanical & Electrical Repair & Maintenance
811120	Automotive Body, Paint, Interior, & Glass Repair
811190	Other Automotive Repair & Maintenance (including oil change & lubrication shops & car washes)
811210	Electronic & Precision Equipment Repair & Maintenance
811310	Commercial & Industrial Machinery & Equipment (except Automotive & Electronic) Repair & Maintenance
811410	Home & Garden Equipment & Appliance Repair & Maintenance
811420	Reupholstery & Furniture Repair
811430	Footwear & Leather Goods Repair
811490	Other Personal & Household Goods Repair & Maintenance

Personal and Laundry Services
Code	
812111	Barber Shops
812112	Beauty Salons
812113	Nail Salons
812190	Other Personal Care Services (including diet & weight reducing centers)
812210	Funeral Homes & Funeral Services
812220	Cemeteries & Crematories
812310	Coin-Operated Laundries & Drycleaners
812320	Drycleaning & Laundry Services (except Coin-Operated)
812330	Linen & Uniform Supply
812910	Pet Care (except Veterinary) Services
812920	Photofinishing
812930	Parking Lots & Garages
812990	All Other Personal Services

Religions, Grantmaking, Civic, Professional, and Similar Organizations
Code	
813000	Religious, Grantmaking, Civic, Professional, & Similar Organizations (including condominium and homeowners associations)

INSTRUCTIONS

The Combined Business Tax Registration Application (Form FR-500) is to be completed by a business or consumer who is registering with the Government of the District of Columbia, Office of Tax and Revenue and the Department of Employment Services (DOES) for the following taxes or payment:

• Corporation Franchise Tax Return (Form D-20)
• Unincorporated Business Franchise Tax Return (Form D-30)
• Employer Withholding Tax Return (Form FR-900 series)
• Sales and Use Tax Return (Form FR-800 series)
• Personal Property Tax Return (Form FP-31)
• Street Vendor Payment
• Gross Receipts Tax
• Unemployment Compensation Tax (Registered by DOES)

PART I

The following general instructions are to assist you in completing Form FR-500.

• **All questions in Parts I through VI must be answered. If not applicable, write "N/A" in the answer block.**
• **Although there is duplication of some information requested in Part I and Part VI, both parts must be completed. Part VI will be processed separately from Parts I through V-1 and V-2.**
• **All questions requesting a date must be answered with the month, day and year.**
• **Sign the application at the end of Parts V-2 and VI.**
• **Return only the signed original completed application form. Do not send copies.**
• **Enter your Federal Employer Identification Number.**
• **Enter your Social Security Number.**
• **Enter the correct Business Activity Code from the list of codes provided.**

PART II
D.C. TAX REQUIREMENTS
Corporation Franchise Tax
Unincorporated Business Franchise Tax

Corporation Franchise Tax — A Corporation Franchise Tax Return (Form D-20) is required of every corporation engaging in or carrying on a trade or business in the District of Columbia and/or receiving income from sources within the District of Columbia. A Form D-20 must be filed by the 15th day of the third month following the close of the corporation's taxable year. If the amount of tax owed is less than $100 the minimum amount of $100 is required to be paid.

Unincorporated Business Franchise Tax — An Unincorporated Business Franchise Tax Return (Form D-30) is required of every unincorporated business (ex, sole proprietor, joint venture, etc.) engaging in or carrying on any trade or business in the District of Columbia, deriving rental income, and/or receiving other income from sources within the District, whose gross receipts exceed $12,000. A Form D-30 must be filed annually by the 15th day of the fourth month following the close of the business' taxable year. If the amount owed is less than $100 the minimum amount of $100 is required to be paid.

Partnership Return of Income (D-65) — Partnerships which are not required to file a Form D-30 (for whatever reason) must file a Form D-65.

Non-profit Organizations — Organizations which are subject to tax on unrelated business income are required to file a Form D-20, Corporation Franchise Tax return. The due date for this filing is the 15th day of the fifth month after the close of the organization's tax year.

PART III
Employer Withholding Tax

Employer Withholding Tax — A Form FR-900 must be filed by every employer doing business in the District and having D.C. resident employees. The employer is required to register and withhold District of Columbia income tax from the wages of such employees. Form FR-900M must be filed monthly by the 20th day of the month following the period being reported on, unless notified by the Office of Tax and Revenue that an annual return (Form FR-900A) may be filed. The FR-900A is to be filed on or before January 20th of the subsequent year.

PART IV
Sales and Use Tax

Sales Tax — Any individual engaging in business in the District of Columbia must collect District of Columbia sales tax from the purchaser on: sales of tangible personal property delivered to a customer in D.C.; certain foods and drinks sold at retail; certain services, rental and leasing of tangible personal property; rental of rooms to transients; admissions to certain public events that take place in D.C.; and the service of parking, storing or keeping motor vehicles or trailers in D.C. A Sales and Use Tax Return (Form FR-800M) must be filed monthly by the 20th day of the month following the reporting period, unless notified by the Office of Tax and Revenue that an annual return (Form FR-800A) may be filed. The FR-800A is to be filed on or before January 20th of the subsequent year.

The promoter of a Special Event must provide a list of the participants (the individuals who must collect District of Columbia sales tax from the purchasers of any goods sold at the event). The list should contain the name, address and telephone number of each participant, the name and date(s) of the event and whether the participant is a street vendor. Please refer to the Special Event Registration Application (Form FR-500B) for additional information.

Use Tax — The use tax is imposed at the same rate as the sales tax on the purchase or rental of tangible personal property for the purpose of use, storage or consumption in the District by a buyer who did not pay a sales tax to the District or any other taxing jurisdiction at the time of the purchase or rental of the property.

For more information on Sales and Use Taxes, obtain a copy of the publication *General Information – Sales and Use Taxes* (FR-379) from the Customer Service Center. You may either visit the Center at 941 North Capitol St., N.E. (first floor), Washington, D.C. or you may call 202-727-4TAX (4829).

PART V-1
Personal Property Tax

Personal Property Tax — A Personal Property Tax Return (Form FP-31) is required to be filed by every business owning or holding in trust any tangible personal property tax (ex. furniture, computers, fixtures, books, etc.) located in or having a taxable situs in the District of Columbia and which is used or is available for use in a trade, business or office held for business purposes, including property kept in storage or held for rent or which is leased to third parties, including governmental agencies, under a "lease-purchase agreement." A Form FP-31 must be filed and the tax paid on or before July 31st of each year based upon the remaining cost (current value) of all tangible personal property owned as of July 1st.

Railroad companies operating rolling stock, parlor cars and sleeping cars in the District over any railroad line, must file Form FP-32 (Railroad Tangible Property Return) by July 31st of each year, on property owned on July 1st. Also, every railroad company whose lines run through the District, must report by July 31st of each year, on Form FP-33 (Railroad Company Report), and any other company whose cars run on their D.C. tracks, must file Form FP-34 (Rolling Stock Tax Return) together with full payment of the tax owed.

Part V-2
Gross Receipts Tax

Gross Receipts Tax — Utilities, telecommunication companies providing long distance service, companies providing cable television, satellite relay or distribution of video or radio transmission to subscribers and paying customers, heating oil delivery companies, commercial mobile service providers and non-public utility sellers of natural or artificial gas are subject to the Gross Receipts Tax.

Companies subject to the Gross Receipts Tax must submit a monthly report of their gross receipts from District of Columbia sources. Gross receipts should be reported by filing Form FP-27 for utilities, Form FP-27T for telecommunication companies, Form FP-27C for cable television, satellite relay, video distribution and radio transmission companies, Form FP-27NAG for non-public utility sellers of natural or artificial gas, Form FP-27M for commercial mobile service providers and Form FP-27H for heating oil delivery companies. Companies must file the proper form by the 20th of the month following the period being reported.

PAYMENT REQUIREMENT FOR STREET VENDORS

Every street vendor who holds a Class A license, Class B license, Class C non-food license or Class C food license issued by the District of Columbia, Department of Consumer and Regulatory Affairs must register with the Office of Tax and Revenue, make an initial payment of $125 (credited against the $375 due the 1st quarter) and thereafter submit quarterly installment payments of $375 using a vendor payment coupon. These quarterly payments are in lieu of collecting and remitting sales tax for each immediately preceding three-month period. Vendors holding such licenses must complete Parts I, II and VI of this application. If a holder of an annual street vending license surrenders his/her license, prior to the close of a quarter, the quarterly payment is pro-rated based on the number of months, or fraction of a month, that the license is held during the quarter. Payment is due on or before the 20th day of every January, April, July and October.

A holder of only a Class A **temporary license** or a Class B **temporary license** must make a $125 payment in lieu of collecting and remitting sales tax. The payment is due on or before the 10th day following the expiration date of the temporary license. Payments must be made in cash, certified check, cashier's check, or money order.

NOTE: Every street vendor who is licensed by the D.C. Department of Consumer and Regulatory Affairs is required to make vendor payment(s) regardless of the amount of sales, if any, the street vendor makes during the year.

If you have any questions regarding the above tax requirements, contact the Office of Tax and Revenue, 941 North Capitol Street, N.E., Washington, D.C. 20002; or call (202) 727-4TAX (4829). First time applicants must mail an original application.

PART VI
UNEMPLOYMENT COMPENSATION TAX REGISTRATION

Unemployment Compensation Tax — Employers who hire one or more persons to perform services in the District of Columbia are required to register for Unemployment Compensation Taxes. Domestic/household employers who pay cash remuneration of $500 or more in any calendar quarter are also required to register and file reports. A non-profit organization that has been granted exemption from the payment of FUTA taxes under Section 501(c)(3) of the Internal Revenue Code may elect to reimburse the D.C. Office of Unemployment Compensation in lieu of paying taxes.

ITEM 16 OF PART VI SHOULD BE COMPLETED BY NON-PROFIT ORGANIZATIONS ONLY. If you are exempt from federal unemployment taxes, check the appropriate box and include a copy of the Internal Revenue Service exemption letter.

A non-profit organization has two options to finance Unemployment Insurance Coverage:

1. Payment of contributions at the rate assigned by the D.C. Department of Employment Services. The rate is applied to the taxable wages earned by each employee during a calendar year. Contributions are paid on a calendar quarter basis.

OR

2. Reimbursement of the trust fund. At the end of each calendar quarter, the employer is billed for unemployment benefits paid to its former employees during the quarter.

PERCENTAGE OF ASSETS ACQUIRED. Enter appropriate information in item 15 of Part VI of the form. List any prior D.C. ID number issued to you or to the business.

If you are a new employer acquiring your business from a predecessor, answer the appropriate questions or state whether this is a change in the type of business such as individual ownership, partnership or corporation which is changing its entity. This information is necessary to determine your experience rate. If changing the trade name, include the former trade name.

Questions concerning liability or financing options for Unemployment Compensation Taxes should be directed to the D.C. Department of Employment Services, Office of Unemployment Compensation, Division of Tax, 609 H St., N.E., Room 362, Washington, D.C. 20002 or telephone (202) 698-7550. The facsimile number is (202) 698-5706.

CERTIFICATE OF RESALE
DISTRICT OF COLUMBIA SALES AND USE TAX

TO: FROM:

SELLER			PURCHASER		
TRADE NAME (IF ANY)			TRADE NAME (IF ANY)		
SELLER'S STREET ADDRESS			PURCHASER'S STREET ADDRESS		
CITY	STATE	ZIP CODE	CITY	STATE	ZIP CODE
NOTE: SELLER MUST KEEP THIS CERTIFICATE			D.C.CERTIFICATE OF REGISTRATION NUMBER		

I certify that all tangible personal property and services purchased from you are for resale or rental either in the same form or for incorporation as a material part of other property being produced for resale or rental.

This certificate shall be considered a part of each order we shall give, provided the order contains our D.C. Certificate of Registration number and will continue in force until revoked by written notice to you.

AUTHORIZED SIGNATURE	TITLE	DATE

INSTRUCTIONS

This certificate is not valid unless it contains the purchaser's District of Columbia Sales and Use Tax Registration Number. It must be signed by the owner or authorized officer and must be dated.

If the issuer of the certificate buys from the seller items which do not qualify for tax exemption he/she should advise the seller to charge the appropriate tax on such items. Otherwise, the purchaser is required to report use tax directly to the Office of Tax & Revenue

The seller must retain all Certificates of Resale on file to substantiate exemptions in the event of an audit of his/her D.C. Sales and Use Tax returns.

Purchasers who are located outside the District of Columbia and who make no retail sales in the District may, upon application, be issued a D.C. Certificate of Registration in order that they may furnish a Certificate of Resale for items intended for resale outside the District.

Form **8850**
(Rev. October 2002)
Department of the Treasury
Internal Revenue Service

Pre-Screening Notice and Certification Request for the Work Opportunity and Welfare-to-Work Credits

▶ See separate instructions.

OMB No. 1545-1500

Job applicant: Fill in the lines below and check any boxes that apply. Complete only this side.

Your name _____   Social security number ▶ _____

Street address where you live _____

City or town, state, and ZIP code _____

Telephone number (___) ___ - _____

If you are under age 25, enter your date of birth (month, day, year) ___ / ___ / ___

Work Opportunity Credit

1 ☐ Check here if you received a conditional certification from the state employment security agency (SESA) or a participating local agency for the work opportunity credit.

2 ☐ Check here if **any** of the following statements apply to you.

- I am a member of a family that has received assistance from Temporary Assistance for Needy Families (TANF) for any 9 months during the last 18 months.

- I am a veteran and a member of a family that received food stamps for at least a 3-month period within the last 15 months.

- I was referred here by a rehabilitation agency approved by the state or the Department of Veterans Affairs.

- I am at least age 18 but **not** age 25 or older and I am a member of a family that:

  a Received food stamps for the last 6 months **or**

  b Received food stamps for at least 3 of the last 5 months, **but** is no longer eligible to receive them.

- Within the past year, I was convicted of a felony or released from prison for a felony **and** during the last 6 months I was a member of a low-income family.

- I received supplemental security income (SSI) benefits for any month ending within the last 60 days.

Welfare-to-Work Credit

3 ☐ Check here if you received a conditional certification from the SESA or a participating local agency for the welfare-to-work credit.

4 ☐ Check here if you are a member of a family that:

- Received TANF payments for at least the last 18 months, **or**

- Received TANF payments for any 18 months beginning after August 5, 1997, **and** the earliest 18-month period beginning after August 5, 1997, ended within the last 2 years, **or**

- Stopped being eligible for TANF payments within the last 2 years because Federal or state law limited the maximum time those payments could be made.

All Applicants

Under penalties of perjury, I declare that I gave the above information to the employer on or before the day I was offered a job, and it is, to the best of my knowledge, true, correct, and complete.

Job applicant's signature ▶   Date   ___ / ___ / ___

For Employer's Use Only

Employer's name _____ Telephone no. (___) ___ - _____ EIN ► _____ ⋮ _____

Street address _____

City or town, state, and ZIP code _____

Person to contact, if different from above _____ Telephone no. (___) ___ - _____

Street address _____

City or town, state, and ZIP code _____

If, based on the individual's age and home address, he or she is a member of group 4 or 6 (as described under **Members of Targeted Groups** in the separate instructions), enter that group number (4 or 6) . . . . ► _____

| Date applicant: | Gave information | / / | Was offered job | / / | Was hired | / / | Started job | / / |

Under penalties of perjury, I declare that I completed this form on or before the day a job was offered to the applicant and that the information I have furnished is, to the best of my knowledge, true, correct, and complete. Based on the information the job applicant furnished on page 1, I believe the individual is a member of a targeted group or a long-term family assistance recipient. I hereby request a certification that the individual is a member of a targeted group or a long-term family assistance recipient.

Employer's signature ► _____   **Title** _____   **Date** _/ _/ _____

Privacy Act and Paperwork Reduction Act Notice

Section references are to the Internal Revenue Code.

Section 51(d)(12) permits a prospective employer to request the applicant to complete this form and give it to the prospective employer. The information will be used by the employer to complete the employer's Federal tax return. Completion of this form is voluntary and may assist members of targeted groups and long-term family assistance recipients in securing employment. Routine uses of this form include giving it to the state employment security agency (SESA), which will contact appropriate sources to confirm that the applicant is a member of a targeted group or a long-term family assistance recipient. This form may also be given to the Internal Revenue Service

for administration of the Internal Revenue laws, to the Department of Justice for civil and criminal litigation, to the Department of Labor for oversight of the certifications performed by the SESA, and to cities, states, and the District of Columbia for use in administering their tax laws. In addition, we may disclose this information to Federal, state, or local agencies that investigate or respond to acts or threats of terrorism or participate in intelligence or counterintelligence activities concerning terrorism.

You are not required to provide the information requested on a form that is subject to the Paperwork Reduction Act unless the form displays a valid OMB control number. Books or records relating to a form or its instructions must be retained as long as their contents may become material in the administration of any Internal Revenue law. Generally, tax returns and return information are confidential, as required by section 6103.

The time needed to complete and file this form will vary depending on individual circumstances. The estimated average time is:

Recordkeeping . . . . 2 hr., 46 min.
Learning about the law or the form . . . . .36 min.
Preparing and sending this form to the SESA . . . . . . .36 min.

If you have comments concerning the accuracy of these time estimates or suggestions for making this form simpler, we would be happy to hear from you. You can write to the Tax Forms Committee, Western Area Distribution Center, Rancho Cordova, CA 95743-0001.

Do not send this form to this address. Instead, see **When and Where To File** in the separate instructions.

Instructions for Form 8850

(Rev. October 2002)

Department of the Treasury
Internal Revenue Service

Pre-Screening Notice and Certification Request for the Work Opportunity and Welfare-to-Work Credits

Section references are to the Internal Revenue Code unless otherwise noted.

General Instructions

Changes To Note

• The categories of high-risk youth and summer youth employees now include qualified individuals who live in renewal communities and begin work for you after December 31, 2001.

• The work opportunity credit and the welfare-to-work credit are now allowed for qualified individuals who begin work for you before January 1, 2004.

Purpose of Form

Employers use Form 8850 to pre-screen and to make a written request to a state employment security agency (SESA) to certify an individual as:

• A member of a targeted group for purposes of qualifying for the work opportunity credit or

• A long-term family assistance recipient for purposes of qualifying for the welfare-to-work credit.

Submitting Form 8850 to the SESA is but one step in the process of qualifying for the work opportunity credit or the welfare-to-work credit. The SESA must certify the job applicant is a member of a targeted group or is a long-term family assistance recipient. After starting work, the employee must meet the minimum number-of-hours-worked requirement for the work opportunity credit or the minimum number-of-hours, number-of-days requirement for the welfare-to-work credit. The employer may elect to take the applicable credit by filing **Form 5884**, Work Opportunity Credit, or **Form 8861**, Welfare-to-Work Credit.

Note: *Do not use Form 8850 with respect to New York Liberty Zone business employees. Certification is not required for these employees. See **Form 8884**, New York Liberty Zone Business Employee Credit, for details.*

Who Should Complete and Sign the Form

The job applicant gives information to the employer on or before the day a job offer is made. This information is entered on Form 8850. Based on the applicant's information, the employer determines whether or not he or she believes the applicant is a member of a targeted group (as defined under **Members of Targeted Groups** on page 2) or a long-term family assistance recipient (as defined under **Welfare-to-Work Job Applicants** on page 2). If the employer believes the applicant is a member of

a targeted group or a long-term family assistance recipient, the employer completes the rest of the form no later than the day the job offer is made. Both the job applicant and the employer must sign Form 8850 no later than the date for submitting the form to the SESA.

Instructions for Employer

When and Where To File

Do not file Form 8850 with the Internal Revenue Service. Instead, file it with the work opportunity tax credit (WOTC) coordinator for your SESA no later than the 21st day after the job applicant begins work for you. You may be able to file Form 8850 electronically. See Announcement 2002-44 for details. You can find Announcement 2002-44 on page 809 of Internal Revenue Bulletin 2002-17 at **www.irs.gov/pub/irs-irbs/irb02-17.pdf**.

To get the name, address, phone and fax numbers, and e-mail address of the WOTC coordinator for your SESA, visit the Department of Labor Employment and Training Administration (ETA) web site at **www.ows.doleta.gov/employ/tax.asp**.

Additional Requirements for Certification

In addition to filing Form 8850, you must complete and send to your state's WOTC coordinator **either**:
• **ETA Form 9062**, Conditional Certification Form, if the job applicant received this form from a participating agency (e.g., the Jobs Corps) **or**
• **ETA Form 9061**, Individual Characteristics Form, if the job applicant did not receive a conditional certification.

You can get ETA Form 9061 from your local public employment service office, or you can download it from the ETA web site at **www.ows.doleta.gov**.

Recordkeeping

Keep copies of Forms 8850, along with any transmittal letters that you submit to your SESA, as long as they may be needed for the administration of the Internal Revenue Code provisions relating to the work opportunity credit and the welfare-to-work credit. Records that support these credits usually must be kept for 3 years from the date any income tax return claiming the credits is due or filed, whichever is later.

Members of Targeted Groups

A job applicant may be certified as a member of a targeted group if he or she is described in one of the following groups.

1. Qualified IV-A recipient. A member of a family receiving assistance under a state plan approved under part A of title IV of the Social Security Act relating to Temporary Assistance for Needy Families (TANF). The assistance must be received for any 9 months during the 18-month period that ends on the hiring date.

2. Qualified veteran. A veteran who is a member of a family receiving assistance under the Food Stamp program for generally at least a 3-month period during the 15-month period ending on the hiring date. See section 51(d)(3). To be considered a **veteran**, the applicant must:

● Have served on active duty (not including training) in the Armed Forces of the United States for more than 180 days or have been discharged for a service-connected disability and

● Not have a period of active duty (not including training) of more than 90 days that ended during the 60-day period ending on the hiring date.

3. Qualified ex-felon. An ex-felon who:

● Has been convicted of a felony under any Federal or state law,

● Is hired not more than 1 year after the conviction or release from prison for that felony, and

● Is a member of a family that had income on an annual basis of 70% or less of the Bureau of Labor Statistics lower living standard during the 6 months preceding the earlier of the month the income determination occurs or the month in which the hiring date occurs.

4. High-risk youth. An individual who is at least 18 but not yet 25 on the hiring date and lives in an empowerment zone, enterprise community, or renewal community.

5. Vocational rehabilitation referral. An individual who has a physical or mental disability resulting in a substantial handicap to employment and who was referred to the employer upon completion of (or while receiving) rehabilitation services under a state plan of employment or a program approved by the Department of Veterans Affairs.

6. Summer youth employee. An individual who:

● Performs services for the employer between May 1 and September 15,

● Is age 16 but not yet age 18 on the hiring date (or if later, on May 1),

● Has never worked for the employer before, and

● Lives in an empowerment zone, enterprise community, or renewal community.

7. Food stamp recipient. An individual who:

● Is at least age 18 but not yet age 25 and

● Is a member of a family that—

a. Has received food stamps for the 6-month period ending on the hiring date or

b. Is no longer eligible for such assistance under section 6(o) of the Food Stamp Act of 1977, but the family received food stamps for at least 3 months of the 5-month period ending on the hiring date.

8. SSI recipient. An individual who is receiving supplemental security income benefits under title XVI of the Social Security Act (including benefits of the type described in section 1616 of the Social Security Act or section 212 of Public Law 93-66) for any month ending within the 60-day period ending on the hiring date.

Empowerment zones, enterprise communities, and renewal communities. For details about rural empowerment zone and enterprise communities, you can access **www.ezec.gov**, call 1-800-645-4712, or contact your SESA. For details on all empowerment zones, enterprise communities, and renewal communities, you can access **http://hud.esri.com/locateservices/ezec**. You can also call HUD at 1-800-998-9999 for details on renewal communities, urban empowerment zones, and urban enterprise communities.

Note: *Parts of Washington, DC, are treated as an empowerment zone. For details, see section 1400 and Notice 98-57, 1998-2 C.B. 671 (you can find Notice 98-57 on page 9 of Internal Revenue Bulletin 1998-47 at* ***www.irs.gov/pub/irs-irbs/irb98-47.pdf***). *Also, there are no areas designated in Puerto Rico, Guam, or any U.S. possession.*

Welfare-to-Work Job Applicants

An individual may be certified as a long-term family assistance recipient if he or she is a member of a family that:

● Has received TANF payments for at least 18 consecutive months ending on the hiring date, **or**

● Receives TANF payments for any 18 months (whether or not consecutive) beginning after August 5, 1997, **and** the earliest 18-month period beginning after August 5, 1997, ended within the last 2 years, **or**

● Stopped being eligible for TANF payments because Federal or state law limits the maximum period such assistance is payable **and** the individual is hired not more than 2 years after such eligibility ended.

U.S. Department of Justice
Immigration and Naturalization Service

OMB No. 1115-0136

Employment Eligibility Verification

Please read instructions carefully before completing this form. The instructions must be available during completion of this form. ANTI-DISCRIMINATION NOTICE: It is illegal to discriminate against work eligible individuals. Employers CANNOT specify which document(s) they will accept from an employee. The refusal to hire an individual because of a future expiration date may also constitute illegal discrimination.

Section 1. Employee Information and Verification. To be completed and signed by employee at the time employment begins.

Print Name: Last _____ First _____ Middle Initial _____ Maiden Name _____

Address (Street Name and Number) _____ Apt. # _____ Date of Birth (month/day/year) _____

City _____ State _____ Zip Code _____ Social Security # _____

I am aware that federal law provides for imprisonment and/or fines for false statements or use of false documents in connection with the completion of this form.

I attest, under penalty of perjury, that I am (check one of the following):
☐ A citizen or national of the United States
☐ A Lawful Permanent Resident (Alien # A _____)
☐ An alien authorized to work until ___/___/___
(Alien # or Admission #)

Employee's Signature _____ Date (month/day/year) _____

Preparer and/or Translator Certification. (To be completed and signed if Section 1 is prepared by a person other than the employee.) I attest, under penalty of perjury, that I have assisted in the completion of this form and that to the best of my knowledge the information is true and correct.

Preparer's/Translator's Signature _____ Print Name _____

Address (Street Name and Number, City, State, Zip Code) _____ Date (month/day/year) _____

Section 2. Employer Review and Verification. To be completed and signed by employer. Examine one document from List A OR examine one document from List B and one from List C, as listed on the reverse of this form, and record the title, number and expiration date, if any, of the document(s)

List A	OR	List B	AND	List C
Document title: _____		_____		_____
Issuing authority: _____		_____		_____
Document #: _____		_____		_____
Expiration Date (if any): ___/___/___		___/___/___		___/___/___
Document #: _____				
Expiration Date (if any): ___/___/___				

CERTIFICATION - I attest, under penalty of perjury, that I have examined the document(s) presented by the above-named employee, that the above-listed document(s) appear to be genuine and to relate to the employee named, that the employee began employment on (month/day/year) ___/___/___ and that to the best of my knowledge the employee is eligible to work in the United States. (State employment agencies may omit the date the employee began employment.)

Signature of Employer or Authorized Representative _____ Print Name _____ Title _____

Business or Organization Name _____ Address (Street Name and Number, City, State, Zip Code) _____ Date (month/day/year) _____

Section 3. Updating and Reverification. To be completed and signed by employer.

A. New Name (if applicable) _____ B. Date of rehire (month/day/year) (if applicable) _____

C. If employee's previous grant of work authorization has expired, provide the information below for the document that establishes current employment eligibility.

Document Title: _____ Document #: _____ Expiration Date (if any): ___/___/___

I attest, under penalty of perjury, that to the best of my knowledge, this employee is eligible to work in the United States, and if the employee presented document(s), the document(s) I have examined appear to be genuine and to relate to the individual.

Signature of Employer or Authorized Representative _____ Date (month/day/year) _____

Form I-9 (Rev. 11-21-91)N Page 2

U.S. Department of Justice
Immigration and Naturalization Service

OMB No. 1115-0136

Employment Eligibility Verification

INSTRUCTIONS
PLEASE READ ALL INSTRUCTIONS CAREFULLY BEFORE COMPLETING THIS FORM.

Anti-Discrimination Notice. It is illegal to discriminate against any individual (other than an alien not authorized to work in the U.S.) in hiring, discharging, or recruiting or referring for a fee because of that individual's national origin or citizenship status. It is illegal to discriminate against work eligible individuals. Employers **CANNOT** specify which document(s) they will accept from an employee. The refusal to hire an individual because of a future expiration date may also constitute illegal discrimination.

Section 1 - Employee.
All employees, citizens and noncitizens, hired after November 6, 1986, must complete Section 1 of this form at the time of hire, which is the actual beginning of employment. **The employer is responsible for ensuring that Section 1 is timely and properly completed.**

Preparer/Translator Certification. The Preparer/Translator Certification must be completed if Section 1 is prepared by a person other than the employee. A preparer/translator may be used only when the employee is unable to complete Section 1 on his/her own. However, the employee must still sign Section 1.

Section 2 - Employer.
For the purpose of completing this form, the term "employer" includes those recruiters and referrers for a fee who are agricultural associations, agricultural employers or farm labor contractors.

Employers must complete Section 2 by examining evidence of identity and employment eligibility within three (3) business days of the date employment begins. If employees are authorized to work, but are unable to present the required document(s) within three business days, they must present a receipt for the application of the document(s) within three business days and the actual document(s) within ninety (90) days. However, if employers hire individuals for a duration of less than three business days, Section 2 must be completed at the time employment begins. **Employers must record: 1)** document title; **2)** issuing authority; **3)** document number, **4)** expiration date, if any; and **5)** the date employment begins. Employers must sign and date the certification. Employees must present original documents. Employers may, but are not required to, photocopy the document(s) presented. These photocopies may only be used for the verification process and must be retained with the I-9. **However, employers are still responsible for completing the I-9.**

Section 3 - Updating and Reverification.
Employers must complete Section 3 when updating and/or reverifying the I-9. Employers must reverify employment eligibility of their employees on or before the expiration date recorded in Section 1. Employers **CANNOT** specify which document(s) they will accept from an employee.

- If an employee's name has changed at the time this form is being updated/ reverified, complete Block A.

- If an employee is rehired within three (3) years of the date this form was originally completed and the employee is still eligible to be employed on the same basis as previously indicated on this form (updating), complete Block B and the signature block.

- If an employee is rehired within three (3) years of the date this form was originally completed and the employee's work authorization has expired **or** if a current employee's work authorization is about to expire (reverification), complete Block B and:
  - examine any document that reflects that the employee is authorized to work in the U.S. (see List A **or** C),
  - record the document title, document number and expiration date (if any) in Block C, and complete the signature block.

Photocopying and Retaining Form I-9. A blank I-9 may be reproduced, provided both sides are copied. The Instructions must be available to all employees completing this form. Employers must retain completed I-9s for three (3) years after the date of hire or one (1) year after the date employment ends, whichever is later.

For more detailed information, you may refer to the INS Handbook for Employers, (Form M-274). You may obtain the handbook at your local INS office.

Privacy Act Notice. The authority for collecting this information is the Immigration Reform and Control Act of 1986, Pub. L. 99-603 (8 USC 1324a).

This information is for employers to verify the eligibility of individuals for employment to preclude the unlawful hiring, or recruiting or referring for a fee, of aliens who are not authorized to work in the United States.

This information will be used by employers as a record of their basis for determining eligibility of an employee to work in the United States. The form will be kept by the employer and made available for inspection by officials of the U.S. Immigration and Naturalization Service, the Department of Labor and the Office of Special Counsel for Immigration Related Unfair Employment Practices.

Submission of the information required in this form is voluntary. However, an individual may not begin employment unless this form is completed, since employers are subject to civil or criminal penalties if they do not comply with the Immigration Reform and Control Act of 1986.

Reporting Burden. We try to create forms and instructions that are accurate, can be easily understood and which impose the least possible burden on you to provide us with information. Often this is difficult because some immigration laws are very complex. Accordingly, the reporting burden for this collection of information is computed as follows: **1)** learning about this form, 5 minutes; **2)** completing the form, 5 minutes; and **3)** assembling and filing (recordkeeping) the form, 5 minutes, for an average of 15 minutes per response. If you have comments regarding the accuracy of this burden estimate, or suggestions for making this form simpler, you can write to the Immigration and Naturalization Service, HQPDI, 425 I Street, N.W., Room 4034, Washington, DC 20536. OMB No. 1115-0136.

EMPLOYERS MUST RETAIN COMPLETED FORM I-9
PLEASE DO NOT MAIL COMPLETED FORM I-9 TO INS

Form I-9 (Rev. 11-21-91)N

LISTS OF ACCEPTABLE DOCUMENTS

LIST A		LIST B		LIST C
Documents that Establish Both Identity and Employment Eligibility	**OR**	**Documents that Establish Identity**	**AND**	**Documents that Establish Employment Eligibility**

LIST A — Documents that Establish Both Identity and Employment Eligibility

1. U.S. Passport (unexpired or expired)
2. Certificate of U.S. Citizenship (INS Form N-560 or N-561)
3. Certificate of Naturalization (INS Form N-550 or N-570)
4. Unexpired foreign passport, with I-551 stamp or attached INS Form I-94 indicating unexpired employment authorization
5. Permanent Resident Card or Alien Registration Receipt Card with photograph (INS Form I-151 or I-551)
6. Unexpired Temporary Resident Card (INS Form I-688)
7. Unexpired Employment Authorization Card (INS Form I-688A)
8. Unexpired Reentry Permit (INS Form I-327)
9. Unexpired Refugee Travel Document (INS Form I-571)
10. Unexpired Employment Authorization Document issued by the INS which contains a photograph (INS Form I-688B)

OR

LIST B — Documents that Establish Identity

1. Driver's license or ID card issued by a state or outlying possession of the United States provided it contains a photograph or information such as name, date of birth, gender, height, eye color and address
2. ID card issued by federal, state or local government agencies or entities, provided it contains a photograph or information such as name, date of birth, gender, height, eye color and address
3. School ID card with a photograph
4. Voter's registration card
5. U.S. Military card or draft record
6. Military dependent's ID card
7. U.S. Coast Guard Merchant Mariner Card
8. Native American tribal document
9. Driver's license issued by a Canadian government authority

For persons under age 18 who are unable to present a document listed above:

10. School record or report card
11. Clinic, doctor or hospital record
12. Day-care or nursery school record

AND

LIST C — Documents that Establish Employment Eligibility

1. U.S. social security card issued by the Social Security Administration (other than a card stating it is not valid for employment)
2. Certification of Birth Abroad issued by the Department of State (Form FS-545 or Form DS-1350)
3. Original or certified copy of a birth certificate issued by a state, county, municipal authority or outlying possession of the United States bearing an official seal
4. Native American tribal document
5. U.S. Citizen ID Card (INS Form I-197)
6. ID Card for use of Resident Citizen in the United States (INS Form I-179)
7. Unexpired employment authorization document issued by the INS (other than those listed under List A)

Illustrations of many of these documents appear in Part 8 of the Handbook for Employers (M-274)

Form **SS-4**
(Rev. December 2001)
Department of the Treasury
Internal Revenue Service

Application for Employer Identification Number

(For use by employers, corporations, partnerships, trusts, estates, churches,
government agencies, Indian tribal entities, certain individuals, and others.)
· See separate instructions for each line. · Keep a copy for your records.

EIN

OMB No. 1545-0003

Type or print clearly.

1 Legal name of entity (or individual) for whom the EIN is being requested	

2 Trade name of business (if different from name on line 1)	**3** Executor, trustee, "care of" name

4a Mailing address (room, apt., suite no. and street, or P.O. box)	**5a** Street address (if different) (Do not enter a P.O. box.)
4b City, state, and ZIP code	**5b** City, state, and ZIP code

6 County and state where principal business is located

7a Name of principal officer, general partner, grantor, owner, or trustor	**7b** SSN, ITIN, or EIN

8a **Type of entity** (check only one box)

☐ Sole proprietor (SSN) _____
☐ Partnership
☐ Corporation (enter form number to be filed) · _____
☐ Personal service corp.
☐ Church or church-controlled organization
☐ Other nonprofit organization (specify) · _____
☐ Other (specify) ·

☐ Estate (SSN of decedent) _____
☐ Plan administrator (SSN) _____
☐ Trust (SSN of grantor) _____
☐ National Guard ☐ State/local government
☐ Farmers' cooperative ☐ Federal government/military
☐ REMIC ☐ Indian tribal governments/enterprises
Group Exemption Number (GEN) · _____

8b If a corporation, name the state or foreign country (if applicable) where incorporated

State	Foreign country

9 **Reason for applying** (check only one box)

☐ Started new business (specify type) · _____
☐ Hired employees (Check the box and see line 12.)
☐ Compliance with IRS withholding regulations
☐ Other (specify) ·

☐ Banking purpose (specify purpose) · _____
☐ Changed type of organization (specify new type) · _____
☐ Purchased going business
☐ Created a trust (specify type) · _____
☐ Created a pension plan (specify type) · _____

10 Date business started or acquired (month, day, year)	**11** Closing month of accounting year

12 First date wages or annuities were paid or will be paid (month, day, year). **Note:** *If applicant is a withholding agent, enter date income will first be paid to nonresident alien. (month, day, year)* . . . .

13 Highest number of employees expected in the next 12 months. **Note:** *If the applicant does not expect to have any employees during the period, enter "-0-."*	Agricultural	Household	Other

14 Check **one** box that best describes the principal activity of your business. ☐ Health care & social assistance ☐ Wholesale–agent/broker

☐ Construction ☐ Rental & leasing ☐ Transportation & warehousing ☐ Accommodation & food service ☐ Wholesale–other ☐ Retail
☐ Real estate ☐ Manufacturing ☐ Finance & insurance ☐ Other (specify)

15 Indicate principal line of merchandise sold; specific construction work done; products produced; or services provided.

16a Has the applicant ever applied for an employer identification number for this or any other business? . . . . . ☐ **Yes** ☐ **No**
Note: *If "Yes," please complete lines 16b and 16c.*

16b If you checked "Yes" on line 16a, give applicant's legal name and trade name shown on prior application if different from line 1 or 2 above.
Legal name · Trade name ·

16c Approximate date when, and city and state where, the application was filed. Enter previous employer identification number if known.

Approximate date when filed (mo., day, year)	City and state where filed	Previous EIN

Third Party Designee	Complete this section **only** if you want to authorize the named individual to receive the entity's EIN and answer questions about the completion of this form.	
	Designee's name	Designee's telephone number (include area code) ( )
	Address and ZIP code	Designee's fax number (include area code) ( )

Under penalties of perjury, I declare that I have examined this application, and to the best of my knowledge and belief, it is true, correct, and complete.

Applicant's telephone number (include area code) ( )

Name and title (type or print clearly) ·

Applicant's fax number (include area code) ( )

Signature · Date ·

For Privacy Act and Paperwork Reduction Act Notice, see separate instructions. Cat. No. 16055N Form **SS-4** (Rev. 12-2001)

Do I Need an EIN?

File Form SS-4 if the applicant entity does not already have an EIN but is required to show an EIN on any return, statement, or other document.[1] **See also the separate instructions for each line on Form SS-4.**

IF the applicant...	AND...	THEN...
Started a new business	Does not currently have (nor expect to have) employees	Complete lines 1, 2, 4a- 6, 8a, and 9- 16c.
Hired (or will hire) employees, including household employees	Does not already have an EIN	Complete lines 1, 2, 4a- 6, 7a- b (if applicable), 8a, 8b (if applicable), and 9- 16c.
Opened a bank account	Needs an EIN for banking purposes only	Complete lines 1- 5b, 7a- b (if applicable), 8a, 9, and 16a- c.
Changed type of organization	Either the legal character of the organization or its ownership changed (e.g., you incorporate a sole proprietorship or form a partnership)[2]	Complete lines 1- 16c (as applicable).
Purchased a going business[3]	Does not already have an EIN	Complete lines 1- 16c (as applicable).
Created a trust	The trust is other than a grantor trust or an IRA trust[4]	Complete lines 1- 16c (as applicable).
Created a pension plan as a plan administrator[5]	Needs an EIN for reporting purposes	Complete lines 1, 2, 4a- 6, 8a, 9, and 16a- c.
Is a foreign person needing an EIN to comply with IRS withholding regulations	Needs an EIN to complete a Form W-8 (other than Form W-8ECI), avoid withholding on portfolio assets, or claim tax treaty benefits[6]	Complete lines 1- 5b, 7a- b (SSN or ITIN optional), 8a- 9, and 16a- c.
Is administering an estate	Needs an EIN to report estate income on Form 1041	Complete lines 1, 3, 4a- b, 8a, 9, and 16a- c.
Is a withholding agent for taxes on non-wage income paid to an alien (i.e., individual, corporation, or partnership, etc.)	Is an agent, broker, fiduciary, manager, tenant, or spouse who is required to file **Form 1042,** Annual Withholding Tax Return for U.S. Source Income of Foreign Persons	Complete lines 1, 2, 3 (if applicable), 4a- 5b, 7a- b (if applicable), 8a, 9, and 16a- c.
Is a state or local agency	Serves as a tax reporting agent for public assistance recipients under Rev. Proc. 80-4, 1980-1 C.B. 581[7]	Complete lines 1, 2, 4a- 5b, 8a, 9, and 16a- c.
Is a single-member LLC	Needs an EIN to file **Form 8832,** Classification Election, for filing employment tax returns, **or** for state reporting purposes[8]	Complete lines 1- 16c (as applicable).
Is an S corporation	Needs an EIN to file **Form 2553,** Election by a Small Business Corporation[9]	Complete lines 1- 16c (as applicable).

[1] For example, a sole proprietorship or self-employed farmer who establishes a qualified retirement plan, or is required to file excise, employment, alcohol, tobacco, or firearms returns, must have an EIN. **A partnership, corporation, REMIC (real estate mortgage investment conduit), nonprofit organization (church, club, etc.), or farmers' cooperative must use an EIN for any tax-related purpose even if the entity does not have employees.**

[2] However, **do not** apply for a new EIN if the existing entity only **(a)** changed its business name, **(b)** elected on Form 8832 to change the way it is taxed (or is covered by the default rules), or **(c)** terminated its partnership status because at least 50% of the total interests in partnership capital and profits were sold or exchanged within a 12-month period. (The EIN of the terminated partnership should continue to be used. See Regulations section 301.6109-1(d)(2)(iii).)

[3] Do not use the EIN of the prior business unless you became the "owner" of a corporation by acquiring its stock.

[4] However, IRA trusts that are required to file **Form 990-T,** Exempt Organization Business Income Tax Return, must have an EIN.

[5] A plan administrator is the person or group of persons specified as the administrator by the instrument under which the plan is operated.

[6] Entities applying to be a Qualified Intermediary (QI) need a QI-EIN even if they already have an EIN. **See Rev. Proc. 2000-12.**

[7] See also *Household employer* on page 4. (**Note:** State or local agencies may need an EIN for other reasons, e.g., hired employees.)

[8] Most LLCs **do not** need to file Form 8832. See **Limited liability company (LLC)** on page 4 for details on completing Form SS-4 for an LLC.

[9] An existing corporation that is electing or revoking S corporation status should use its previously-assigned EIN.

Instructions for Form SS-4
(Rev. December 2001)
Application for Employer Identification Number
Section references are to the Internal Revenue Code unless otherwise noted.

 Department of the Treasury
Internal Revenue Service

General Instructions

Use these instructions to complete **Form SS-4,** Application for Employer Identification Number. Also see **Do I Need an EIN?** on page 2 of Form SS-4.

Purpose of Form

Use Form SS-4 to apply for an employer identification number (EIN). An EIN is a nine-digit number (for example, 12-3456789) assigned to sole proprietors, corporations, partnerships, estates, trusts, and other entities for tax filing and reporting purposes. The information you provide on this form will establish your business tax account.

 *An EIN is for use in connection with your business activities only. Do **not** use your EIN in place of your social security number (SSN).*

File only one Form SS-4. Generally, a sole proprietor should file only one Form SS-4 and needs only one EIN, regardless of the number of businesses operated as a sole proprietorship or trade names under which a business operates. However, if the proprietorship incorporates or enters into a partnership, a new EIN is required. Also, each corporation in an affiliated group must have its own EIN.

EIN applied for, but not received. If you do not have an EIN by the time a **return** is due, write "Applied For" and the date you applied in the space shown for the number. **Do not** show your social security number (SSN) as an EIN on returns.

If you do not have an EIN by the time a **tax deposit** is due, send your payment to the Internal Revenue Service Center for your filing area as shown in the instructions for the form that you are are filing. Make your check or money order payable to the **"United States Treasury"** and show your name (as shown on Form SS-4), address, type of tax, period covered, and date you applied for an EIN.

Related Forms and Publications

The following **forms** and **instructions** may be useful to filers of Form SS-4:
- **Form 990-T,** Exempt Organization Business Income Tax Return
- **Instructions for Form 990-T**
- **Schedule C (Form 1040),** Profit or Loss From Business
- **Schedule F (Form 1040),** Profit or Loss From Farming
- **Instructions for Form 1041 and Schedules A, B, D, G, I, J, and K-1,** U.S. Income Tax Return for Estates and Trusts

- **Form 1042,** Annual Withholding Tax Return for U.S. Source Income of Foreign Persons
- **Instructions for Form 1065,** U.S. Return of Partnership Income
- **Instructions for Form 1066,** U.S. Real Estate Mortgage Investment Conduit (REMIC) Income Tax Return
- **Instructions for Forms 1120 and 1120-A**
- **Form 2553,** Election by a Small Business Corporation
- **Form 2848,** Power of Attorney and Declaration of Representative
- **Form 8821,** Tax Information Authorization
- **Form 8832,** Entity Classification Election
  For more **information** about filing Form SS-4 and related issues, see:
- **Circular A,** Agricultural Employer's Tax Guide (Pub. 51)
- **Circular E,** Employer's Tax Guide (Pub. 15)
- **Pub. 538,** Accounting Periods and Methods
- **Pub. 542,** Corporations
- **Pub. 557,** Exempt Status for Your Organization
- **Pub. 583,** Starting a Business and Keeping Records
- **Pub. 966,** EFTPS: Now a Full Range of Electronic Choices to Pay All Your Federal Taxes
- **Pub. 1635,** Understanding Your EIN
- **Package 1023,** Application for Recognition of Exemption
- **Package 1024,** Application for Recognition of Exemption Under Section 501(a)

How To Get Forms and Publications

Phone. You can order forms, instructions, and publications by phone 24 hours a day, 7 days a week. Just call 1-800-TAX-FORM (1-800-829-3676). You should receive your order or notification of its status within 10 workdays.

Personal computer. With your personal computer and modem, you can get the forms and information you need using the IRS Web Site at **www.irs.gov** or File Transfer Protocol at **ftp.irs.gov.**

CD-ROM. For small businesses, return preparers, or others who may frequently need tax forms or publications, a CD-ROM containing over 2,000 tax products (including many prior year forms) can be purchased from the National Technical Information Service (NTIS).

To order **Pub. 1796,** Federal Tax Products on CD-ROM, call **1-877-CDFORMS** (1-877-233-6767) toll free or connect to **www.irs.gov/cdorders.**

Tax Help for Your Business

IRS-sponsored Small Business Workshops provide information about your Federal and state tax obligations. For information about workshops in your area, call 1-800-829-1040 and ask for your Taxpayer Education Coordinator.

How To Apply

You can apply for an EIN by telephone, fax, or mail depending on how soon you need to use the EIN.

Application by Tele-TIN. Under the Tele-TIN program, you can receive your EIN by telephone and use it immediately to file a return or make a payment. To receive an EIN by telephone, IRS suggests that you complete Form SS-4 so that you will have all relevant information available. Then call the Tele-TIN number at 1-866-816-2065. (International applicants must call 215-516-6999.) Tele-TIN hours of operation are 7:30 a.m. to 5:30 p.m. The person making the call must be authorized to sign the form or be an authorized designee. See **Signature** and **Third Party Designee** on page 6. Also see the **TIP** below.

An IRS representative will use the information from the Form SS-4 to establish your account and assign you an EIN. Write the number you are given on the upper right corner of the form and sign and date it. Keep this copy for your records.

If requested by an IRS representative, mail or fax (facsimile) the signed Form SS-4 (including any Third Party Designee authorization) **within 24 hours** to the Tele-TIN Unit at the service center address provided by the IRS representative.

(TIP) *Taxpayer representatives can use Tele-TIN to apply for an EIN on behalf of their client and request that the EIN be faxed to their **client** on the same day. (**Note:** By utilizing this procedure, you are authorizing the IRS to fax the EIN without a cover sheet.)*

Application by Fax-TIN. Under the Fax-TIN program, you can receive your EIN by fax within 4 business days. Complete and fax Form SS-4 to the IRS using the Fax-TIN number listed below for your state. A long-distance charge to callers outside of the local calling area will apply. Fax-TIN numbers can only be used to apply for an EIN. **The numbers may change without notice.** Fax-TIN is available 24 hours a day, 7 days a week.

Be sure to provide your fax number so that IRS can fax the EIN back to you. (**Note:** By utilizing this procedure, you are authorizing the IRS to fax the EIN without a cover sheet.)

Do not call Tele-TIN for the same entity because duplicate EINs may be issued. See **Third Party Designee** on page 6.

Application by mail. Complete Form SS-4 at least 4 to 5 weeks before you will need an EIN. Sign and date the application and mail it to the service center address for your state. You will receive your EIN in the mail in approximately 4 weeks. See also **Third Party Designee** on page 6.

Call 1-800-829-1040 to verify a number or to ask about the status of an application by mail.

If your principal business, office or agency, or legal residence in the case of an individual, is located in:	Call the Tele-TIN or Fax-TIN number shown or file with the "Internal Revenue Service Center" at:
Connecticut, Delaware, District of Columbia, Florida, Georgia, Maine, Maryland, Massachusetts, New Hampshire, New Jersey, New York, North Carolina, Ohio, Pennsylvania, Rhode Island, South Carolina, Vermont, Virginia, West Virginia	Attn: EIN Operation Holtsville, NY 00501 Tele-TIN 866-816-2065 Fax-TIN 631-447-8960
Illinois, Indiana, Kentucky, Michigan	Attn: EIN Operation Cincinnati, OH 45999 Tele-TIN 866-816-2065 Fax-TIN 859-669-5760
Alabama, Alaska, Arizona, Arkansas, California, Colorado, Hawaii, Idaho, Iowa, Kansas, Louisiana, Minnesota, Mississippi, Missouri, Montana, Nebraska, Nevada, New Mexico, North Dakota, Oklahoma, Oregon, Puerto Rico, South Dakota, Tennessee, Texas, Utah, Washington, Wisconsin, Wyoming	Attn: EIN Operation Philadelphia, PA 19255 Tele-TIN 866-816-2065 Fax-TIN 215-516-3990
If you have no legal residence, principal place of business, or principal office or agency in any state:	Attn: EIN Operation Philadelphia, PA 19255 Tele-TIN 215-516-6999 Fax-TIN 215-516-3990

Specific Instructions

Print or type all entries on Form SS-4. Follow the instructions for each line to expedite processing and to avoid unnecessary IRS requests for additional information. Enter "N/A" (nonapplicable) on the lines that do not apply.

Line 1—Legal name of entity (or individual) for whom the EIN is being requested. Enter the legal name of the entity (or individual) applying for the EIN exactly as it appears on the social security card, charter, or other applicable legal document.

Individuals. Enter your first name, middle initial, and last name. If you are a sole proprietor, enter your individual name, not your business name. Enter your business name on line 2. Do not use abbreviations or nicknames on line 1.

Trusts. Enter the name of the trust.

Estate of a decedent. Enter the name of the estate.

Partnerships. Enter the legal name of the partnership as it appears in the partnership agreement.

Corporations. Enter the corporate name as it appears in the corporation charter or other legal document creating it.

Plan administrators. Enter the name of the plan administrator. A plan administrator who already has an EIN should use that number.

Line 2—Trade name of business. Enter the trade name of the business if different from the legal name. The trade name is the "doing business as " (DBA) name.

 Use the full legal name shown on line 1 on all tax returns filed for the entity. (However, if you enter a trade name on line 2 and choose to use the trade name instead of the legal name, enter the trade name on **all returns** *you file.) To prevent processing delays and errors,* **always** *use the legal name only (or the trade name only) on* **all** *tax returns.*

Line 3—Executor, trustee, "care of" name. Trusts enter the name of the trustee. Estates enter the name of the executor, administrator, or other fiduciary. If the entity applying has a designated person to receive tax information, enter that person's name as the "care of" person. Enter the individual's first name, middle initial, and last name.

Lines 4a-b—Mailing address. Enter the mailing address for the entity's correspondence. If line 3 is completed, enter the address for the executor, trustee or "care of" person. Generally, this address will be used on all tax returns.

 File **Form 8822,** *Change of Address, to report any subsequent changes to the entity's mailing address.*

Lines 5a-b—Street address. Provide the entity's physical address **only** if different from its mailing address shown in lines 4a-b. **Do not** enter a P.O. box number here.

Line 6—County and state where principal business is located. Enter the entity's primary **physical** location.

Lines 7a-b—Name of principal officer, general partner, grantor, owner, or trustor. Enter the first name, middle initial, last name, and SSN of **(a)** the principal officer if the business is a corporation, **(b)** a general partner if a partnership, **(c)** the owner of an entity that is disregarded as separate from its owner (disregarded entities owned by a corporation enter the corporation's name and EIN), or **(d)** a grantor, owner, or trustor if a trust.

If the person in question is an **alien individual** with a previously assigned individual taxpayer identification number (ITIN), enter the ITIN in the space provided and submit a copy of an official identifying document. If necessary, complete **Form W-7,** Application for IRS Individual Taxpayer Identification Number, to obtain an ITIN.

You are **required** to enter an SSN, ITIN, or EIN unless the only reason you are applying for an EIN is to make an entity classification election (see Regulations section 301.7701-1 through 301.7701-3) and you are a nonresident alien with no effectively connected income from sources within the United States.

Line 8a—Type of entity. Check the box that best describes the type of entity applying for the EIN. If you are an alien individual with an ITIN previously assigned to you, enter the ITIN in place of a requested SSN.

 This is not an election for a tax classification of an entity. See **"Limited liability company (LLC)"** *on page 4.*

Other. If not specifically mentioned, check the "Other" box, enter the type of entity and the type of return, if any, that will be filed (for example, "Common Trust Fund, Form 1065" or "Created a Pension Plan"). Do not enter "N/A." If you are an alien individual applying for an EIN, see the **Lines 7a-b** instructions above.

● **Household employer.** If you are an individual, check the "Other" box and enter "Household Employer" and your SSN. If you are a state or local agency serving as a tax reporting agent for public assistance recipients who become household employers, check the "Other" box and enter "Household Employer Agent." If you are a trust that qualifies as a household employer, you do not need a separate EIN for reporting tax information relating to household employees; use the EIN of the trust.

● **QSub.** For a qualified subchapter S subsidiary (QSub) check the "Other" box and specify "QSub."

● **Withholding agent.** If you are a withholding agent required to file Form 1042, check the "Other" box and enter "Withholding Agent."

Sole proprietor. Check this box if you file Schedule C, C-EZ, or F (Form 1040) and have a qualified plan, or are required to file excise, employment, or alcohol, tobacco, or firearms returns, or are a payer of gambling winnings. Enter your SSN (or ITIN) in the space provided. If you are a nonresident alien with no effectively connected income from sources within the United States, you do not need to enter an SSN or ITIN.

Corporation. This box is for any corporation **other than a personal service corporation.** If you check this box, enter the income tax form number to be filed by the entity in the space provided.

 If you entered **"1120S"** *after the "Corporation" checkbox, the corporation* **must** *file Form 2553* **no later than the 15th day of the 3rd month of the tax year the election is to take effect.** *Until Form 2553 has been received and approved, you will be considered a Form 1120 filer. See the Instructions for Form 2553.*

Personal service corp. Check this box if the entity is a personal service corporation. An entity is a personal service corporation for a tax year only if:
● The principal activity of the entity during the testing period (prior tax year) for the tax year is the performance of personal services substantially by employee-owners, and
● The employee-owners own at least 10% of the fair market value of the outstanding stock in the entity on the last day of the testing period.

Personal services include performance of services in such fields as health, law, accounting, or consulting. For more information about personal service corporations, see the Instructions for Forms 1120 and 1120-A and Pub. 542.

Other nonprofit organization. Check this box if the nonprofit organization is other than a church or church-controlled organization and specify the type of nonprofit organization (for example, an educational organization).

 *If the organization also seeks tax-exempt status, you **must** file either Package 1023 or Package 1024. See Pub. 557 for more information.*

If the organization is covered by a group exemption letter, enter the four-digit **group exemption number (GEN).** (Do not confuse the GEN with the nine-digit EIN.) If you do not know the GEN, contact the parent organization. Get Pub. 557 for more information about group exemption numbers.

Plan administrator. If the plan administrator is an individual, enter the plan administrator's SSN in the space provided.

REMIC. Check this box if the entity has elected to be treated as a real estate mortgage investment conduit (REMIC). See the Instructions for Form 1066 for more information.

Limited liability company (LLC). An LLC is an entity organized under the laws of a state or foreign country as a limited liability company. For Federal tax purposes, an LLC may be treated as a partnership or corporation or be disregarded as an entity separate from its owner.

By **default,** a domestic LLC with only one member is **disregarded** as an entity separate from its owner and must include all of its income and expenses on the owner's tax return (e.g., **Schedule C (Form 1040)**). Also by default, a domestic LLC with two or more members is treated as a partnership. A domestic LLC may file Form 8832 to avoid either default classification and elect to be classified as an association taxable as a corporation. For more information on entity classifications (including the rules for foreign entities), see the instructions for Form 8832.

*Do not file Form 8832 if the LLC accepts the default classifications above. **However, if the LLC will be electing S Corporation status, it must timely file both Form 8832 and Form 2553.***

Complete Form SS-4 for LLCs as follows:
• A single-member, domestic LLC that accepts the default classification (above) does not need an EIN and generally should not file Form SS-4. Generally, the LLC should use the name and EIN of its **owner** for all Federal tax purposes. However, the reporting and payment of employment taxes for employees of the LLC may be made using the name and EIN or **either** the owner or the LLC as explained in Notice 99-6, 1999-1 C.B. 321. You can find Notice 99-6 on page 12 of Internal Revenue Bulletin 1999-3 at **www.irs.gov. (Note:** If the LLC-applicant indicates in box 13 that it has employees or expects to have employees, the owner (whether an individual or other entity) of a single-member domestic LLC will also be assigned its own EIN (if it does not

already have one) even if the LLC will be filing the employment tax returns.)
• A single-member, domestic LLC that accepts the default classification (above) and wants an EIN for filing employment tax returns (see above) or non-Federal purposes, such as a state requirement, must check the "Other" box and write "Disregarded Entity" or, when applicable, "Disregarded Entity—Sole Proprietorship" in the space provided.
• A multi-member, domestic LLC that accepts the default classification (above) must check the "Partnership" box.
• A domestic LLC that will be filing Form 8832 to elect corporate status must check the "Corporation" box and write in "Single-Member" or "Multi-Member" immediately below the "form number" entry line.

Line 9—Reason for applying. Check only **one** box. Do not enter "N/A."

Started new business. Check this box if you are starting a new business that requires an EIN. If you check this box, enter the type of business being started. **Do not** apply if you already have an EIN and are only adding another place of business.

Hired employees. Check this box if the existing business is requesting an EIN because it has hired or is hiring employees and is therefore required to file employment tax returns. **Do not** apply if you already have an EIN and are only hiring employees. For information on employment taxes (e.g., for family members), see Circular E.

You may be required to make electronic deposits of all depository taxes (such as employment tax, excise tax, and corporate income tax) using the Electronic Federal Tax Payment System (EFTPS). See section 11, Depositing Taxes, of Circular E and Pub. 966.

Created a pension plan. Check this box if you have created a pension plan and need an EIN for reporting purposes. Also, enter the type of plan in the space provided.

Check this box if you are applying for a trust EIN when a new pension plan is established. In addition, check the "Other" box in line 8a and write "Created a Pension Plan" in the space provided.

Banking purpose. Check this box if you are requesting an EIN for banking purposes only, and enter the banking purpose (for example, a bowling league for depositing dues or an investment club for dividend and interest reporting).

Changed type of organization. Check this box if the business is changing its type of organization for example, the business was a sole proprietorship and has been incorporated or has become a partnership. If you check this box, specify in the space provided (including available space immediately below) the type of change made. For example, "From Sole Proprietorship to Partnership."

Purchased going business. Check this box if you purchased an existing business. **Do not** use the former owner's EIN unless you became the "owner" of a corporation by acquiring its stock.

Created a trust. Check this box if you created a trust, and enter the type of trust created. For example, indicate if the trust is a nonexempt charitable trust or a split-interest trust.

Exception. Do **not** file this form for certain grantor-type trusts. The trustee does not need an EIN for the trust if the trustee furnishes the name and TIN of the grantor/owner and the address of the trust to all payors. See the Instructions for Form 1041 for more information.

 Do not check this box if you are applying for a trust EIN when a new pension plan is established. Check "Created a pension plan."

Other. Check this box if you are requesting an EIN for any other reason; and enter the reason. For example, a newly-formed state government entity should enter "Newly-Formed State Government Entity" in the space provided.

Line 10—Date business started or acquired. If you are starting a new business, enter the starting date of the business. If the business you acquired is already operating, enter the date you acquired the business. Trusts should enter the date the trust was legally created. Estates should enter the date of death of the decedent whose name appears on line 1 or the date when the estate was legally funded.

Line 11—Closing month of accounting year. Enter the last month of your accounting year or tax year. An accounting or tax year is usually 12 consecutive months, either a calendar year or a fiscal year (including a period of 52 or 53 weeks). A calendar year is 12 consecutive months ending on December 31. A fiscal year is either 12 consecutive months ending on the last day of any month other than December or a 52-53 week year. For more information on accounting periods, see Pub. 538.

Individuals. Your tax year generally will be a calendar year.

Partnerships. Partnerships must adopt one of the following tax years:
- The tax year of the majority of its partners,
- The tax year common to all of its principal partners,
- The tax year that results in the least aggregate deferral of income, or
- In certain cases, some other tax year.
See the Instructions for Form 1065 for more information.

REMICs. REMICs must have a calendar year as their tax year.

Personal service corporations. A personal service corporation generally must adopt a calendar year unless:
- It can establish a business purpose for having a different tax year, or
- It elects under section 444 to have a tax year other than a calendar year.

Trusts. Generally, a trust must adopt a calendar year except for the following:
- Tax-exempt trusts,
- Charitable trusts, and
- Grantor-owned trusts.

Line 12—First date wages or annuities were paid or will be paid. If the business has or will have employees, enter the date on which the business began or will begin to pay wages. If the business does not plan to have employees, enter "N/A."

Withholding agent. Enter the date you began or will begin to pay income (including annuities) to a nonresident alien. This also applies to individuals who are required to file Form 1042 to report alimony paid to a nonresident alien.

Line 13—Highest number of employees expected in the next 12 months. Complete each box by entering the number (including zero ("-0-")) of "Agricultural," "Household," or "Other" employees expected by the applicant in the next 12 months. For a definition of agricultural labor (farmwork), see Circular A.

Lines 14 and 15. Check the **one** box in line 14 that best describes the principal activity of the applicant's business. Check the "Other" box (and specify the applicant's principal activity) if none of the listed boxes applies.

Use line 15 to describe the applicant's principal line of business in more detail. For example, if you checked the "Construction" box in line 14, enter additional detail such as "General contractor for residential buildings" in line 15.

 Do not complete lines 14 and 15 if you entered zero "(-0-)" in line 13.

Construction. Check this box if the applicant is engaged in erecting buildings or other structures, (e.g., streets, highways, bridges, tunnels). The term "Construction" also includes special trade contractors, (e.g., plumbing, HVAC, electrical, carpentry, concrete, excavation, etc. contractors).

Real estate. Check this box if the applicant is engaged in renting or leasing real estate to others; managing, selling, buying or renting real estate for others; or providing related real estate services (e.g., appraisal services).

Rental and leasing. Check this box if the applicant is engaged in providing tangible goods such as autos, computers, consumer goods, or industrial machinery and equipment to customers in return for a periodic rental or lease payment.

Manufacturing. Check this box if the applicant is engaged in the mechanical, physical, or chemical transformation of materials, substances, or components into new products. The assembling of component parts of manufactured products is also considered to be manufacturing.

Transportation & warehousing. Check this box if the applicant provides transportation of passengers or cargo; warehousing or storage of goods; scenic or sight-seeing transportation; or support activities related to these modes of transportation.

Finance & insurance. Check this box if the applicant is engaged in transactions involving the creation, liquidation, or change of ownership of financial assets and/or facilitating such financial transactions;

underwriting annuities/insurance policies; facilitating such underwriting by selling insurance policies; or by providing other insurance or employee-benefit related services.

Health care and social assistance. Check this box if the applicant is engaged in providing physical, medical, or psychiatric care using licensed health care professionals or providing social assistance activities such as youth centers, adoption agencies, individual/family services, temporary shelters, etc.

Accommodation & food services. Check this box if the applicant is engaged in providing customers with lodging, meal preparation, snacks, or beverages for immediate consumption.

Wholesale–agent/broker. Check this box if the applicant is engaged in arranging for the purchase or sale of goods owned by others or purchasing goods on a commission basis for goods traded in the wholesale market, usually between businesses.

Wholesale–other. Check this box if the applicant is engaged in selling goods in the wholesale market generally to other businesses for resale on their own account.

Retail. Check this box if the applicant is engaged in selling merchandise to the general public from a fixed store; by direct, mail-order, or electronic sales; or by using vending machines.

Other. Check this box if the applicant is engaged in an activity not described above. Describe the applicant's principal business activity in the space provided.

Lines 16a-c. Check the applicable box in line 16a to indicate whether or not the entity (or individual) applying for an EIN was issued one previously. Complete lines 16b and 16c **only** if the "Yes" box in line 16a is checked. If the applicant previously applied for **more than one** EIN, write "See Attached" in the empty space in line 16a and attach a separate sheet providing the line 16b and 16c information for each EIN previously requested.

Third Party Designee. Complete this section **only** if you want to authorize the named individual to receive the entity's EIN and answer questions about the completion of Form SS-4. The designee's authority terminates at the time the EIN is assigned and released to the designee. **You must complete the signature area for the authorization to be valid.**

Signature. When required, the application must be signed by **(a)** the individual, if the applicant is an individual, **(b)** the president, vice president, or other principal officer, if the applicant is a corporation, **(c)** a responsible and duly authorized member or officer having knowledge of its affairs, if the applicant is a partnership, government entity, or other unincorporated organization, or **(d)** the fiduciary, if the applicant is a trust or an estate. Foreign applicants may have any duly-authorized person, (e.g., division manager), sign Form SS-4.

Privacy Act and Paperwork Reduction Act Notice. We ask for the information on this form to carry out the Internal Revenue laws of the United States. We need it to comply with section 6109 and the regulations thereunder which generally require the inclusion of an employer identification number (EIN) on certain returns, statements, or other documents filed with the Internal Revenue Service. If your entity is required to obtain an EIN, you are required to provide all of the information requested on this form. Information on this form may be used to determine which Federal tax returns you are required to file and to provide you with related forms and publications.

We disclose this form to the Social Security Administration for their use in determining compliance with applicable laws. We may give this information to the Department of Justice for use in civil and criminal litigation, and to the cities, states, and the District of Columbia for use in administering their tax laws. We may also disclose this information to Federal, state, or local agencies that investigate or respond to acts or threats of terrorism or participate in intelligence or counterintelligence activities concerning terrorism.

We will be unable to issue an EIN to you unless you provide all of the requested information which applies to your entity. Providing false information could subject you to penalties.

You are not required to provide the information requested on a form that is subject to the Paperwork Reduction Act unless the form displays a valid OMB control number. Books or records relating to a form or its instructions must be retained as long as their contents may become material in the administration of any Internal Revenue law. Generally, tax returns and return information are confidential, as required by section 6103.

The time needed to complete and file this form will vary depending on individual circumstances. The estimated average time is:

Recordkeeping	6 min.
Learning about the law or the form	22 min.
Preparing the form	46 min.
Copying, assembling, and sending the form to the IRS	20 min.

If you have comments concerning the accuracy of these time estimates or suggestions for making this form simpler, we would be happy to hear from you. You can write to the Tax Forms Committee, Western Area Distribution Center, Rancho Cordova, CA 95743-0001. **Do not** send the form to this address. Instead, see **How To Apply** on page 2.

Form **SS-8**

(Rev. January 2001)

Department of the Treasury
Internal Revenue Service

Determination of Worker Status
for Purposes of Federal Employment Taxes
and Income Tax Withholding

OMB No. 1545-0004

| Name of firm (or person) for whom the worker performed services | Worker's name |

| Firm's address (include street address, apt. or suite no., city, state, and ZIP code) | Worker's address (include street address, apt. or suite no., city, state, and ZIP code) |

| Trade name | Telephone number (include area code) ( ) | Worker's social security number |

| Telephone number (include area code) ( ) | Firm's employer identification number | Worker's employer identification number (if any) |

Important Information Needed To Process Your Request

If this form is being completed by the worker, the IRS must have your permission to disclose your name to the firm. Do you object to disclosing your name and the information on this form to the firm? . . . . ☐ **Yes** ☐ **No**
If you answered "Yes" or did not check a box, stop here. The IRS cannot act on your request and a determination will not be issued.

You must answer ALL items OR mark them "Unknown" or "Does not apply." If you need more space, attach another sheet.

A This form is being completed by: ☐ Firm ☐ Worker; for services performed _____ to _____ .
(beginning date) _(ending date)_

B Explain your reason(s) for filing this form (e.g., you received a bill from the IRS, you believe you received a Form 1099 or Form W-2 erroneously, you are unable to get worker's compensation benefits, you were audited or are being audited by the IRS). ----------

C Total number of workers who performed or are performing the same or similar services _____ .

D How did the worker obtain the job? ☐ Application ☐ Bid ☐ Employment Agency ☐ Other (specify) _____

E Attach copies of all supporting documentation (contracts, invoices, memos, Forms W-2, Forms 1099, IRS closing agreements, IRS rulings, etc.). In addition, please inform us of any current or past litigation concerning the worker's status. If no income reporting forms (Form 1099-MISC or W-2) were furnished to the worker, enter the amount of income earned for the year(s) at issue $ _____ .

F Describe the firm's business. ----------

G Describe the work done by the worker and provide the worker's job title. ----------

H Explain why you believe the worker is an employee or an independent contractor. ----------

I Did the worker perform services for the firm before getting this position? . . . . ☐ **Yes** ☐ **No** ☐ **N/A**
If "Yes," what were the dates of the prior service? ----------
If "Yes," explain the differences, if any, between the current and prior service. ----------

J If the work is done under a written agreement between the firm and the worker, attach a copy (preferably signed by both parties). Describe the terms and conditions of the work arrangement. ----------

For Privacy Act and Paperwork Reduction Act Notice, see page 5. Cat. No. 16106T Form **SS-8** (Rev. 1-2001)

Part I   Behavioral Control

1 What specific training and/or instruction is the worker given by the firm? ....

2 How does the worker receive work assignments? ....

3 Who determines the methods by which the assignments are performed? ....

4 Who is the worker required to contact if problems or complaints arise and who is responsible for their resolution? ....

5 What types of reports are required from the worker? Attach examples. ....

6 Describe the worker's daily routine (i.e., schedule, hours, etc.). ....

7 At what location(s) does the worker perform services (e.g., firm's premises, own shop or office, home, customer's location, etc.)? ....

8 Describe any meetings the worker is required to attend and any penalties for not attending (e.g., sales meetings, monthly meetings, staff meetings, etc.). ....

9 Is the worker required to provide the services personally? . . . . ☐ **Yes** ☐ **No**

10 If substitutes or helpers are needed, who hires them? ....

11 If the worker hires the substitutes or helpers, is approval required? . . . . ☐ **Yes** ☐ **No**
   If "Yes," by whom? ....

12 Who pays the substitutes or helpers? ....

13 Is the worker reimbursed if the worker pays the substitutes or helpers? . . . . ☐ **Yes** ☐ **No**
   If "Yes," by whom? ....

Part II   Financial Control

1 List the supplies, equipment, materials, and property provided by each party:
   The firm ....
   The worker ....
   Other party ....

2 Does the worker lease equipment? . . . . ☐ **Yes** ☐ **No**
   If "Yes," what are the terms of the lease? (Attach a copy or explanatory statement.) ....

3 What expenses are incurred by the worker in the performance of services for the firm? ....

4 Specify which, if any, expenses are reimbursed by:
   The firm ....
   Other party ....

5 Type of pay the worker receives: ☐ Salary   ☐ Commission   ☐ Hourly Wage   ☐ Piece Work
   ☐ Lump Sum   ☐ Other (specify) ....
   If type of pay is commission, and the firm guarantees a minimum amount of pay, specify amount $ _____ .

6 If the worker is paid by a firm other than the one listed on this form for these services, enter name, address, and employer identification number of the payer. ....

7 Is the worker allowed a drawing account for advances? . . . . ☐ **Yes** ☐ **No**
   If "Yes," how often? ....
   Specify any restrictions. ....

8 Whom does the customer pay? . . . . ☐ Firm   ☐ Worker
   If worker, does the worker pay the total amount to the firm? ☐ **Yes** ☐ **No** If "No," explain. ....

9 Does the firm carry worker's compensation insurance on the worker? . . . . ☐ **Yes** ☐ **No**

10 What economic loss or financial risk, if any, can the worker incur beyond the normal loss of salary (e.g., loss or damage of equipment, material, etc.)? ....

Part III Relationship of the Worker and Firm

1 List the benefits available to the worker (e.g., paid vacations, sick pay, pensions, bonuses). ----------

2 Can the relationship be terminated by either party without incurring liability or penalty? . . . . ☐ **Yes** ☐ **No**
If "No," explain your answer. ----------

3 Does the worker perform similar services for others? . . . . ☐ **Yes** ☐ **No**
If "Yes," is the worker required to get approval from the firm? . . . . ☐ **Yes** ☐ **No**

4 Describe any agreements prohibiting competition between the worker and the firm while the worker is performing services or during any later period. Attach any available documentation. ----------

5 Is the worker a member of a union? . . . . ☐ **Yes** ☐ **No**

6 What type of advertising, if any, does the worker do (e.g., a business listing in a directory, business cards, etc.)? Provide copies, if applicable.

7 If the worker assembles or processes a product at home, who provides the materials and instructions or pattern? ----------

8 What does the worker do with the finished product (e.g., return it to the firm, provide it to another party, or sell it)? ----------

9 How does the firm represent the worker to its customers (e.g., employee, partner, representative, or contractor)? ----------

10 If the worker no longer performs services for the firm, how did the relationship end? ----------

Part IV For Service Providers or Salespersons- Complete this part if the worker provided a service directly to customers or is a salesperson.

1 What are the worker's responsibilities in soliciting new customers? ----------

2 Who provides the worker with leads to prospective customers? ----------

3 Describe any reporting requirements pertaining to the leads. ----------

4 What terms and conditions of sale, if any, are required by the firm? ----------

5 Are orders submitted to and subject to approval by the firm? . . . . ☐ **Yes** ☐ **No**

6 Who determines the worker's territory? ----------

7 Did the worker pay for the privilege of serving customers on the route or in the territory? . . . . ☐ **Yes** ☐ **No**
If "Yes," whom did the worker pay? ----------
If "Yes," how much did the worker pay? . . . . $ _____

8 Where does the worker sell the product (e.g., in a home, retail establishment, etc.)? ----------

9 List the product and/or services distributed by the worker (e.g., meat, vegetables, fruit, bakery products, beverages, or laundry or dry cleaning services). If more than one type of product and/or service is distributed, specify the principal one. ----------

10 Does the worker sell life insurance full time? . . . . ☐ **Yes** ☐ **No**
11 Does the worker sell other types of insurance for the firm? . . . . ☐ **Yes** ☐ **No**
If "Yes," enter the percentage of the worker's total working time spent in selling other types of insurance. . . . _____%

12 If the worker solicits orders from wholesalers, retailers, contractors, or operators of hotels, restaurants, or other similar establishments, enter the percentage of the worker's time spent in the solicitation. . . . . _____%

13 Is the merchandise purchased by the customers for resale or use in their business operations? . . . . ☐ **Yes** ☐ **No**
Describe the merchandise and state whether it is equipment installed on the customers' premises. ----------

Part V Signature (see page 4)

Under penalties of perjury, I declare that I have examined this request, including accompanying documents, and to the best of my knowledge and belief, the facts presented are true, correct, and complete.

Signature ▶ _____ Title ▶ _____ Date ▶ _____
(Type or print name below)

General Instructions

Section references are to the Internal Revenue Code unless otherwise noted.

Purpose

Firms and workers file Form SS-8 to request a determination of the status of a worker for purposes of Federal employment taxes and income tax withholding.

A Form SS-8 determination may be requested only in order to resolve Federal tax matters. The taxpayer requesting a determination must file an income tax return for the years under consideration before a determination can be issued. If Form SS-8 is submitted for a tax year for which the statute of limitations on the tax return has expired, a determination letter will not be issued. The statute of limitations expires 3 years from the due date of the tax return or the date filed, whichever is later.

The IRS does not issue a determination letter for proposed transactions or on hypothetical situations. We may, however, issue an information letter when it is considered appropriate.

Definition

Firm. For the purposes of this form, the term "firm" means any individual, business enterprise, organization, state, or other entity for which a worker has performed services. The firm may or may not have paid the worker directly for these services. **If the firm was not responsible for payment for services, please be sure to complete question 6 in Part II of Form SS-8.**

The SS-8 Determination Process

The IRS will acknowledge the receipt of your Form SS-8. Because there are usually two (or more) parties who could be affected by a determination of employment status, the IRS attempts to get information from all parties involved by sending those parties blank Forms SS-8 for completion. The case will be assigned to a technician who will review the facts, apply the law, and render a decision. The technician may ask for additional information before rendering a decision. The IRS will generally issue a formal determination to the firm or payer (if that is a different entity), and will send a copy to the worker. A determination letter applies only to a worker (or a class of workers) requesting it, and the decision is binding on the IRS. In certain cases, a formal determination will not be issued; instead, an information letter may be issued. Although an information letter is advisory only and is not binding on the IRS, it may be used to assist the worker to fulfill his or her Federal tax obligations. This process takes approximately 120 days.

Neither the SS-8 determination process nor the review of any records in connection with the determination constitutes an examination (audit) of any Federal tax return. If the periods under consideration have previously been examined, the SS-8 determination process will not constitute a reexamination under IRS reopening procedures. Because this is not an examination of any Federal tax return, the appeal rights available in connection with an examination do not apply to an SS-8 determination. However, if you disagree with a determination and you have additional information concerning the work relationship that you believe was not previously considered, you may request that the determining office reconsider the determination.

Completing Form SS-8

Please answer all questions as completely as possible. Attach additional sheets if you need more space. Provide information for all years the worker provided services for the firm. Determinations are based on the entire relationship between the firm and the worker.

Additional copies of this form may be obtained by calling 1-800-TAX-FORM (1-800-829-3676) or from the IRS Web Site at **www.irs.gov.**

Fee

There is no fee for requesting an SS-8 determination letter.

Signature

The Form SS-8 must be signed and dated by the taxpayer. A stamped signature will not be accepted.

The person who signs for a corporation must be an officer of the corporation who has personal knowledge of the facts. If the corporation is a member of an affiliated group filing a consolidated return, it must be signed by an officer of the common parent of the group.

The person signing for a trust, partnership, or limited liability company must be, respectively, a trustee, general partner, or member-manager who has personal knowledge of the facts.

Where To File

Send the completed Form SS-8 to the address listed below for the firm's location. However, for cases involving Federal agencies, send the form to the Internal Revenue Service, Attn: CC:CORP:T:C, Ben Franklin Station, P.O. Box 7604, Washington, DC 20044.

Firm's location:	Send to:
Alaska, Arizona, Arkansas, California, Colorado, Hawaii, Idaho, Illinois, Iowa, Kansas, Minnesota, Missouri, Montana, Nebraska, Nevada, New Mexico, North Dakota, Oklahoma, Oregon, South Dakota, Texas, Utah, Washington, Wisconsin, Wyoming, American Samoa, Guam, Puerto Rico, U.S. Virgin Islands	Internal Revenue Service SS-8 Determinations P.O. Box 1231 Stop 4106 AUCSC Austin, TX 78767
Alabama, Connecticut, Delaware, District of Columbia, Florida, Georgia, Indiana, Kentucky, Louisiana, Maine, Maryland, Massachusetts, Michigan, Mississippi, New Hampshire, New Jersey, New York, North Carolina, Ohio, Pennsylvania, Rhode Island, South Carolina, Tennessee, Vermont, Virginia, West Virginia, all other locations not listed	Internal Revenue Service SS-8 Determinations 40 Lakemont Road Newport, VT 05855-1555

Instructions for Workers

If you are requesting a determination for more than one firm, complete a separate Form SS-8 for each firm.

 Form SS-8 is not a claim for refund of social security and Medicare taxes or Federal income tax withholding.

If you are found to be an employee, you are responsible for filing an amended return for any corrections related to this decision. A determination that a worker is an employee does not necessarily reduce any current or prior tax liability. For more information, call 1-800-829-1040.

Time for filing a claim for refund. Generally, you must file your claim for a credit or refund within 3 years from the date your original return was filed or within 2 years from the date the tax was paid, whichever is later.

Form SS-8 does not prevent the expiration of the time in which a claim for a refund must be filed. If you are concerned about a refund, and the statute of limitations for filing a claim for refund for the year(s) at issue has not yet expired, you should file **Form 1040X,** Amended U.S. Individual Income Tax Return, to protect your statute of limitations. File a separate Form 1040X for each year.

On the Form 1040X you file, do not complete lines 1 through 24 on the form. Write "Protective Claim" at the top of the form, sign and date it. In addition, you should enter the following statement in Part II, Explanation of Changes to Income, Deductions, and Credits: "Filed Form SS-8 with the Internal Revenue Service Office in (Austin, TX; Newport, VT; or Washington, DC; as appropriate). By filing this protective claim, I reserve the right to file a claim for any refund that may be due after a determination of my employment tax status has been completed."

Filing Form SS-8 does not alter the requirement to timely file an income tax return. Do not delay filing your tax return in anticipation of an answer to your SS-8 request. You must file an income tax return for related tax years before a determination can be issued. In addition, if applicable, do not delay in responding to a request for payment while waiting for a determination of your worker status.

Instructions for Firms

If a **worker** has requested a determination of his or her status while working for you, you will receive a request from the IRS to complete a Form SS-8. In cases of this type, the IRS usually gives each party an opportunity to present a statement of the facts because any decision will affect the employment tax status of the parties. Failure to respond to this request will not prevent the IRS from issuing an information letter to the worker based on the information he or she has made available so that the worker may fulfill his or her Federal tax obligations. However, the information that you provide is extremely valuable in determining the status of the worker.

If **you** are requesting a determination for a particular class of worker, complete the form for **one** individual who is representative of the class of workers whose status is in question. If you want a written determination for more than one class of workers, complete a separate Form SS-8 for one worker from each class whose status is typical of that class. A written determination for any worker will apply to other workers of the same class if the facts are not materially different for these workers. Please provide a list of names and addresses of all workers potentially affected by this determination.

If you have a reasonable basis for not treating a worker as an employee, you may be relieved from having to pay employment taxes for that worker under section 530 of the 1978 Revenue Act. However, this relief provision cannot be considered in conjunction with a Form SS-8 determination because the determination does not constitute an examination of any tax return. For more information regarding section 530 of the 1978 Revenue Act and to determine if you qualify for relief under this section, you may visit the IRS Web Site at **www.irs.gov**.

Privacy Act and Paperwork Reduction Act Notice. We ask for the information on this form to carry out the Internal Revenue laws of the United States. This information will be used to determine the employment status of the worker(s) described on the form. Subtitle C, Employment Taxes, of the Internal Revenue Code imposes employment taxes on wages. Sections 3121(d), 3306(a), and 3401(c) and (d) and the related regulations define employee and employer for purposes of employment taxes imposed under Subtitle C. Section 6001 authorizes the IRS to request information needed to determine if a worker(s) or firm is subject to these taxes. Section 6109 requires you to provide your taxpayer identification number. Neither workers nor firms are required to request a status determination, but if you choose to do so, you must provide the information requested on this form. Failure to provide the requested information may prevent us from making a status determination. If any worker or the firm has requested a status determination, and you are being asked to provide information for use in that determination, you are not required to provide the requested information. However, failure to provide such information will prevent the IRS from considering it in making the status determination. Providing false or fraudulent information may subject you to penalties. Routine uses of this information include providing it to the Department of Justice for use in civil and criminal litigation, to the Social Security Administration for the administration of social security programs, and to cities, states, and the District of Columbia for the administration of their tax laws. We may also provide this information to the affected worker(s) or the firm as part of the status determination process.

You are not required to provide the information requested on a form that is subject to the Paperwork Reduction Act unless the form displays a valid OMB control number. Books or records relating to a form or its instructions must be retained as long as their contents may become material in the administration of any Internal Revenue law. Generally, tax returns and return information are confidential, as required by section 6103.

The time needed to complete and file this form will vary depending on individual circumstances. The estimated average time is: **Recordkeeping,** 22 hrs.; **Learning about the law or the form,** 47 min.; and **Preparing and sending the form to the IRS,** 1 hr., 11 min. If you have comments concerning the accuracy of these time estimates or suggestions for making this form simpler, we would be happy to hear from you. You can write to the Tax Forms Committee, Western Area Distribution Center, Rancho Cordova, CA 95743-0001. **Do not** send the tax form to this address. Instead, see **Where To File** on page 4.

Form W-4 (2003)

Purpose. Complete Form W-4 so that your employer can withhold the correct Federal income tax from your pay. Because your tax situation may change, you may want to refigure your withholding each year.

Exemption from withholding. If you are exempt, complete only lines 1, 2, 3, 4, and 7 and sign the form to validate it. Your exemption for 2003 expires February 16, 2004. See **Pub. 505**, Tax Withholding and Estimated Tax.

Note: *You cannot claim exemption from withholding if: (a) your income exceeds $750 and includes more than $250 of unearned income (e.g., interest and dividends) and (b) another person can claim you as a dependent on their tax return.*

Basic instructions. If you are not exempt, complete the **Personal Allowances Worksheet** below. The worksheets on page 2 adjust your withholding allowances based on itemized deductions, certain credits, adjustments to income, or two-earner/two-job situations. Complete all worksheets that apply. **However, you may claim fewer (or zero) allowances.**

Head of household. Generally, you may claim head of household filing status on your tax return only if you are unmarried and pay more than 50% of the costs of keeping up a home for yourself and your dependent(s) or other qualifying individuals. See line **E** below.

Tax credits. You can take projected tax credits into account in figuring your allowable number of withholding allowances. Credits for child or dependent care expenses and the child tax credit may be claimed using the **Personal Allowances Worksheet** below. See **Pub. 919,** How Do I Adjust My Tax Withholding? for information on converting your other credits into withholding allowances.

Nonwage income. If you have a large amount of nonwage income, such as interest or dividends, consider making estimated tax payments using **Form 1040-ES,** Estimated Tax for Individuals. Otherwise, you may owe additional tax.

Two earners/two jobs. If you have a working spouse or more than one job, figure the total number of allowances you are entitled to claim on all jobs using worksheets from only one Form W-4. Your withholding usually will be most accurate when all allowances are claimed on the Form W-4 for the highest paying job and zero allowances are claimed on the others.

Nonresident alien. If you are a nonresident alien, see the **Instructions for Form 8233** before completing this Form W-4.

Check your withholding. After your Form W-4 takes effect, use Pub. 919 to see how the dollar amount you are having withheld compares to your projected total tax for 2003. See Pub. 919, especially if your earnings exceed $125,000 (Single) or $175,000 (Married).

Recent name change? If your name on line 1 differs from that shown on your social security card, call 1-800-772-1213 for a new social security card.

Personal Allowances Worksheet (Keep for your records.)

A	Enter "1" for **yourself** if no one else can claim you as a dependent	**A** _____
B	Enter "1" if: • You are single and have only one job; or	
	• You are married, have only one job, and your spouse does not work; or	**B** _____
	• Your wages from a second job or your spouse's wages (or the total of both) are $1,000 or less.	
C	Enter "1" for your **spouse.** But, you may choose to enter "-0-" if you are married and have either a working spouse or more than one job. (Entering "-0-" may help you avoid having too little tax withheld.)	**C** _____
D	Enter number of **dependents** (other than your spouse or yourself) you will claim on your tax return	**D** _____
E	Enter "1" if you will file as **head of household** on your tax return (see conditions under **Head of household** above) .	**E** _____
F	Enter "1" if you have at least $1,500 of **child or dependent care expenses** for which you plan to claim a credit . .	**F** _____
	(**Note:** Do **not** include child support payments. See **Pub. 503**, Child and Dependent Care Expenses, for details.)	
G	**Child Tax Credit** (including additional child tax credit):	
	• If your total income will be between $15,000 and $42,000 ($20,000 and $65,000 if married), enter "1" for each eligible child plus **1 additional** if you have three to five eligible children or **2 additional** if you have six or more eligible children.	
	• If your total income will be between $42,000 and $80,000 ($65,000 and $115,000 if married), enter "1" if you have one or two eligible children, "2" if you have three eligible children, "3" if you have four eligible children, or "4" if you have five or more eligible children.	**G** _____
H	Add lines A through G and enter total here. **Note:** This may be different from the number of exemptions you claim on your tax return. •	**H** _____

For accuracy, complete all worksheets that apply.
- If you plan to **itemize or claim adjustments to income** and want to reduce your withholding, see the **Deductions and Adjustments Worksheet** on page 2.
- If you have **more than one job** or are **married and you and your spouse both work** and the combined earnings from all jobs exceed $35,000, see the **Two-Earner/Two-Job Worksheet** on page 2 to avoid having too little tax withheld.
- If **neither** of the above situations applies, **stop here** and enter the number from line H on line 5 of Form W-4 below.

---------------------------- Cut here and give Form W-4 to your employer. Keep the top part for your records. ----------------------------

---

Form **W-4**
Department of the Treasury
Internal Revenue Service

Employee's Withholding Allowance Certificate

• **For Privacy Act and Paperwork Reduction Act Notice, see page 2.**

OMB No. 1545-0010

2003

1 Type or print your first name and middle initial	Last name		2 Your social security number

Home address (number and street or rural route)	**3** ☐ Single ☐ Married ☐ Married, but withhold at higher Single rate.
City or town, state, and ZIP code	**Note:** If married, but legally separated, or spouse is a nonresident alien, check the "Single" box.
	4 If your last name differs from that shown on your social security card, check here. You must call 1-800-772-1213 for a new card. • ☐

5	Total number of allowances you are claiming (from line **H** above **or** from the applicable worksheet on page 2)	**5** _____
6	Additional amount, if any, you want withheld from each paycheck	**6** $ _____
7	I claim exemption from withholding for 2003, and I certify that I meet **both** of the following conditions for exemption:	
	• Last year I had a right to a refund of **all** Federal income tax withheld because I had **no** tax liability **and**	
	• This year I expect a refund of **all** Federal income tax withheld because I expect to have **no** tax liability.	
	If you meet both conditions, write "Exempt" here . . . . ▸	**7**

Under penalties of perjury, I certify that I am entitled to the number of withholding allowances claimed on this certificate, or I am entitled to claim exempt status.

Employee's signature
(Form is not valid
unless you sign it.) ▸ _____   Date ▸ _____

8 Employer's name and address (Employer: Complete lines 8 and 10 only if sending to the IRS.)	**9** Office code (optional)	**10** Employer identification number

Form W-4 (2003)   Page **2**

Deductions and Adjustments Worksheet

Note: *Use this worksheet **only** if you plan to itemize deductions, claim certain credits, or claim adjustments to income on your 2003 tax return.*

1   Enter an estimate of your 2003 itemized deductions. These include qualifying home mortgage interest, charitable contributions, state and local taxes, medical expenses in excess of 7.5% of your income, and miscellaneous deductions. (For 2003, you may have to reduce your itemized deductions if your income is over $139,500 ($69,750 if married filing separately). See **Worksheet 3** in Pub. 919 for details.) . . . . **1** $ _____

2   Enter: \{ $7,950 if married filing jointly or qualifying widow(er)
          $7,000 if head of household
          $4,750 if single
          $3,975 if married filing separately \} . . . . **2** $ _____

3   **Subtract** line 2 from line 1. If line 2 is greater than line 1, enter "-0-" . . . . **3** $ _____

4   Enter an estimate of your 2003 adjustments to income, including alimony, deductible IRA contributions, and student loan interest   **4** $ _____

5   **Add** lines 3 and 4 and enter the total. Include any amount for credits from **Worksheet 7** in Pub. 919 . . **5** $ _____

6   Enter an estimate of your 2003 nonwage income (such as dividends or interest) . . . . **6** $ _____

7   **Subtract** line 6 from line 5. Enter the result, but not less than "-0-" . . . . **7** $ _____

8   **Divide** the amount on line 7 by $3,000 and enter the result here. Drop any fraction . . . . **8** _____

9   Enter the number from the **Personal Allowances Worksheet,** line H, page 1 . . . . **9** _____

10   **Add** lines 8 and 9 and enter the total here. If you plan to use the **Two-Earner/Two-Job Worksheet,** also enter this total on line 1 below. Otherwise, **stop here** and enter this total on Form W-4, line 5, page 1 . **10** _____

Two-Earner/Two-Job Worksheet

Note: *Use this worksheet **only** if the instructions under line H on page 1 direct you here.*

1   Enter the number from line H, page 1 (or from line 10 above if you used the **Deductions and Adjustments Worksheet**)   **1** _____

2   Find the number in **Table 1** below that applies to the **lowest** paying job and enter it here . . . . . **2** _____

3   If line 1 is **more than or equal to** line 2, subtract line 2 from line 1. Enter the result here (if zero, enter "-0-") and on Form W-4, line 5, page 1. **Do not** use the rest of this worksheet . . . . **3** _____

Note: *If line 1 is **less than** line 2, enter "-0-" on Form W-4, line 5, page 1. Complete lines 4-9 below to calculate the additional withholding amount necessary to avoid a year-end tax bill.*

4   Enter the number from line 2 of this worksheet . . . . **4** _____

5   Enter the number from line 1 of this worksheet . . . . **5** _____

6   **Subtract** line 5 from line 4 . . . . **6** _____

7   Find the amount in **Table 2** below that applies to the **highest** paying job and enter it here . . . . . **7** $ _____

8   **Multiply** line 7 by line 6 and enter the result here. This is the additional annual withholding needed . . **8** $ _____

9   Divide line 8 by the number of pay periods remaining in 2003. For example, divide by 26 if you are paid every two weeks and you complete this form in December 2002. Enter the result here and on Form W-4, line 6, page 1. This is the additional amount to be withheld from each paycheck . . . . **9** $ _____

Table 1: Two-Earner/Two-Job Worksheet

Married Filing Jointly				All Others			
If wages from **LOWEST** paying job are-	Enter on line 2 above	If wages from **LOWEST** paying job are-	Enter on line 2 above	If wages from **LOWEST** paying job are-	Enter on line 2 above	If wages from **LOWEST** paying job are-	Enter on line 2 above
$0 - $4,000	0	44,001 - 50,000	8	$0 - $6,000	0	75,001 - 100,000	8
4,001 - 9,000	1	50,001 - 60,000	9	6,001 - 11,000	1	100,001 - 110,000	9
9,001 - 15,000	2	60,001 - 70,000	10	11,001 - 18,000	2	110,001 and over	10
15,001 - 20,000	3	70,001 - 90,000	11	18,001 - 25,000	3		
20,001 - 25,000	4	90,001 - 100,000	12	25,001 - 29,000	4		
25,001 - 33,000	5	100,001 - 115,000	13	29,001 - 40,000	5		
33,001 - 38,000	6	115,001 - 125,000	14	40,001 - 55,000	6		
38,001 - 44,000	7	125,001 and over	15	55,001 - 75,000	7		

Table 2: Two-Earner/Two-Job Worksheet

Married Filing Jointly		All Others	
If wages from **HIGHEST** paying job are-	Enter on line 7 above	If wages from **HIGHEST** paying job are-	Enter on line 7 above
$0 - $50,000	$450	$0 - $30,000	$450
50,001 - 100,000	800	30,001 - 70,000	800
100,001 - 150,000	900	70,001 - 140,000	900
150,001 - 270,000	1,050	140,001 - 300,000	1,050
270,001 and over	1,200	300,001 and over	1,200

IRS Form **8300**
(Rev. December 2001)
OMB No. 1545-0892
Department of the Treasury
Internal Revenue Service

Report of Cash Payments Over $10,000 Received in a Trade or Business

▶ See instructions for definition of cash.
▶ Use this form for transactions occurring after December 31, 2001. Do not use prior versions after this date.
For Privacy Act and Paperwork Reduction Act Notice, see page 4.

FinCEN Form **8300**
(December 2001)
OMB No. 1506-0018
Department of the Treasury
Financial Crimes
Enforcement Network

1 Check appropriate box(es) if: **a** ☐ Amends prior report; **b** ☐ Suspicious transaction.

Part I — Identity of Individual From Whom the Cash Was Received

2 If more than one individual is involved, check here and see instructions . . . . ▶ ☐

3 Last name

4 First name

5 M.I.

6 Taxpayer identification number

7 Address (number, street, and apt. or suite no.)

8 Date of birth . ▶ (see instructions) M M D D Y Y Y Y

9 City

10 State

11 ZIP code

12 Country (if not U.S.)

13 Occupation, profession, or business

14 Document used to verify identity: **a** Describe identification ▶
b Issued by
c Number

Part II — Person on Whose Behalf This Transaction Was Conducted

15 If this transaction was conducted on behalf of more than one person, check here and see instructions . . . . . ▶ ☐

16 Individual's last name or Organization's name

17 First name

18 M.I.

19 Taxpayer identification number

20 Doing business as (DBA) name (see instructions)

Employer identification number

21 Address (number, street, and apt. or suite no.)

22 Occupation, profession, or business

23 City

24 State

25 ZIP code

26 Country (if not U.S.)

27 Alien identification: **a** Describe identification ▶
b Issued by
c Number

Part III — Description of Transaction and Method of Payment

28 Date cash received
M M D D Y Y Y Y

29 Total cash received
$ .00

30 If cash was received in more than one payment, check here . . . . ▶ ☐

31 Total price if different from item 29
$ .00

32 Amount of cash received (in U.S. dollar equivalent) (must equal item 29) (see instructions):

a U.S. currency $ _____ .00 (Amount in $100 bills or higher $ _____ .00)
b Foreign currency $ _____ .00 (Country ▶ _____)
c Cashier's check(s) $ _____ .00
d Money order(s) $ _____ .00
e Bank draft(s) $ _____ .00
f Traveler's check(s) $ _____ .00

Issuer's name(s) and serial number(s) of the monetary instrument(s) ▶ _____

33 Type of transaction

a ☐ Personal property purchased
b ☐ Real property purchased
c ☐ Personal services provided
d ☐ Business services provided
e ☐ Intangible property purchased
f ☐ Debt obligations paid
g ☐ Exchange of cash
h ☐ Escrow or trust funds
i ☐ Bail received by court clerks
j ☐ Other (specify) ▶

34 Specific description of property or service shown in 33. (Give serial or registration number, address, docket number, etc.) ▶

Part IV — Business That Received Cash

35 Name of business that received cash

36 Employer identification number

37 Address (number, street, and apt. or suite no.)

Social security number

38 City

39 State

40 ZIP code

41 Nature of your business

42 Under penalties of perjury, I declare that to the best of my knowledge the information I have furnished above is true, correct, and complete.

Signature ▶ _____ Authorized official

Title ▶ _____

43 Date of signature M M D D Y Y Y Y

44 Type or print name of contact person

45 Contact telephone number
( )

IRS Form **8300** (Rev. 12-2001)

Cat. No. 62133S

FinCEN Form **8300** (12-2001)

Multiple Parties
(Complete applicable parts below if box 2 or 15 on page 1 is checked)

Part I Continued- **Complete if box 2 on page 1 is checked**

3 Last name	4 First name	5 M.I.	6 Taxpayer identification number

7 Address (number, street, and apt. or suite no.)	8 Date of birth . ▶ (see instructions) M M D D Y Y Y Y

9 City	10 State	11 ZIP code	12 Country (if not U.S.)	13 Occupation, profession, or business

14 Document used to verify identity: **a** Describe identification ▶ _____
b Issued by _____ **c** Number .

3 Last name	4 First name	5 M.I.	6 Taxpayer identification number

7 Address (number, street, and apt. or suite no.)	8 Date of birth . ▶ (see instructions) M M D D Y Y Y Y

9 City	10 State	11 ZIP code	12 Country (if not U.S.)	13 Occupation, profession, or business

14 Document used to verify identity: **a** Describe identification ▶ _____
b Issued by _____ **c** Number

Part II Continued- **Complete if box 15 on page 1 is checked**

16 Individual's last name or Organization's name	17 First name	18 M.I.	19 Taxpayer identification number

20 Doing business as (DBA) name (see instructions)	Employer identification number

21 Address (number, street, and apt. or suite no.)	22 Occupation, profession, or business

23 City	24 State	25 ZIP code	26 Country (if not U.S.)

27 Alien identification: **a** Describe identification ▶ _____
b Issued by _____ **c** Number

16 Individual's last name or Organization's name	17 First name	18 M.I.	19 Taxpayer identification number

20 Doing business as (DBA) name (see instructions)	Employer identification number

21 Address (number, street, and apt. or suite no.)	22 Occupation, profession, or business

23 City	24 State	25 ZIP code	26 Country (if not U.S.)

27 Alien identification: **a** Describe identification ▶ _____
b Issued by _____ **c** Number

Section references are to the Internal Revenue Code unless otherwise noted.

Changes To Note

• Section 6050I (26 United States Code (U.S.C.) 6050I) and 31 U.S.C. 5331 require that certain information be reported to the IRS and the Financial Crimes Enforcement Network (FinCEN). This information must be reported on **IRS/FinCEN Form 8300.**

• Item 33 box **i** is to be checked **only** by clerks of the court; box **d** is to be checked by bail bondsmen. See the instructions on page 4.

• For purposes of section 6050I and 31 U.S.C. 5331, the word "cash" and "currency" have the same meaning. See **Cash** under **Definitions** below.

General Instructions

Who must file. Each person engaged in a trade or business who, in the course of that trade or business, receives more than $10,000 in cash in one transaction or in two or more related transactions, must file Form 8300. Any transactions conducted between a payer (or its agent) and the recipient in a 24-hour period are related transactions. Transactions are considered related even if they occur over a period of more than 24 hours if the recipient knows, or has reason to know, that each transaction is one of a series of connected transactions.

Keep a copy of each Form 8300 for 5 years from the date you file it.

Clerks of Federal or State courts must file Form 8300 if more than $10,000 in cash is received as bail for an individual(s) charged with certain criminal offenses. For these purposes, a clerk includes the clerk's office or any other office, department, division, branch, or unit of the court that is authorized to receive bail. If a person receives bail on behalf of a clerk, the clerk is treated as receiving the bail. See the instructions for **Item 33** on page 4.

If multiple payments are made in cash to satisfy bail and the initial payment does not exceed $10,000, the initial payment and subsequent payments must be aggregated and the information return must be filed by the 15th day after receipt of the payment that causes the aggregate amount to exceed $10,000 in cash. In such cases, the reporting requirement can be satisfied either by sending a single written statement with an aggregate amount listed or by furnishing a copy of each Form 8300 relating to that payer. Payments made to satisfy separate bail requirements are not required to be aggregated. See Treasury Regulations section 1.6050I-2.

Casinos must file Form 8300 for nongaming activities (restaurants, shops, etc.).

Voluntary use of Form 8300. Form 8300 may be filed voluntarily for any suspicious transaction (see **Definitions**) for use by FinCEN and the IRS, even if the total amount does not exceed $10,000.

Exceptions. Cash is not required to be reported if it is received:

• By a financial institution required to file **Form 4789,** Currency Transaction Report.

• By a casino required to file (or exempt from filing) **Form 8362,** Currency Transaction Report by Casinos, if the cash is received as part of its gaming business.

• By an agent who receives the cash from a principal, if the agent uses all of the cash within 15 days in a second transaction that is reportable on Form 8300 or on Form 4789, and discloses all the information necessary to complete Part II of Form 8300 or Form 4789 to the recipient of the cash in the second transaction.

• In a transaction occurring entirely outside the United States. See **Pub. 1544,** Reporting Cash Payments Over $10,000 (Received in a Trade or Business), regarding transactions occurring in Puerto Rico, the Virgin Islands, and territories and possessions of the United States.

• In a transaction that is not in the course of a person's trade or business.

When to file. File Form 8300 by the 15th day after the date the cash was received. If that date falls on a Saturday, Sunday, or legal holiday, file the form on the next business day.

Where to file. File the form with the Internal Revenue Service, Detroit Computing Center, P.O. Box 32621, Detroit, MI 48232.

Statement to be provided. You must give a written statement to each person named on a required Form 8300 on or before January 31 of the year following the calendar year in which the cash is received. The statement must show the name, telephone number, and address of the information contact for the business, the aggregate amount of reportable cash received, and that the information was furnished to the IRS. Keep a copy of the statement for your records.

Multiple payments. If you receive more than one cash payment for a single transaction or for related transactions, you must report the multiple payments any time you receive a total amount that exceeds $10,000 within any 12-month period. Submit the report within 15 days of the date you receive the payment that causes the total amount to exceed $10,000. If more than one report is required within 15 days, you may file a combined report. File the combined report no later than the date the earliest report, if filed separately, would have to be filed.

Taxpayer identification number (TIN). You must furnish the correct TIN of the person or persons from whom you receive the cash and, if applicable, the person or persons on whose behalf the transaction is being conducted. **You may be subject to penalties for an incorrect or missing TIN.**

The TIN for an individual (including a sole proprietorship) is the individual's social security number (SSN). For certain resident aliens who are not eligible to get an SSN and nonresident aliens who are required to file tax returns, it is an IRS Individual Taxpayer Identification Number (ITIN). For other persons, including corporations, partnerships, and estates, it is the employer identification number (EIN).

If you have requested but are not able to get a TIN for one or more of the parties to a transaction within 15 days following the transaction, file the report and attach a statement explaining why the TIN is not included.

Exception: *You are not required to provide the TIN of a person who is a nonresident alien individual or a foreign organization* **if** *that person does not have income effectively connected with the conduct of a U.S. trade or business* **and** *does not have an office or place of business, or fiscal or paying agent, in the United States. See Pub. 1544 for more information.*

Penalties. You may be subject to penalties if you fail to file a correct and complete Form 8300 on time and you cannot show that the failure was due to reasonable cause. You may also be subject to penalties if you fail to furnish timely a correct and complete statement to each person named in a required report. A minimum penalty of $25,000 may be imposed if the failure is due to an intentional or willful disregard of the cash reporting requirements.

Penalties may also be imposed for causing, or attempting to cause, a trade or business to fail to file a required report; for causing, or attempting to cause, a trade or business to file a required report containing a material omission or misstatement of fact; or for structuring, or attempting to structure, transactions to avoid the reporting requirements. These violations may also be subject to criminal prosecution which, upon conviction, may result in imprisonment of up to 5 years or fines of up to $250,000 for individuals and $500,000 for corporations or both.

Definitions

Cash. The term "cash" means the following:

• U.S. and foreign coin and currency received in any transaction.

• A cashier's check, money order, bank draft, or traveler's check having a face amount of $10,000 or less that is received in a **designated reporting transaction** (defined below), or that is received in any transaction in which the recipient knows that the instrument is being used in an attempt to avoid the reporting of the transaction under either section 6050I or 31 U.S.C. 5331.

Note: *Cash does not include a check drawn on the payer's own account, such as a personal check, regardless of the amount.*

Designated reporting transaction. A retail sale (or the receipt of funds by a broker or other intermediary in connection with a retail sale) of a consumer durable, a collectible, or a travel or entertainment activity.

Retail sale. Any sale (whether or not the sale is for resale or for any other purpose) made in the course of a trade or business if that trade or business principally consists of making sales to ultimate consumers.

Consumer durable. An item of tangible personal property of a type that, under ordinary usage, can reasonably be expected to remain useful for at least 1 year, and that has a sales price of more than $10,000.

Collectible. Any work of art, rug, antique, metal, gem, stamp, coin, etc.

Travel or entertainment activity. An item of travel or entertainment that pertains to a single trip or event if the combined sales price of the item and all other items relating to the same trip or event that are sold in the same transaction (or related transactions) exceeds $10,000.

Exceptions. A cashier's check, money order, bank draft, or traveler's check is not considered received in a designated reporting transaction if it constitutes the proceeds of a bank loan or if it is received as a payment on certain promissory notes, installment sales contracts, or down payment plans. See Pub. 1544 for more information.

Person. An individual, corporation, partnership, trust, estate, association, or company.

Recipient. The person receiving the cash. Each branch or other unit of a person's trade or business is considered a separate recipient unless the branch receiving the cash (or a central office linking the branches), knows or has reason to know the identity of payers making cash payments to other branches.

Transaction. Includes the purchase of property or services, the payment of debt, the exchange of a negotiable instrument for cash, and the receipt of cash to be held in escrow or trust. A single transaction may not be broken into multiple transactions to avoid reporting.

Suspicious transaction. A transaction in which it appears that a person is attempting to cause Form 8300 not to be filed, or to file a false or incomplete form. The term also includes any transaction in which there is an indication of possible illegal activity.

Specific Instructions

You must complete all parts. However, you may skip Part II if the individual named in Part I is conducting the transaction on his or her behalf only. **For voluntary reporting of suspicious transactions, see Item 1 below.**

Item 1. If you are amending a prior report, check box 1a. Complete the appropriate items with the correct or amended information only. Complete all of Part IV. Staple a copy of the original report to the amended report.

To voluntarily report a suspicious transaction (see **Definitions**), check box 1b. You may also telephone your local IRS Criminal Investigation Division or call 1-800-800-2877.

Part I

Item 2. If two or more individuals conducted the transaction you are reporting, check the box and complete Part I for any one of the individuals. Provide the same information for the other individual(s) on the back of the form. If more than three individuals are involved, provide the same information on additional sheets of paper and attach them to this form.

Item 6. Enter the taxpayer identification number (TIN) of the individual named. See **Taxpayer identification number (TIN)** on page 3 for more information.

Item 8. Enter eight numerals for the date of birth of the individual named. For example, if the individual's birth date is July 6, 1960, enter 07 06 1960.

Item 13. Fully describe the nature of the occupation, profession, or business (for example, "plumber," "attorney," or "automobile dealer"). Do not use general or nondescriptive terms such as "businessman" or "self-employed."

Item 14. You must verify the name and address of the named individual(s). Verification must be made by examination of a document normally accepted as a means of identification when cashing checks (for example, a driver's license, passport, alien registration card, or other official document). In item 14a, enter the type of document examined. In item 14b, identify the issuer of the document. In item 14c, enter the document's number. For example, if the individual has a Utah driver's license, enter "driver's license" in item 14a, "Utah" in item 14b, and the number appearing on the license in item 14c.

Part II

Item 15. If the transaction is being conducted on behalf of more than one person (including husband and wife or parent and child), check the box and complete Part II for any one of the persons. Provide the same information for the other person(s) on the back of the form. If more than three persons are involved, provide the same information on additional sheets of paper and attach them to this form.

Items 16 through 19. If the person on whose behalf the transaction is being conducted is an individual, complete items 16, 17, and 18. Enter his or her TIN in item 19. If the individual is a sole proprietor and has an employer identification number (EIN), you must enter both the SSN and EIN in item 19. If the person is an organization, put its name as shown on required tax filings in item 16 and its EIN in item 19.

Item 20. If a sole proprietor or organization named in items 16 through 18 is doing business under a name other than that entered in item 16 (e.g., a "trade" or "doing business as (DBA)" name), enter it here.

Item 27. If the person is not required to furnish a TIN, complete this item. See **Taxpayer Identification Number (TIN)** on page 3. Enter a description of the type of official document issued to that person in item 27a (for example, "passport"), the country that issued the document in item 27b, and the document's number in item 27c.

Part III

Item 28. Enter the date you received the cash. If you received the cash in more than one payment, enter the date you received the payment that caused the combined amount to exceed $10,000. See **Multiple payments** under General Instructions for more information.

Item 30. Check this box if the amount shown in item 29 was received in more than one payment (for example, as installment payments or payments on related transactions).

Item 31. Enter the total price of the property, services, amount of cash exchanged, etc. (for example, the total cost of a vehicle purchased, cost of catering service, exchange of currency) if different from the amount shown in item 29.

Item 32. Enter the dollar amount of each form of cash received. Show foreign currency amounts in U.S. dollar equivalent at a fair market rate of exchange available to the public. **The sum of the amounts must equal item 29.** For cashier's check, money order, bank draft, or traveler's check, provide the name of the issuer and the serial number of each instrument. Names of all issuers and all serial numbers involved must be provided. If necessary, provide this information on additional sheets of paper and attach them to this form.

Item 33. Check the appropriate box(es) that describe the transaction. If the transaction is not specified in boxes a- i, check box j and briefly describe the transaction (for example, "car lease," "boat lease," "house lease," or "aircraft rental"). If the transaction relates to the receipt of bail by a court clerk, check box **i**, "Bail received by court clerks." This box is **only** for use by court clerks. If the transaction relates to cash received by a bail bondsman, check box **d**, "Business services provided."

Part IV

Item 36. If you are a sole proprietorship, you must enter your SSN. If your business also has an EIN, you must provide the EIN as well. All other business entities must enter an EIN.

Item 41. Fully describe the nature of your business, for example, "attorney" or "jewelry dealer." Do not use general or nondescriptive terms such as "business" or "store."

Item 42. This form must be signed by an individual who has been authorized to do so for the business that received the cash.

Privacy Act and Paperwork Reduction Act Notice. Except as otherwise noted, the information solicited on this form is required by the Internal Revenue Service (IRS) and the Financial Crimes Enforcement Network (FinCEN) in order to carry out the laws and regulations of the United States Department of the Treasury. Trades or businesses, except for clerks of criminal courts, are required to provide the information to the IRS and FinCEN under both section 6050I and 31 U.S.C. 5331. Clerks of criminal courts are required to provide the information to the IRS under section 6050I. Section 6109 and 31 U.S.C. 5331 require that you provide your social security number in order to adequately identify you and process your return and other papers. The principal purpose for collecting the information on this form is to maintain reports or records where such reports or records have a high degree of usefulness in criminal, tax, or regulatory investigations or proceedings, or in the conduct of intelligence or counterintelligence activities, by directing the Federal Government's attention to unusual or questionable transactions.

While such information is invaluable with regards to the purpose of this form, you are not required to provide information as to whether the reported transaction is deemed suspicious. No penalties or fines will be assessed for failure to provide such information, even if you determine that the reported transaction is indeed suspicious in nature. Failure to provide all other requested information, or the provision of fraudulent information, may result in criminal prosecution and other penalties under Title 26 and Title 31 of the United States Code.

Generally, tax returns and return information are confidential, as stated in section 6103. However, section 6103 allows or requires the IRS to disclose or give the information requested on this form to others as described in the Code. For example, we may disclose your tax information to the Department of Justice, to enforce the tax laws, both civil and criminal, and to cities, states, the District of Columbia, U.S. commonwealths or possessions, and certain foreign governments to carry out their tax laws. We may disclose your tax information to the Department of Treasury and contractors for tax administration purposes; and to other persons as necessary to obtain information which we cannot get in any other way in order to determine the amount of or to collect the tax you owe. We may disclose your tax information to the Comptroller General of the United States to permit the Comptroller General to review the IRS. We may disclose your tax information to Committees of Congress; Federal, state, and local child support agencies; and to other Federal agencies for the purposes of determining entitlement for benefits or the eligibility for and the repayment of loans. We may also disclose this information to Federal agencies that investigate or respond to acts or threats of terrorism or participate in intelligence or counterintelligence activities concerning terrorism.

FinCEN may provide the information collected through this form to those officers and employees of the Department of the Treasury who have a need for the records in the performance of their duties. FinCEN may also refer the records to any other department or agency of the Federal Government upon the request of the head of such department or agency and may also provide the records to appropriate state, local, and foreign criminal law enforcement and regulatory personnel in the performance of their official duties.

You are not required to provide the information requested on a form that is subject to the Paperwork Reduction Act unless the form displays a valid OMB control number. Books or records relating to a form or its instructions must be retained as long as their contents may become material in the administration of any law under Title 26 or Title 31.

The time needed to complete this form will vary depending on individual circumstances. The estimated average time is 21 minutes. If you have comments concerning the accuracy of this time estimate or suggestions for making this form simpler, you can write to the Tax Forms Committee, Western Area Distribution Center, Rancho Cordova, CA 95743-0001. **Do not** send this form to this office. Instead, see **Where To File** on page 3.

APPLICATION FOR EMPLOYMENT

We consider applicants for all positions without regard to race, color, religion, sex, national origin, age, marital or veteran status, the presence of a non-job-related medical condition or handicap, or any other legally protected status. Proof of citizenship or immigration status will be required upon employment.

(PLEASE TYPE OR PRINT)

Position Applied For	Date of Application

Last Name	First Name	Middle Name or Initial

Is there any other information regarding your name that will be needed to check work or school records? ❑ Yes ❑ No

Address	Number Street	City	State	Zip Code

Telephone Number(s) [indicate home or work]	Social Security Number

Date Available:_____   Are you available: ❑ Full Time   ❑ Part Time   ❑ Weekends

Are you 18 years of age or older?   ❑ Yes   ❑ No

Have you been convicted of a felony within the past 7 years?   ❑ Yes   ❑ No

Conviction will not necessarily disqualify an applicant from employment.
If Yes, attach explanation.

Can you produce documents proving you are authorized to work in the United States? ❑ Yes   ❑ No

Education

	High School	Undergraduate	Graduate
School Name & Location			
Years Completed	1 2 3 4	1 2 3 4	1 2 3 4
Diploma / Degree			
Course of Study			

State any additional information you feel may be helpful to us in considering your application (such as any specialized training; skills; apprenticeships; honors received; professional, trade, business or civic organizations or activities; job-related military training or experience; foreign language abilities; etc.)

_____

_____

_____

_____

Employment Experience

Start with your present or last job. Include any job-related military service assignments and voluntary activities. You may exclude organizations which indicate race, color, religion, gender, national origin, handicap, or other protected status.

1.

Employer Name & Address	Dates Employed	Job Title/Duties
	Hourly Rate/Salary	
May we contact this employer? ❑ Yes ❑ No Employer Phone	Hours Per Week	
Supervisor		
Reason for Leaving		

2.

Employer Name & Address	Dates Employed	Job Title/Duties
	Hourly Rate/Salary	
Employer Phone	Hours Per Week	
Supervisor		
Reason for Leaving		

3.

Employer Name & Address	Dates Employed	Job Title/Duties
	Hourly Rate/Salary	
Employer Phone	Hours Per Week	
Supervisor		
Reason for Leaving		

References: Name   Occupation   Address   Phone #   Relationship   Years known

1. _____
2. _____
3. _____

If you need additional space, continue on a separate sheet of paper.

Applicant's Statement

I certify that the information given on this application is true and complete to the best of my knowledge. I authorize investigation of all statements contained in this application, and understand that false or misleading information given in my application or interview(s) may result in discharge.

I understand and acknowledge that, unless otherwise defined by applicable law, any employment relationship with this organization is "at will," which means that I may resign at any time and the employer may discharge me at any time with or without cause. I further understand that this "at will" employment relationship may not be changed orally, by any written document, or by conduct, unless such change is specifically acknowledged in writing by an authorized executive of this organization.

_____   _____

Signature of Applicant   Date

INDEX